World Wisdom
The Library of Perennial Philosophy

The Library of Perennial Philosophy is dedicated to the exposition of the timeless Truth underlying the diverse religions. This Truth, often referred to as the *Sophia Perennis*—or Perennial Wisdom—finds its expression in the revealed Scriptures as well as in the writings of the great sages and the artistic creations of the traditional worlds.

The Heart of Plotinus: The Essential Enneads appears as one of our selections in the Perennial Philosophy series.

The Perennial Philosophy Series

In the beginning of the twentieth century, a school of thought arose which has focused on the enunciation and explanation of the Perennial Philosophy. Deeply rooted in the sense of the sacred, the writings of its leading exponents establish an indispensable foundation for understanding the timeless Truth and spiritual practices which live in the heart of all religions. Some of these titles are companion volumes to the Treasures of the World's Religions series, which allows a comparison of the writings of the great sages of the past with the perennialist authors of our time.

THE HEART OF PLOTINUS
PLOTINUS
The Essential Enneads

including

Porphyry's *On the Cave of the Nymphs*

Edited by

Algis Uždavinys

Foreword by
Jay Bregman

World Wisdom

The Heart of Plotinus: The Essential Enneads
© 2009 World Wisdom, INC.

Most recent printing indicated by last digit below:

10 9 8 7 6 5 4 3 2

Library of Congress Cataloging-in-Publication Data

The heart of Plotinus : the essential Eneads including Porphyry's On the cave of
the nymphs / edited by Algis Uždavinys ; foreword by Jay Bregman.
    p. cm. -- (The library of perennial philosophy)
Includes bibliographical references and index.
    ISBN 978-1-933316-69-7 (pbk. : alk. paper) 1. Plotinus. 2. Plotinus. Enneads.
3. Porphyry, ca. 234-ca. 305. 4. Porphyry, ca. 234-ca. 305. Peri tou en Odysseia
ton nymphon antrou. I. Uždavinys, Algis.
    B693.Z7H37 2009
    186'.4--dc22

                                                                    2009005786

Printed on acid-free paper in the USA.

For information address World Wisdom, INC.
P.O. Box 2682, Bloomington, Indiana 47402-2682

www.worldwisdom.com

CONTENTS

FOREWORD

The American Transcendentalist, Ralph Waldo Emerson, included Plotinus (204-270 C.E.) and Porphyry (235-305 C.E.) in "the high priesthood of pure reason, the *Trismegisti* . . . of the old religion . . . which makes the sanctities of Christianity look parvenus and popular."[1] Ironically, the Neoplatonic version of religious Hellenism has had a seminal influence on Christianity, most notably on the works of Augustine of Hippo in the Latin West and Dionysius the Areopagite in the Greek East. A Neoplatonic underground, as it were, continued this tradition in Byzantium and the Middle Ages, and openly re-emerged in the Christian Neoplatonism of the Renaissance through such figures as Marsilio Ficino and Pico della Mirandola. The Romantic Movement was also significantly Neoplatonic, Plotinus being one of its major sources.

In England, the isolated Thomas Taylor translated their works, and even tried to revive their non-Christian Hellenic religion. Plotinus, though more interested in philosophy than cultic worship, was nevertheless a religious philosopher primarily concerned with the soul's origin in, and return to, the divine First Principle; while Porphyry was involved in the preservation of the ancient myths and rites, as understood Neoplatonically. *On the Cave of the Nymphs*, printed herein in Taylor's translation, represents an attempt to interpret a passage of Greek "sacred scripture" from Homer's *Odyssey* according to allegorical Neoplatonic principles. Taylor's influence was most pronounced in North America,[2] where a group of later Transcendentalists, learning of his works through Emerson and his friend A. Bronson Alcott, became Taylor's "dis-

---

[1] "Intellect", in *The Complete Works of Ralph Waldo Emerson*, ed. Edward W. Emerson (Boston: Houghton Mifflin, 1903-4), Vol. 7, p. 204.

[2] On the reception of Thomas Taylor in America see Jay Bregman, "The Neoplatonic Revival in North America," *Hermathena: A Trinity College Dublin Review*, No. CXLIX, Winter 1990, pp. 99-119.

ciples", as it were. The Hegelian influence on nineteenth century philosophy still provided them with a friendly atmosphere, despite the contemporary rise of materialism and naturalism. Subsequently, philosophy in the twentieth century—especially in the analytic Anglophone world—moved away from absolute idealism and from metaphysics of any kind. Outside of certain artistic and theological circles, Neoplatonic thought was peripheralized; some classical scholars and religious thinkers even saw it as a garbled and vague "perversion" of Plato.

The significant work of several pioneers in the Anglophone world has changed that perception: Plotinus has (from a Western perspective) come to be regarded as the greatest philosopher between Aristotle and Aquinas. Among these pioneers was Stephen MacKenna, an Irish journalist who devoted his life to making a magnificent poetic translation of Plotinus' *Enneads*, chosen here by Algis Uždavinys as a most compelling introduction to the thought of Plotinus, one that draws the reader in through the boldness of its metaphor and imagery. Through some uncanny intuition, the philosophically and philologically untrained MacKenna grasped the gist of his beloved "Plotty," and turned his soaring metaphysical vision into poetry.

Algis Uždavinys, in characteristic fashion, has chosen some of the most important and the most beautiful and inspiring works from the *Enneads* of Plotinus. The passages are organized according to an ascending order presented in Porphyry's editing of his teacher's writings, which takes the reader from the virtues, primarily practiced for the purification of the individual soul, through the dialectic of ascent, all the way to Beauty itself. Indeed, *Ennead* I.6 ("On Beauty"), which is a gloss on Plato's *Symposium*, celebrates (unlike Plato himself) aesthetic imaginative perception and has been an inspiration to artists. Plotinus' celebrated anti-Gnostic treatise, *Ennead* II.9 ("Against the Gnostics"), maintains the traditional Hellenic love of the visible cosmos (on its own level): he chides the "acosmic gnostics" in his lecture room for arrogantly despising its magnificence.

From Plotinus' *Ennead* III we get a glimpse of his somber Stoic-flavored view of Providence, more on Love and Plato's *Symposium*, as well as his justly famous account of the "effortless" contemplation of Nature, in her concrete realization of the spatio-temporal realm. *Ennead* IV presents—perhaps most difficult for Plotinus—the problems of the soul, its connection with the body, and its descent into the material world, conceived both as a natural and necessary occurrence and as the result of a willful and self-defining "falling" away from higher perfection. Yet part of the soul never leaves the noetic realm, the "place" of *nous* or divine intellect. *Ennead* V.8 ("On the Intelligible Beauty") represents one of the most beautiful sections in Plotinus, in which the noetic realm is described not in terms of abstract and "ethereal" Platonic Forms, but as a living interpenetrating universe, boiling with life. So intense, we are reminded of the visionary "imaginal world" of the Islamic Neoplatonists, with its emerald cities and angelic spirits and concretized Ideas. And as Algis shows in his excellent introduction, Plotinus had a major influence on medieval Islamic, as well as Jewish and Christian, thought.

Finally we are brought to the One, the ultimate first principle, beyond thought and conception, which can only be known through negation, and the negation of negation. Yet we must somehow conceive of it as connected with the divine intellect and as the cause of the universe. And mystical union with the One is the final goal of the soul; the reason behind its desire (*eros*) for beauty. Plotinus, in *Ennead* VI, attempts to work out a metaphysics in which the One, as the highest hypostasis, is somehow responsible, out of abundance, for the procession of Intellect and then through Intellect, Soul (these making up the three hypostases) and through Soul, Nature and the visible cosmos. All three exist in each individual soul. We are each of us an intelligible world in miniature. If we can recognize this and purify ourselves, "carve our own statue," and find our higher soul, which remains in the noetic world, we reach a stage of illumination. This penultimate stage prepares us for union with the One; for which we can only wait, as one waits for the sunrise. As Emerson says in his poem "Brahma," "find me

The Heart of Plotinus

and turn thy back on Heaven!" Emerson, a great reader of Plotinus, who was a major influence on his thought, was also attracted to Hindu and other Eastern scriptures: he was aware of the parallels in these texts. Emerson's Plato combined the One of Asia, with the Many of Europe.

Hilary Armstrong, the leading twentieth century Plotinus scholar in the Anglophone world, was fond of pointing out that for Westerners interested in, and seeking bridges toward, Eastern thought, one of the best ways is to read and understand Plotinus and the ancient Neoplatonists. Not the least valuable thing about this volume is how well Algis Uždavinys understands the significance of those connections. In his introductory remarks he shows the influences of Neoplatonism on both East and West; he also connects it with the Perennial Philosophy. It should also be said that he uses, and uses well, the works of the best recent and contemporary scholars of Neoplatonism. His remarks are accurate, helpful, and up-to-date. Generally his introduction manages to cover clearly and in a few pages the most salient points and philosophical issues within Neoplatonic thought. Further, Algis' short introductions to each section of text are of great help to the novice reader who might need some guidance through the often opaque-seeming expression of ideas.

A bonus in this edition is the Thomas Taylor translation of Porphyry. Loved in North America, he was also a great inspiration on Taylor's friend, William Blake, whose typically visionary "Arlington Court Painting" depicts the "Cave of the Nymphs" in Homer, but *as Porphyry saw it*![3] This work is a fine example of late antique philosophical/spiritual allegory, which is also of literary interest. A serious reading of this tract, including the introduction and notes, will enable the reader to acquire a good grasp of the Neoplatonic way of looking at things, and perhaps even cultivate

---

[3] Reproduced as Plate 18 in *Thomas Taylor the Platonist: Selected Writings*, eds. George Mills Harper and Kathleen Raine (Princeton, NJ: Princeton University Press, 1969); see also therein, Kathleen Raine, "Thomas Taylor in England," pp. 3-48 and George Mills Harper, "Thomas Taylor in America," pp. 49-102.

in a concrete experiential way, "that way of seeing, which all have and few make use of."

One friend of MacKenna, whose extensive correspondence with him has been published, was E.R. Dodds, late Regius Professor of Greek at Oxford. Dodds encouraged MacKenna in his work and helped where he could. He is, notably, the founder of modern Anglophone Neoplatonic studies.[4] It was Dodds who recommended A.H Armstrong to the Loeb Classical Library, as the best English translator of Plotinus. Hilary Armstrong was both a serious Classicist *and* a very liberal Christian Platonist. His translation reflects a grasp of the spirit as well as the letter of Plotinus. He was also able to use a better critical edition of the text than the one available to MacKenna. The reader who wishes to continue the study of Plotinus, would do well—after undergoing the poetic initiation of MacKenna's translation—to carefully work through the entire text in the Armstrong edition.

It was through the recommendation of Hilary Armstrong that I first came to know Algis Uždavinys. He has attended meetings of the International Society for Neoplatonic Studies since 2002. He is a serious and scholarly student of Neoplatonism who is also devoted to promoting Neoplatonism as a living experientially significant tradition. Today, in an era of revived religious conflict, we need the tolerant vision provided by the Neoplatonic sensibility. The Neoplatonist Nicholas of Cusa's Renaissance notion of many rites but only one ultimate religious truth, and the Florentine Neoplatonists' inclusion of all traditions as part of a universal "primal revelation" coeval with the Mosaic, is sorely lacking in our allegedly post-Enlightenment "post-modern" world. The notion that "there can not be only one path to penetrate such a great mystery"—presented to the late fourth century Christian emperors by the Roman senator, Symmachus,[5] the Hellenic philosopher and

---

[4] The scholarly consensus is that the founding text for modern Anglophone Neoplatonic scholarship is *Proclus: The Elements of Theology*, ed. and trans. E.R. Dodds (Oxford: Clarendon Press, 1933; 2nd ed., 1965).

[5] Pierre Hadot quotes Symmachus: "What matters the path of wisdom by which

rhetorician, Themistius, and other tolerant adherents of Greek and Roman religion, by then theologically Neoplatonic—is one that should be broadcast loud and clear to our world. The connection of such attitudes with Neoplatonism, and exposure to the spiritual thought of the Hellenic Neoplatonists Plotinus and Porphyry, may in some small way help us out in the current crisis.

Jay Bregman
Professor of History
The University of Maine

each person seeks the truth? One cannot reach such a great mystery by a single path (*'uno itinere non potest pervenire ad tam grande secretum'*)" (Pierre Hadot, *The Veil of Isis: An Essay on the History of the Idea of Nature*, trans. Michael Chase [Cambridge, MA/London: Belknap Press of Harvard University Press, 2006], p. 71 and n. 11). Hilary Armstrong liked to say "I am a *non uno itiner* ('not a single path') man"; that for Western creatures there was Biblical revelation (and Neoplatonism), for Eastern creatures there was the Buddha, and a temple of Isis in our world would be like a Hindu temple. A good example of his religious inclusiveness may be found is his articles, "The Way and the Ways: Religious Tolerance and Intolerance in the Fourth Century A.D." and "Itineraries in Late Antiquity," in A. H. Armstrong, *Hellenic and Christian Studies* (Hampshire, UK/Brookfield, VT: Variorum Reprints, 1990), XIII and XIV.

THE PHILOSOPHY OF
PLOTINUS THE EGYPTIAN

Plotinus and His Master Ammonius

Plotinus (A.D. 204-270) is sometimes regarded as the greatest philosopher in the period between Aristotle and Proclus, though the later Platonists based their teachings rather on the metaphysics of Iamblichus and Syrianus. In this respect, they did not share the modern opinion of the "radical originality" and exceptional status of Plotinus, customarily viewed by the Western classicists as the founder of a reinterpreted version of Platonism that came to be known as "Neoplatonism." This term itself appears to have originated in the eighteenth century as a derisory label invented by Protestant scholars who regarded Neoplatonism as the root and source of all kinds of evils, attributing (as did Johann Lorenz von Mosheim) the invention of such a philosophy to the Devil himself. Even such philosophers as Leibniz declared that Plotinus, in his vain craving for the mystical and marvelous, had corrupted the teaching of Plato. The Protestant theologians were highly suspicious of the "corrupting" influence of Neoplatonism on Christianity. Thus, as E.N. Tigerstedt has pointed out:

> The separation of Platonism from Neoplatonism seems to have been inspired by the wish to dissociate Plato from his later followers, who were regarded as anti-Christian, and thus maintain the venerable view of Plato as *anima naturaliter christiana*.[1]

---

[1] E.N. Tigerstedt, *The Decline and Fall of the Neoplatonic Interpretation of Plato: An Outline and Some Observations* (Helsinki: Societas Scientiarum Fennica, 1974), p. 49.

The "younger Platonists," or "Neoplatonists," were those who, "inflated by metaphysical dreams" and "wild enthusiasm," opposed Plato to Christ and "tried to crush Christianity."

In the strict sense, the label "Neoplatonism" is used to describe that form of Platonism which started with Plotinus, though "Neoplatonism" may also refer to the much earlier transformations of Platonism, including so-called "Middle Platonism." All philosophers now classified as "Middle Platonists" (e.g., Antiochus of Ascalon, Gaius, Atticus, Calvenus Taurus, Alcinous) and "Neoplatonists" (Plotinus, Amelius, Porphyry) regarded themselves as Platonists pure and simple. Their different interpretations of Plato were based partly on oral teachings, partly on the written works, both viewed as containing an esoteric wisdom reserved only for the initiated. Though the basic Neoplatonic doctrines may be collected from an attentive and creative reading of Plato's dialogues, the later Platonists carried Platonic doctrines somewhat further and developed them into a more carefully elaborated metaphysics and mysticism.

According to J.N. Findlay, they brought out Plato's doctrines "from hinting incompletness to expository fullness and coherence," freeing them from tiresome stylistic and argumentative (if not "sophistic") reflexes. Arguing that Plotinus and his master Ammonius represented no serious deviation from Plato (who had only an inexplicit metaphysical system or, rather, program of investigation), he says:

> I see comparatively little development in the treatises of Plotinus. They are the varying exposition of an already established body of doctrine, to which Plotinus may have made some brilliant additions, but whose basic pattern had been previously laid down.[2]

As Plotinus himself clearly attested (though antitraditional scholars regard this assertion as an outrageous lie):

---

[2] J.N. Findlay, "The Neoplatonism of Plato," in *The Significance of Neoplatonism*, ed. R. Baine Harris (Norfolk: ISNS, 1976), p. 25.

So that what we say represents no novelty, and was said not now, but long ago, though in inexplicit fashion. Our present exposition is merely an exegesis of what was then said, and relies for its proof of antiquity on the writings of Plato himself (*Enn.* V.1.8).

The Neoplatonists dealt with the noetic and ineffable realities which in the ancient civilizations were expressed in the language of myth and sacramental theurgic rites. However, they were unwilling to sacrifice rational philosophical discourse, trying thereby to maintain the conceptual precision characteristic of Hellenic thought. Thus, seemingly contradictory statements were unavoidable, and different metaphysical formulations—based on the esoteric interpretation of ancient "theologians" (Homer, Hesiod, Orpheus, the Egyptian and Chaldean priests) and philosophers (Pythagoras, Parmenides, Plato, and Aristotle)—might appear equally inadequate where the realm of first principles is concerned.

Since the divine truths were very imperfectly expressible, Plotinus, being at the same time a mystic and a rationalist, partly adopted an aporetic approach to philosophy. The term "mystic" is here used not in the sense of "irrational," or "devoid of reason"; a "mystic" is one who follows the anagogic path of the spiritual or philosophical "mysteries" to the Ultimate Reality, to be finally united with God or His Attributes. And a "rationalist" (in the traditional sense of this word) is one who possesses, and identifies himself with, the "rational" and therefore "immortal" part of his soul, and thus regards the intelligible world, or the realm of noetic archetypes, as more real than the physical world of images which, nevertheless, are part of the ordered metastructure that mirrors its intelligible paradigms.

It is usually maintained that Plotinus "has gathered the legacy of nearly eight centuries of Greek philosophy into a magnificently unified synthesis."[3] However, he saw himself as a faithful inter-

[3] Maria Luisa Gatti, "Plotinus: The Platonic Tradition and the Foundation of Neoplatonism," in *The Cambridge Companion to Plotinus*, ed. Lloyd P. Gerson (Cam-

preter of Plato, the supreme master, who possessed the whole truth already, like other inspired teachers and divine messengers. Plotinus clearly understood that he himself belonged to the long chain of tradition (*paradosis*), constituted by the brethren of the golden race. According to Porphyry, the oracle of Apollo presented Plotinus (who seemed ashamed of being in the mortal body) as one pure of soul, ever striving towards the divine:

> The oracle says that he was mild and kind, most gentle and attractive, and we knew ourselves that he was like this. It says too that he sleeplessly kept his soul pure and ever strove towards the divine which he loved with all his soul, and did everything to be delivered and "escape from the bitter wave of blood-drinking life here." So to this god-like man above all, who often raised himself in thought—according to the ways Plato teaches in the *Symposium*, to the First and Transcendent God—that God appeared who has neither shape nor any intelligible form, but is throned above Intellect and all the intelligibles (*Vita Plot.* 23).

According to Eunapius (*Vita Soph.* 455) and David (*In Isagog.* 91.23ff), Plotinus was born in Lycopolis, Upper Egypt, in A.D. 204 or 205. Lycopolis (modern Asyut, ancient Egyptian *Zawty*) was the capital of the 13th nome of Upper Egypt, situated between 1. Akhmim (ancient Egyptian Ipu or Khen-min, Coptic Khmin, Greek Khemmis or Panopolis), the famous center of alchemy and Pythagorean philosophy, in the south, and 2. Hermopolis (modern el-Ashmunein, ancient Khmun, Khemmenu), the town of Hermes, Egyptian Thoth, the god of wisdom, sacred rites, philosophy and theurgy, in the north. Thoth was an undisputed master of all knowledge, the patron of scribes, doctors, magicians, and architects who built the sanctuaries of the gods. In Graeco-Roman times, Hermopolis became a center of pilgrimage for Egyptians, Greeks, and Romans, worshipers of Hermes Trismegistus, or Thoth. This god is sometimes regarded as a substitute of Ra (the solar Intellect, later turned into the second hypostasis of Plotinus), and equated with his heart and demiurgic *logos*. Lycopolis had the famous temple of the local god Upawet (Wepwawet), "the Opener of the Ways," the mystagogue of initiates and the guide through the Osirian Underworld (Duat), sometimes equated with the jackal-headed god Anubis.

We cannot be certain about Plotinus' racial origin. He may either be a Greek, or a member of a Hellenized Egyptian family, like that of the priest Aurelius Petearbeschinis, a thoroughly Hellenized man of letters from Panopolis (Akhmim). Plotinus, who was exceedingly reticent regarding his life, is called "the Egyptian" by Proclus (*Plat. Theol.* I.1). At the age of twenty-eight Plotinus became interested in philosophy. He came to Alexandria and, after trying different teachers of philosophy, encountered Ammonius (c. A.D. 175-242), scornfully nicknamed "Saccas" by the later Christian authors, though the Neoplatonists themselves never used this disdainful label, meaning "porter." From that day Plotinus "followed Ammonius continuously, and under his guidance made such progress in philosophy that he became eager to investigate that practiced among the Persians and that perfected by the Indians" (*Vita Plot.* 3).

Ammonius wrote nothing and very little is known about him and his teaching. John Dillon argues that, in the person of Ammonius (who is "little more than a charismatic purveyor of Numenian Neopythagoreanism") Plotinus came into contact with the so-called "Neopythagorean underground":[4] "The great respect that he generated in his pupils for the wisdom of the East is also in line with Numenius."[5] A.H. Armstrong, who assiduously rejects that Plotinus was influenced by any Hermetic teaching or by the ancient solar theologies through the intermediary of Ammonius, says: "The chief claim to distinction of Plotinus' master, the myste-

---

[4] John Dillon, *The Middle Platonists: A Study of Platonism 80 B.C. to A.D. 220*, revised edition with new afterword (London: Duckworth, 1996), pp. 383 and 381.

[5] Ibid., p. 383.

rious Ammonius Saccas, was to have reconciled Plato and Aristotle, and in this he was following a well-established tradition."[6]

Numenius, the second century A.D. Pythagorean and Platonic philosopher, is connected with the Syrian city of Apamea in the Orontes valley where Amelius Gentilianus of Tuscany, the chief pupil of Plotinus and admirer of Numenius, went to live just before his master Plotinus passed away. Numenius based his "perennial philosophy" not only on the teachings of Pythagoras and Plato, but also on the doctrines of the Brahmans, Jews, Magi, and Egyptians (fr. 10). He employed the technique of symbolic and allegorical exegesis, explaining the war between Atlantis and the Athenians recounted by Plato in *Timaeus* (23d ff), for example, as a battle between the wise followers of Athena (the noble and rational souls) and the irrational subjects of Poseidon involved with generation (Proclus, *In Tim.* I.76.30ff).

According to John Dillon, the fragments of Numenius' *On the Good* "gives the impression much more of an Hermetic dialogue than of a Platonic one": the main speaker in this treatise reminds one of Hermes instructing his spiritual "son" Tat.[7] When Plotinus was accused of appropriating the ideas of Numenius or even plagiarizing him, Amelius wrote a book in his defense called *On the Difference between the Doctrines of Plotinus and Numenius.* According to Porphyry the Phoenician (whose native name was Malchus), some people not only thought that Plotinus "was making a show on a basis of plagiarism from Numenius," but also considered that,

> he was a big driveller and despised him because they did not understand what he meant and because he was so completely free from the staginess and windy rant of the professional speechifier: his lectures were like conversations, and he was not quick to make clear to anybody the compelling logical coherence of his discourse (*Vita Plot.* 18).

[6] A.H. Armstrong, *The Architecture of the Intelligible Universe in the Philosophy of Plotinus* (Amsterdam: Adolf M. Hakkert, 1967), pp. 7 and 57.

[7] John Dillon, *The Middle Platonists*, p. 383.

Plotinus belonged to the inner circle of Ammonius' school in Alexandria. Longinus, Erennius, and Origen the Platonist (who produced two works, *On Daimons* and *That the King is the Only Maker*) were also initiates of Ammonius. It is, however, doubtful that the Christian Origen was really Ammonius' pupil at all. The later and, as a rule, less informed authors (including the Church historian Eusebius, who perhaps misunderstood or simply distorted the attestations of Porphyry) sometimes failed to distinguish between the two Origens. Erennius is otherwise unknown, but Longinus, who respected Plotinus while rejecting some of his teachings about the location of the Forms within the Intellect, is known as a learned literary critic and teacher of Porphyry at Athens before he joined Plotinus. Later Longinus became the minister of Arab Queen Zenobia (Zaynab) of Palmyra and was executed when the Romans destroyed Zenobia's state in Syria.

Though Ammonius himself is sometimes described as the most learned scholar of the day, he remains for us "a shadowy figure, who wrote not at all and of whom we know next to nothing."[8] The oral and, to a certain extent, esoteric character of Ammonius' teachings is attested by Porphyry, who says:

> After Philip had become Emperor he (Plotinus) came to Rome, at the age of forty. Erennius, Origen, and Plotinus had made an agreement not to disclose any of the doctrines of Ammonius which he had revealed to them in his lectures. Plotinus kept the agreement, and, though he held conferences with people who came to him, maintained silence about the doctrines of Ammonius. Errenius was the first to break the agreement, and Origen followed his lead. . . . Plotinus for a long time continued to write nothing, but began to base his lectures on his studies with Ammonius. So he continued for ten complete years, admitting people to study with him, but writing nothing (*Vita Plot.* 3).

---

[8] Denis O'Brien, "Plotinus and the Secrets of Ammonius," *Hermathena: A Trinity College Dublin Review*, no. CLVII, winter 1994, p. 137.

From this account it is clear that the pupils of Ammonius bound themselves not to reveal their master's doctrines. We do not know what kind of secrets Porphyry had in mind, but E.R. Dodds argues that the obvious supposition—identifying the hidden doctrines of Ammonius as teachings of the ineffable One and mystical union with the One—is perhaps wrong.[9] However, the mysterious or esoteric character of Ammonius' instructions concerning the philosophical purification and ascent of the soul to the divine is not to be underestimated.

The "secrets" of ancient mystery cults and those of Pythagorean philosophy (e.g., the doctrines regarding the immortality of the soul, reincarnation, separation of the soul from the body, elevation, and deification) were "an open secret." They were more related to spiritual initiation, the ineffable vision, or the real divine presence, than to doctrinal exposition at the level of discursive reasoning. As Peter Kingsley has pointed out,

> true esoteric teaching aims not at filling the disciple or pupil with mere fascinating theories but with opportunities for making these ideas and theories real in his own experience. Romantic notions of an esoteric text as a document containing earth-shattering statements that need locking away from the profane are naïve and vastly oversimplistic. The fact is that hardly anyone would recognize such a text for what it is, let alone know how to use it.[10]

Some scholars, following R.H. Schwyzer, are convinced that the argument regarding Ammonius' doctrines consisted in not putting them into written form, because they were oral teachings. In fact, Porphyry explicitly states that Plotinus had drawn on the teachings of Ammonius for a long time before he began to write, by which time the agreement had already been broken by Erennius

---

[9] E.R. Dodds, "Numenius and Ammonius," *Les sources de Plotin: Entretiens sur l'Antiquite classique, No.5* (Vandroeuvres-Geneve, 1960), pp. 27-28.

[10] Peter Kingsley, *Ancient Philosophy, Mystery, and Magic: Empedocles and Pythagorean Tradition* (Oxford: Clarendon Press, 1995), pp. 369-370.

and Origen.[11] However, Richard Goulet thinks that the oral teachings of Ammonius were not revealed in the early lectures which Plotinus gave in Rome.[12] Even the written lectures were not yet given out to everybody but only to those who had been carefully selected beforehand, since the school of Plotinus in Rome also had its inner circle. The most important members of this inner circle were Amelius, Eustachius, and Porphyry.

The later Neoplatonic tradition tends to emphasize the role of Ammonius in the rediscovery of true Platonism after a long period of its not being properly understood. According to the Alexandrian philosopher Hierocles (whose treatise *On Providence* is presented in a summary by the Byzantine writer Photius), Ammonius belonged to the Golden Chain of Platonism. To describe those philosophers who rediscovered the divine philosophy, Hierocles uses the expression *hiera genea* (the golden race). He believed that Ammonius had purified true philosophy (which is regarded as a revelation) and restored harmony between the views of Aristotle and Plato. Thus Ammonius is introduced by the epithet "divine" (*theodidaktos*) (Photius, *Bibl.* III.112; 172a). As Dominic J. O'Meara has pointed out, Ammonius, according to Hierocles, "emerges as having accomplished what had been an essentially Numenian mission: the restoral of unanimity (*homodoxia*) of Platonism through the purification of a contentious and degraded tradition."[13]

Proclus assigned this role of "rediscoverer" to Plotinus, saying that the divine philosophy shone forth through the grace of the gods: the divine mysteries, established by the gods and guarded by the gods themselves, were in the course of time revealed to such exceptional men as Plato, who may be justly called the high priest and the chief mystagogue of those participating in the mysteries of the pure souls (*Plat. Theol.* I.1). Plotinus the Egyptian, he says,

---

[11] Denis O'Brien, "Plotinus and the Secrets of Ammonius," p. 119.

[12] Ibid., p. 118.

[13] Dominic J. O'Meara, *Pythagoras Revived: Mathematics and Philosophy in Late Antiquity* (Oxford: Clarendon Press, 1997), p. 113.

belongs to this "divine chorus" of true priests and hierophants, who are the exegetes of the divine mysteries of Plato and the promoters of the true interpretation of the blessed visions into which they have been initiated. Hence, the Golden Chain of philosophers (which transcends the boundaries of space and time) transmits these mysteries of "the most unadulterated and the purest light of the truth" (*to gnesiotaton kai katharotaton tes aletheias phos*) to future generations.[14] If the role of Plotinus is somewhat crucial in this chain of transmission, as Proclus has suggested, he may then be regarded as a founder of "Neoplatonism," understood in the hieratic sense of "revival" or "return" to the revealed principles of "divine philosophy" (*theia philosophia*).

Plotinus and His School in Rome

In A.D. 243 Plotinus decided to make contact with the sages of Persia and India in order to study their philosophy. On leaving Alexandria, he joined an expedition of the Emperor Gordian III to Persia against the great Shahanshah, the "king of kings," Shapur I. The Sassanian Empire, founded in A.D. 224, was notably unreceptive to Western (Graeco-Roman) influences and supported a rigid Zoroastrian orthodoxy, though Mesopotamia (where the Sassanian capital Ctesiphon became a new center of learning) was an area of many different creeds and "philosophies." The newly arisen religious teacher Mani (A.D. 216-277) was present in the opposing Persian army. However, the Roman Emperor was assassinated in Mesopotamia by his own troops and Plotinus (who supposedly had been in close relations with the Emperor) escaped death by fleeing to Antioch.

After his failure to reach the East—he had perhaps intended to go as far as Afghanistan and the Indus valley where a veneer of Greek (or Graeco-Buddhist) civilization still covered large areas up

[14] John Glucker, *Antiochus and the Late Academy* (Gottingen: Vanderhoeck and Ruprecht, 1978), p. 313.

to the first-second centuries A.D.—Plotinus established himself in Rome in A.D. 245. During his first years in Rome, Plotinus lectured on the philosophy of Ammonius, giving only oral instruction until A.D. 253 when his pupils (the wider circle of Plotinus' school was made up of Roman senators and local aristocracy) persuaded him to commit his lectures to writing. Among Plotinus' patrons were the Emperor Gallienus (whose sole rule extends from A.D. 260 to 268) and his wife Salonina.

Porphyry describes the living ambience of Plotinus as follows:

> Another of his companions was Zethus, an Arab by race, who married the daughter of Theodosius, a friend of Ammonius. He was another medical man and a close friend of Plotinus, who kept trying to divert him from the affairs of state in which he was active and influential. Plotinus was on terms of great intimacy with him and used to go and stay at his place in the country, six miles from Minturnae. This had formerly belonged to Castricius, surnamed Firmus, who was the greatest lover of beauty of all of us and venerated Plotinus. . . . A good many members of the Senate also attended his lectures, of whom Marcellus Orrontius and Sabinillus worked hardest at philosophy. There was also Rogatianus, a senator, who advanced so far in renunciation of public life that he gave up all his property, dismissed all his servants, and resigned his rank.
> . . . There were women, too, who were greatly devoted to philosophy: Gemina, in whose house he lived, and her daughter Gemina, who had the same name as her mother, and Amphiclea, who became the wife of Ariston, son of Iamblichus. Many men and women of the highest rank, on the approach of death, brought him their children, both boys and girls, and entrusted them to him along with all their property, considering that he would be a holy and god-like guardian (*Vita Plot.* 7; 9).

Porphyry the Phoenician stayed with Plotinus only for the six years from A.D. 263 to 268. Plotinus started to write on the subjects that came up in the meetings of the school in the first year of Gallienus (A.D. 253) and produced twenty-one treatises until the appearance of Porphyry, who arrived from Greece with Antonius of Rhodes. Only a few people had received copies of Plotinus' treatises at that time. According to Porphyry, "The issuing of cop-

ies was still a difficult and anxious business, not at all simple and
easy; those who received them were most carefully scrutinized"
(*Vita Plot.* 4).

No less than thirty years after the master's death in A.D. 270
these and other treatises were arranged by Porphyry into six groups
of nine each. This arrangement ignored the actual chronological
order in which the works were written, and so the division into
fifty-four treatises is somewhat artificial. Some treatises were split
up in order to make six enneads, thus giving the title *Enneads* to
the whole collection. The number nine is prominent in ancient
Egyptian theology where the gods are grouped into the Enneads.
The Ennead (*pesedjet*) of Heliopolis represented the structure
of the noetic cosmos constituted by four ontological levels: 1.
Atum, 2. Shu and Tefnut, 3. Geb and Nut, 4. Osiris, Isis, Seth,
and Nephtys. The nine gods (*neteru*) of the great Ennead represent
the intelligible paradigms for the world of manifestation. Further,
according to the Pythagoreans:

> The ennead is the greatest of the numbers within the decad and
> is an unsurpassable limit. At any rate, it marks the end of the
> formation of specific identities. . . . That number admits nothing
> beyond the ennead, but rather everything circles around within
> it, is clear from the so-called recurrences: there is natural pro-
> gression up to it, but after it there is repetition. . . . Hence they
> called it "Oceanus" and "horizon," because it encompasses both
> of these locations and has them within itself.[15]

The Plotinian treatises, as arranged by Porphyry, represent a movement from the earthly realm to the noetic cosmos and the ineffable
One, the supreme God. Thus, the *Enneads* begin with human
goods, proceed to the topics of the physical world, the soul, and
the intelligible reality, and finally reach the One, or the Good.

---

[15] *The Theology of Arithmetic: On the Mystical, Mathematical, and Cosmological
Symbolism of the First Ten Numbers. Attributed to Iamblichus*, trans. Robin Water-
field (Grand Rapids: Phanes Press, 1988), p. 105.

In A.D. 268 the Emperor Gallienus, the main patron of Plotinus, was assassinated and Porphyry, following the advice of Plotinus, departed to Sicily. At the same time an illness from which Plotinus had suffered became worse and he left Rome for Campania, where he died in A.D. 270 in the presence of the physician Eustochius of Alexandria, his devoted disciple. Porphyry describes the last days of his master as follows:

> When the plague broke out and his masseurs died he . . . contracted acute diphtheria. While I was with him no symptoms of this kind appeared, but after I left on my voyage his disease increased. . . . When he was on the point of death, Eustochius told us—as Eustochius had been staying at Puteoli and was late in coming to see him—that Plotinus said, "I have been waiting a long time for you." Then he said, "Try to bring back the god in us to the divine in the All" and, as a snake crept under the bed on which he was lying and disappeared into a hole in the wall, he breathed his last. It was the end of the second year of the reign of Claudius, and according to Eustochius he was sixty-six years old. At the time of his death I, Porphyry, was staying at Lilybaeum, Amelius was at Apamea in Syria, and Castricius was in Rome; only Eustochius was with him (*Vita Plot.* 2).

After the master's death Amelius asked Apollo where the soul of Plotinus had gone and received an oracle that Plotinus had joined the chorus of the blessed ones:

> But now that you have been freed from this tabernacle (*skenos*) and have left the tomb (*sema*) which held your heavenly (*daimonines*) soul, you come at once to the company of heaven, where winds of delight blow, where is affection and desire that charms the sight, full of pure joy, brimming with streams of immortality from the gods which carry the allurements of the Loves, and sweet breeze and the windless brightness of high heaven. There dwell Minos and Rhadamanthus, brethren of the golden race of great Zeus, there righteous Aeacus and Plato, the sacred power, and noble Pythagoras and all who have set the dance of immortal love and won kinship with spirits most blessed, there where the heart keeps festival in everlasting joy. O blessed one, you have borne so many contests and now move among holy spirits, crowned with mighty life (*Vita Plot.* 22).

Plotinus and the Tradition of Hellenic Philosophy

Plotinus is an heir to the great philosophies of the ancient Graeco-Roman world, namely, those of Pythagoras, Plato, and, to a lesser extent, of Aristotle and the Stoics. Hellenic philosophy itself is based on the reinterpreted and rationalized legacy of the Egyptian, Mesopotamian, Syrian, and Anatolian civilizations. It stems from the Orphic and Pythagorean initiations, the mysteries of Osiris, and the ancient solar theologies. This fact is not recognized by most modern Western scholars, who have systematically misunderstood early Hellenic philosophy and failed to take into account its close initial relations with cultic liturgies, theurgic rites, and mythological traditions. According to Peter Kingsley, "Almost everything that's thought certain and sure about early Western philosophy is unsure, and will become even more insecure as the years go by."[16]

Plotinus' philosophy, which embraces and synthesizes traditional Platonic cosmogony, psychology, and mystagogy, is rarely explicit and never articulated in strictly defined theorems. Basing himself on the oral instructions of Ammonius, Plotinus produced and developed a philosophical discourse aimed at liberation from the realm of becoming and the realization of one's true divine identity. In this respect he depended principally on the tradition of "divine philosophy" transmitted by his master Ammonius and his unknown predecessors. Lloyd P. Gerson thus rightly observes that Plotinus was neither original in calling the first Principle of reality "the One," nor in making the Forms, or Ideas, internal to the divine Intellect, nor even in distinguishing the mortal empirical self from the immortal noetic Self, tantamount to one's true inmost nature.[17]

---

[16] Peter Kingsley, *In the Dark Places of Wisdom* (Inverness: The Golden Sufi Center, 1999), p. 38.

[17] Lloyd P. Gerson, "Introduction," in *The Cambridge Companion to Plotinus* (Cambridge: Cambridge University Press, 1996), p. 7.

The transcendent and ineffable One is the source (*arche*) of all beings and the ultimate goal of philosophizing. Since the One "fills all things," it is "everywhere" and "nowhere." The supreme Principle transcends Being and Intellect, which constitute the second divine hypostasis. In this respect the Neoplatonic One is analogous to the ancient Egyptian Nun (or the hidden Amun), the ineffable Principle from which the solar Intellect, Atum-Ra, emerges along with the entire noetic cosmos. Thus, the three Plotinian hypostases, namely, the One (*to hen*), Intellect (*nous*), and Soul (*psuche*) are close to the Egyptian theological triads such as Nun, Atum-Ra, Osiris, or Amun, Ra, Ptah. According to Plotinus, Hesiod's three gods—Ouranos, Kronos, and Zeus—are also equivalent to those metaphysical principles: Ouranos represents the One, Kronos the Intellect, Zeus the Soul. The mutilation of Ouranos in the Hesiod myth may be interpreted as Intellect's return towards the One, and the binding of Kronos in chains means that Intellect keeps the pure Ideas apart from matter.[18]

The concept of the Neoplatonic One is related to the exegesis of Plato's *Parmenides*, which underlies the whole Plotinian metaphysics. According to the testimony of Simplicius (*In Phys.* 231.7-24), who depends in this respect on Porphyry, the Pythagorean philosopher Moderatus (first century A.D.) discerned different ontological levels of reality, which correspond to the eight hypotheses raised in Plato's *Parmenides*. He related the One Beyond Being to hypothesis one, and the One True Being to hypothesis two, basing this view upon a metaphysical interpretation of the second part of the *Parmenides*. According to Moderatus, Plato

> following the Pythagoreans, declares that the first One is above Being and all essence, while the second One—which is the truly existent (*ontos on*) and the object of intellection (*noeton*)—he says is the Forms; the third, which is the soul-realm (*psuchikon*), par-

---

[18] Pierre Hadot, "Ouranos, Kronos, and Zeus in Plotinus' Treatise Against the Gnostics," in *Neoplatonism and Early Christian Thought: Essays in Honour of A.H. Armstrong*, eds. H.J. Blumenthal and R.A. Marcus (London: Variorum, 1981), p. 129.

ticipates (*metechei*) in The One and the Forms, while the lowest nature comes after it, that of the sense realm, does not even participate, but receives order by reflection from those others. . . .[19]

The metaphysical interpretation of the first three or four hypotheses of Plato's *Parmenides* conducted by Moderatus leads to the three main hypostases of Plotinus. However, though this triadic metaphysical structure is supposedly deduced from Plato's text, one cannot maintain that such a division of divine reality is the result of some semiotic game unrelated to the ancient theologies and the structure of reality itself. It seems that Plotinus philosophically articulated and synthesized metaphysical teachings already discussed by Thrasyllus, Moderatus, Numenius, Cronius, and his own master Ammonius. Porphyry cites Longinius saying as follows:

> Plotinus, it would seem, has expounded the principles of Pythagorean and Platonic philosophy more clearly than anyone before him. The works of Numenius and Cronius and Moderatus and Thrasyllus come nowhere near the accuracy of Plotinus' treatises on the same subjects (*Vita Plot.* 20).

Harold Tarrant maintains that Plotinus' influence springs less from any new approach to Platonic exegesis (since the Middle Platonists and Neopythagoreans are forerunners of the Neoplatonists in all respects except in certain metaphysical details and distinctly symbolical interpretations) than from Plotinus' ability to make this exegesis inseparable from his personal mystical and philosophical life. Therefore he was able to provide a much more fresh and detailed account of the Pythagorean and Platonic principles turned into the living experience of the intelligible realities.[20]

Plotinus concentrated himself not on the Socratic aporias and ironies, but on the mystical and metaphysical side of Plato's teaching,

---

[19] John M. Dillon, "General Introduction," in *Proclus' Commentary on Plato's Parmenides* (Princeton: Princeton University Press, 1987), p. xxvi.

[20] Harold Tarrant, *Thrasyllan Platonism* (Ithaca and London: Cornell University Press, 1993), p. 177.

further elaborated and developed in order to repel the Peripatetic and Stoic assault. Thus certain doctrines of Aristotle are crucial for understanding the Plotinian concept of the divine Intellect and the Soul, including some aspects of his physics. Likewise, in spite of a rather critical attitude towards Stoicism, the Stoic accounts of God, *logos*, soul, and nature have all influenced the Plotinian version of Platonism. According to Porphyry, Plotinus' writings

> are full of concealed Stoic and Peripatetic doctrines. Aristotle's *Metaphysics*, in particular, is concentrated in them. . . . In the meetings of the school he used to have the commentaries read, perhaps of Severus, perhaps of Cronius or Numenius or Gaius or Atticus, and among the Peripatetics of Aspasius, Alexander, Adrastus, and others that were available. But he did not just speak straight out of these books but took a distinctive personal line in his consideration, and brought the intellect of Ammonius (*ton Ammoniou pheron noun*) to bear on the investigations in hand (*Vita Plot.* 14.4-17).

Whereas Plotinus used Aristotle to understand and defend Plato, later Neoplatonists (starting already with Porphyry) explicitly declared that, correctly interpreted, Aristotle's philosophy agrees both with Plato's and Plotinus' thought.[21] For example, they held that the eventual purpose of embarking on a study of Aristotle (regarded as a representative of the Lesser Mysteries by Syrianus and Proclus) is to be carried up to the divine Intellect and finally to the ineffable One, though this goal may be achieved only through the Greater Mysteries of Platonic philosophy.

The Plotinian exegesis of Plato is not simply commentary: the philosopher of Lycopolis searched for a single purpose beyond the different intentions of Plato's various texts, thus providing an integral metaphysical interpretation of them. The scattered passages from the *Timaeus*, the *Republic*, the *Parmenides*, the II and VI Epistles (frequently separated from their immediate context),

---

[21] Pierre Hadot, "The Harmony of Plotinus and Aristotle according to Porphyry," in *Aristotle Transformed: The Ancient Commentators and their Influence*, ed. Richard Sorabji (Ithaca and New York: Cornell University Press, 1990), p. 131.

when properly understood, according to Plotinus, teach the doctrine of the three divine hypostases, which serve as a foundation of his ontology and are described in the *Enn.* V.1. Being very selective, Plotinus did not concern himself with following the letter of his master's writings; he thus never cites Plato directly or takes passages in their context, but tries instead to reveal an inner and presumably true intention of Platonic philosophy—its essential meaning.

Plotinus eliminated the so-called Socratic irony and politics from philosophy, at the same time turning any kind of Pythagorean or Platonic dualism into an extreme, both transcendent and immanent, monism, thus praising the supreme Unity from which everything derives and to which everything comes back. Like Plato, but unlike Iamblichus, Plotinus maintains that the soul's purification, ascent, and union with the divine is accomplished primarily through philosophy, accompanied by self-disciple, dialectic, and virtues, though discursive reasoning is rather limited and must finally be transcended, since the vision of truth culminates in mystical union, which is ineffable.

Accordingly, Plotinus transposed Hellenic philosophy into a new key, or rather related it back to the initial mystical vein—not so much by introducing the mystical experience itself (which is partly determined by the particular mythological, cosmological, and religious framework and not always identical to the subjective "experience" in the late Protestant sense), but by relating the hierarchy of metaphysical realities with states of consciousness. In this respect he follows the ancient tradition (known in its different forms from Ramesside Egypt to Upanishadic India) of an inner ascent, transformation, and restoration of one's real divine identity, adapting it to the categories of Hellenic "rationalism" represented by Platonic dialectic and Peripatetic metaphysics. However, his "rationalism" has nothing in common with modern "rationalism." Thus, if the term "rationalism" is understood in its modern deviated sense, we could scarcely label Plotinus as a "rationalist" and thus fully agree with Frithjof Schuon, who says:

It is a mistake to see in Socrates, Plato, and Aristotle the fathers of rationalism, or even of modern thought generally; no doubt they reasoned—Shankara and Ramanuja did so as well—but they never said that reasoning is the alpha and omega of intelligence and of truth, nor *a fortiori* that our experience or our tastes determine thought and have priority over intellectual intuition and logic, *quod absit.*[22]

R.T. Wallis argues that Plotinus' account of consciousness forms a remarkable contrast both with Classical Greek thought and with the Cartesian identification of consciousness with "mental activity."[23] For Plotinus, human "surface consciousness is only one of several levels of awareness," like one particular Sufi *maqam*, or station, which excludes a number of other states and stations. The true reality and one's real divine self-consciousness lies within, away from the sensible world. In this respect Plotinus is a conceptualizer of the ancient anagogic and meditative practices, now partly demythologized and put into the terms of Hellenic logic and scientific theory:

From their earliest days Greek philosophy and science had drawn freely on the ideas of the Near East, which they had habitually given new meaning by organizing them in a conceptual system hitherto lacking, and it is therefore to be expected that the Neoplatonists should have done the same.[24]

However, John Dillon emphasizes that Plotinus' philosophical position arose logically from his acute questioning of the second century A.D. Platonic tradition. This assertion is directed against the "comfortable" attitude that Plotinus' postulation of the transcendent first Principle beyond Being and Intellect is some sort of

[22] Frithjof Schuon, *The Transfiguration of Man* (Bloomington: World Wisdom Books, 1995), p. 4.

[23] R.T. Wallis, *Neoplatonism* (London: Duckworth, 1995), p. 5

[24] Ibid., p. 14.

concession to "Oriental irrationalism" and "mysticism."[25] Dillon recognizes that Plotinus was a mystic but argues that he arrives at his doctrines by trying to solve certain long-standing problems within Platonism. Such a one-sided attitude (though perfectly acceptable in its own particular context) likewise "comfortably" ignores both the larger historical framework of the ancient theologies and the universal character of metaphysics, which is neither simply a result of Plato's exegesis, nor an empty semiotic construction based on certain wishful twists of human imagination.

Plotinus provided an important revision of traditional Hellenic metaphysics, actually arriving at a position quite new in relation to Plato as he is usually understood. But Plotinus' insights were nevertheless based on the experience of noetic and supranoetic realities (which are not "invented" at will by Hellenic, Indian, or Egyptian metaphysicians, in spite of the concrete cultural determinations of discourse). In this sense, one should speak rather of perennial truths, revelations, and imaginative perspectives, though these are adapted to the particular recipients, historical frameworks, and theoretical developments of discursive thinking.

The famous Plotinian phrase *phuge monon pros monon* (*Enn.* VI.9.11), usually rendered as "the flight of the alone to the Alone," far from being his own original "invention," is inherited from the ancient mystical tradition. The formula *monos pros monon* is related to the older formula *monos mono* as "private," "secret," thus presupposing an approach to the divine throne in the temple or in the heart. The Egyptian initiate hopes to see the divinity "alone, face-to-face," and this mystical encounter is symbolically repeated (or modeled on) the encounter with the animated divine statue in the temple's holy of holies. The face-to-face revelatory discourse uses an archaic temple language and is to be understood within the theurgic context, since the flight (or ascent) to the divine Light

---

[25] John M. Dillon, "Plotinus at Work on Platonism," *Greece & Rome*, vol. XXXIX, no. 2, October 1992, p. 194.

of Lights is analogous to the Egyptian ritual for self-deification by uniting with the Sun, Amun-Ra.

Maria Luisa Gatti insists that the main differences between the thought of Plato, ancient Platonism, and Plotinus are of a theoretical nature. They consist, firstly, in the doctrine of the procession of the hypostases from the One, which is arranged according to a circular triad, and secondly, in "creative contemplation": "These constitute the key to the systematic reading of the entire Plotinian philosophy."[26] However, both the procession of different levels of being (within the articulated divine realm) and creative contemplation are attested already in the Egyptian solar theology of Heliopolis. The Eye of Atum-Ra is involved in contemplative return thus forming the first intelligible triad of Atum-Shu-Tefnut.

Metaphysics of Plotinus

Although it is usually held that Plotinus inherited two major problems from his predecessors, i.e., a contradiction between the Pythagorean doctrine of the first Principle as an ultimate unity (the One) and the Peripatetic doctrine (going back to Anaxagoras) that the first Principle is the divine Intellect thinking itself, these two perspectives are in fact easily reconcilable, as numerous examples of different ancient theological systems prove. In fact, only those who are bound to formal discursive reasoning can see a contradiction between *Brahma nirguna* and *Brahma saguna*, the ineffable Principle and personal Ishwara, Parama Shiva and Aham, Nun and Atum, or between apophatic and kataphatic ways of approaching God.

Within the framework of Hellenic philosophy, the realization that Intellect cannot be regarded as the ultimate Principle may be the outcome of exegesis (e.g., metaphysical interpretation of Plato's *Parmenides*), or stem from a rigorous analysis of transcendent unity

---

[26] Maria Luisa Gatti, "Plotinus: The Platonic Tradition and the Foundation of Neo-platonism," p. 28.

as the basic reality. However, the designation of God as *epekeina tes ousias* is not simply a "Platonic" but rather a universal (though sometimes esoteric) truth. For Plotinus, the One is not a "negativity" in the profane sense. Although philosophizing about the One has the concrete result of nullifying itself, this attitude, according to John Bussanich, is "neither nihilist nor antiphilosophical, but . . . points to a soteriontology."[27] The One is boiling with activity, though it is viewed as simple and non-composite, i.e., without parts and internal or external relations. The term "One" does not really describe the Principle, which is beyond form; it is therefore false even to say of it that it is one.

Being formless (*amorphon*) and infinite (*apeiron*), the One, as a perfect actuality (*energeia*), contains everything and lacks nothing, thus having the supreme power (*dunamis*) to generate the noetic world. This does not mean that the One is compelled to generate being, life, and intelligence: it simply causes the existence of all manifested reality by the principle that its inexhaustible perfection and freedom (itself beyond necessity) produces by sheer undiminished giving, like water flowing from a source or light radiating from the sun. Since the One is the universal cause of all things, it is not only transcendent but also immanent: its omnipresence fills all things. The final causality of the One is related to the actualization of Intellect and the mystical return of the soul to its source.

The Intellect proceeds from the One like the Egyptian scarab Khepera emerges from the "waters" of Nun. The first stage of procession from the One is a sort of indefiniteness, tantamount both to the Indefinite Dyad of the Pythagoreans (also attested within the Platonic oral tradition) and to "noetic matter." The contemplative reversion upon its source, the One, makes Intellect properly Intellect. Light plays a significant role in the actualization of Intellect through a "generative radiance" of the One. However, since the One is beyond being and form, Intellect cannot grasp it

---

[27] John Bussanich, "Plotinus' Metaphysics of the One," in *The Cambridge Companion to Plotinus* (Cambridge: Cambridge University Press, 1996), p. 24.

but only sees the supreme image of the One. From this fragmental vision arises the multiplicity of Forms or intelligible beings (noetic gods, spiritual lights) and the actuality of pure thought or intellection (*noesis*).

Intellect thus holds One's light within itself. It is filled by the One's power and this plurality of lights, or intellects, is analogous to the spatial plurality of the sphere that is illuminated by the omnipresent power of light. The One's light is broken into multiple unities by Intellect and these unities are also equated to the Forms. Since Intellect proceeds from the One, the generating light of the One is present in its supreme "image," *Nous*, which may be described as the One viewed through intelligible Matter, that is, as pluralized into Forms. According to the conception of imaging, the immanent presence of the higher generating reality is found in its lower manifestations. Thus the sensible world is regarded as a way of viewing Soul through Matter, which is a principle of plurality, sometimes equated to a non-being.

Although Intellect is the image of the One, Plotinus is very much concerned to safeguard the unity and supremacy of the noetic cosmos. J.H. Fielder says that unlike sensible matter, intelligible Matter belongs to Being and has a noetic life: "Intelligible Matter does provide plurality but that plurality is not acknowledged as the source of *Nous'* being a diminished image of the One."[28] For Plotinus, every Form mirrors the whole of Intellect, but from its own perspective. According to A.H. Armstrong, he understands the world of Forms, or *kosmos noetos*, in terms of direct sense-awareness, not reducing it to "the conceptual skeleton to which even the bodily world of our immediate experience here below has to be reduced to be manageable in scientific discourses."[29] Initially (e.g., in Homer) *nous* is associated with "sensation" rather

---

[28] John H. Fielder, "*Chorismos* and Emanation in the Philosophy of Plotinus," in *The Significance of Neoplatonism*, ed. R. Baine Harris (Norfolk: ISNS, 1976), p. 117.

[29] A.H. Armstrong, "Platonic Mirrors," *Eranos 1987, Jahrbuch*, vol. 56 (Insel Verlag Frankfurt am Main, 1989).

than with intellectual thought, being a kind of internal perception which penetrates deeper into the nature of things. In this sense, intellection (*noesis*) is analogous to the Sufi *dhawq*, which means tasted knowledge, mystical intuition.

The divine Intellect contains the totality of true Being and transcends time; therefore on the level of *Nous* there is perfect identity between subject and object as well as complete self-awareness. The objects of Intellect are pure Forms: each member of the noetic world contemplates the whole of that world, being identical both with the entire intelligible realm and with each individual member. Since discursive thought belongs to the lower level of soul, it contemplates the Forms only at a distance and must be content with mental images reflected in a mirror of *phantasia*.

In the Platonic tradition, the status of imagination is usually low, because it is regarded as a faculty of the lower soul, which depends upon sense perception and from which the rational soul must purify itself in the course of ascent (*anagoge*). However, Plotinus admits that imagination stands on the borderline (*methorion*) between the intelligible and the sensible, thus belonging to the Soul's life: "For this reason Nature does not possess even imagination. Intellection (*noesis*) is superior to imagination. Imagination is between the levels of Nature and of Intellection" (*Enn.* IV.4.3).

Thus *phantasia*, being situated between two levels of soul, is receptive of images both from the noetic realm and the sensible world. Accordingly, Plotinus speaks of two imaginations, two imaging faculties. The lower imagination (which ought to be ruled and dominated by the superior soul) involves no synthesis or judgment: it simply takes in the data of sense perception as discrete images. The higher imagination (or imagination in the primary sense, *prote phantasia*) is able to synthesize the data of sense perception and is called *doxa*, "opinion." However, as John Dillon has pointed out, besides synthesizing the reports of the senses, it also mirrors the activities of the divine Intellect:

> In the course of discussion as to why we are not always conscious of the activity of *nous* within us, Plotinus presents *phantasia* as

a mirror for intellectual activity, which only performs properly when the "surface" of the soul, so to speak, is unruffled by passion, and thus "smooth." But when this is broken because the harmony of the body is upset, thought and intellect operate without an image, and then intellectual activity takes place without *phantasia*.[30]

Plotinus is concerned with preserving *phantasia* in the disembodied soul, while at the same time being unable to reject its traditional Platonic designation as the slave of sense perception (*aisthesis*) and the irrational passions. Contrary to Plato's anachronistic attitudes, he recognizes the active and creative use of imagination on the spiritual way. A mystical vision may be achieved through the correct performance of spiritual exercises which involve *phantasmata*, like those described at *Enn.* V.8.9. John Dillon says:

> But in one important respect Plotinus goes beyond, and indeed against, Plato, and that is in the value he places on the artistic imagination—or at least in the imagination of some divinely-inspired artists, such as Pheidias. His doctrine here was a great consolation later to Platonically-minded artists of the Renaissance, such as Michelangelo, to whom Plato would have given short shrift.[31]

For Plotinus, the three divine hypostases are repeated within each individual microcosm, though the higher levels of consciousness are not accessible to all human beings and are actualized only through spiritual and philosophical practice. Therefore *Nous* is attained by turning within and leaving sense-perception behind. The world of Forms, or spiritual lights, is the object of mystical experience, though the "undifferentiated unity" corresponds to the first hypostasis, the One. Nonetheless, R.T. Wallis argues that the distinction between the One and Intellect cannot correspond in any form to the distinction between so-called "theistic" and

[30] John Dillon, "Plotinus and the Transcendent Imagination," in *Religious Imagination*, ed. J.P. Mackey (Edinburgh: University of Edinburgh Press, 1986), p. 56.

[31] Ibid., p. 61.

"monistic" mysticism. We cannot identify the mystical experience of Intellect with the vision of a unity running through the external world, if this unity is opposed to the "introvertive" union with the One.[32] The individual intellect (which in the realm of earthly existence may be veiled or darkened by the passions or ignorance) is an image of Intellect, just as Soul as a whole is an image of Intellect. The Forms of *Nous* are not simply self-subsistent universals but both thinking beings (analogous to the angels of the later Islamic philosophies) and objects of intellection.

All things proceed through productive contemplation (*theoria*) and are in the great contemplative return, which is simply the other side of the creative outgoing from the One. Therefore at every stage of reality the ontological hierarchy is constituted by true and living images, or reflections. The mirror does not just passively receive the reflection, but is active in contemplating, and the movement of contemplation through all the mirroring levels of the universe (*to pan*) is at every level open to the presence of "that which cannot be mirrored or imagined."[33]

Being itself the image of the One, Intellect contains in archetype all kinds of things found at lower levels of the hierarchy, which consists in a series of prototypes and images. Being an image (*eikon*) entails being different from that which is the archetype; the image is thus in some way inferior to the archetype. However, the image necessarily depends on its archetype and is somewhat similar to it. This dependence operates in one direction only, therefore the lower always depends on the higher but not vice versa. The One provides the existence of things, not their *ousia* (essence, or substance), which derives from the second principle, Intellect as the *arche* of Forms. The Forms in Intellect are not an image of Forms in the One, since otherwise Intellect would not have knowledge of Forms, but only of images.

---

[32] Richard T. Wallis, "NOYΣ as Experience," in *The Significance of Neoplatonism*, ed. R. Baine Harris (Norfolk: ISNS, 1976), p. 122.

[33] A.H. Armstrong, *Platonic Mirrors*, p. 172.

The One is the supreme *arche* of all and cannot be deprived of its *energeia* because all multiplicity flows from the superabundance of the One and must be referred back to the One. So, is the Plotinian metaphysics "creationist" or "emanationist"? Lloyd Gerson, who raises this question, says that to think of emanating, irradiating, or flowing in contrast to creating is to make a sort of category mistake:

> For metaphors are not properly contrasted with technical termi-
> nology. If one wants convincing on this point, we need only recall
> that Aquinas sometimes uses the same metaphor in behalf of an
> explanation of creation, not in contrast to it. . . . But Plotinus,
> too, says that the One is perfect and that it acts according to its
> will (*boulesis*). So, whereas Aquinas contrasts the alternatives of
> acting by necessity and acting by will (and intellect), Plotinus
> contrasts acting by necessity and acting on the basis of discursive
> reasoning. . . . So to say that the One acts by necessity could mean
> nothing else but that it acts according to its will.[34]

For Plotinus, Soul is the image of *Nous*, although Soul is frequently regarded as belonging to the realm of Being and Intellect. Every image, in order to be dependent on its archetype, must preserve its unity, structure, and value, which remind us of the existence of a higher reality that is immanently present throughout the plurality of the image. The very being of *eikon* depends upon the inner presence of *paradeigma* that makes it what it is. But Soul, though being an image of *Nous*, also has the characteristic lower intellectual activity of discursive thought, reasoning, reckoning, and planning: she is not, like Intellect, wholly absorbed in contemplation, but is active in forming, animating, and ruling the sensible world as a whole and all of its parts. Since Soul turns to Intellect in her contemplative *epistrophe*, she is united with Intellect and thus keeps the iconic-contemplative relationship which holds together all levels of the cosmos.

[34] Lloyd P. Gerson, "Plotinus' Metaphysics: Emanation or Creation?" *The Review of Metaphysics*, vol. XLVI, no. 3, March 1993, pp. 559-561.

Time appears as the life of Soul, in contrast to the Eternity (*aion*) of Intellect. Analogously, *dianoia*, or discursive reasoning, is contrasted to the non-discursive *noesis* of Intellect. Discursive reasoning and planning are, however, only characteristic of the lower levels of Soul, especially the individual human *psuchai*, which descend from Soul regarded as the third divine hypostasis. Therefore Plotinus distinguishes between 1) the hypostasis Soul, 2) the World-Soul, and 3) the individual soul. Both the World-Soul and the individual souls proceed from Soul the hypostasis. In this descent the separate souls decline from their identity with Intellect through a desire for self-identity.

But Soul cannot descend into Matter in such a way as to be affected by it: the mixing of Soul with Matter is similar to the immanent presence of the light-principle in the sphere. Hence, it cannot be viewed materialistically. Soul is not combined with Matter but is immanently present in it. Thus Soul pervades all things: the universe lies in Soul, which bears it up, and nothing is without a share of Soul. The world is like a net immersed in the living psychic "waters." Plotinus follows both Plato and Aristotle: he accepts Aristotle's sharp distinction of Soul and Intellect, maintaining the transcendence of *Nous*, at the same time preserving their continuity, since in Plato *nous* is *psuche* at its highest level at which the elevated soul (restored to its primeval noetic nature) can contemplate the Forms. Thus, A.H. Armstrong argues:

> All the levels of psychic activity, including the noetic or contemplative, which is not clearly distinguished from the dianoetic and reasoning, are continuous, and there is no break, still less any sense of tension and opposition, between contemplative-rational activity and the external activities which should be directed by it. This applies both to divine and human *psuche*.[35]

---

[35] A.H. Armstrong, "Aristotle in Plotinus: The Continuity and Discontinuity of Psyche and Nous," in *Aristotle and the Later Tradition*, ed. Henry Blumenthal and Howard Robinson (Oxford: Clarendon Press, 1991), p. 117.

Plotinus maintains that soul is present to the body as light is to air. For the rational soul, the ideal is to liken oneself to God, thus leaving the realm of Nature and all sensible phenomena. Nature, regarded as a "power which makes," does not need to reason or inquire: it makes by contemplating Soul and it is in its contemplation that the world is produced. Ultimately, Nature's "wisdom" depends on that of the divine Intellect. If matter can be regarded as "evil" (in no positive sense), this is because it is absolutely non-existent and formless. Nevertheless, it is necessary for the completion of the universe. The existence of Form compels the existence of Matter, since every form requires a substrate in which it is lodged. Therefore just as sensible matter is filled by the immanent presence of Soul, so intelligible Matter is illuminated by the One, taking light from outside itself, and thus providing the matrix in which a higher level of reality may be immanently present. Just as light is weakened through its dispersion in the air, so is form weakened when dispersed into matter.

Mystical Experience, Self-Knowledge, and Union with the One

Plotinus invites us, through philosophical reflection, spiritual meditation, and virtue to reach the divine Intellect and contemplate the beauty of noetic archetypes, or Forms. Thus, according to J.H. Fielder, "one of the functions of the *Enneads* is to be a spiritual guide to this transcendence,"[36] as if piercing through the fog of ignorance or ascending from the dark cave of phenomena to the immortal realm of *Nous*, in order to see the true archetypal Reality of which the world constitutes a partial image. As H.J. Blumenthal says:

[36] John H. Fielder, "*Chorismos* and Emanation in the Philosophy of Plotinus," p. 112.

Reuniting ourselves with this intellect of ours, and ultimately transcending it, by union, or reunion, with whatever lies "above," be it the One or the One and Intellect, remains a fundamental aspiration for Neoplatonists. This is so whether that reunion means turning ourselves away from other preoccupations to our intellect's perpetual activity, as for Plotinus himself, or rising to it as for Iamblichus and those who came after him.[37]

Following Plato (*Phaed.* 67c), Plotinus conceived philosophy as a preparation for death. He also accepted Aristotle's statement that only the life according to intellect (*bios kata noun: Nicomach. Eth.* 118a6) is proper to man. For this reason Porphyry described the aim (*telos*) of philosophy as return to one's real Self which is *Nous*. Hence, the goal of life is to live according to the divine Intellect (*zen kata noun: De abst.* 1.29.4). If the soul wishes to contemplate the ineffable One, the Good, it must be "intellectified" (*nootheisa*) and be reunited with the divine *Nous*, which does not belong to any individual, but is rather universal. As Pierre Hadot has pointed out:

> Thus, we could say that the mystical experience of the soul consists in living the life of the divine Intellect and in associating itself with the immediate experience of the presence of the Good, as lived by the Intellect. In other words, the summit of the mystical experience of the soul is the mystical experience of the Intellect itself with which the soul has succeeded, for a moment, in identifying.[38]

The mystical experience in Platonism and Neoplatonism is implicitly based on the Eleusinian model, because both the term "mystical" itself (which, for Plotinus, designates simply the "hidden meaning") and the notion of the experience of God as an

[37] Henry J. Blumenthal, "On Soul and Intellect," in *The Cambridge Companion to Plotinus*, ed. Lloyd P. Gerson (Cambridge: Cambridge University Press, 1996), p. 100.

[38] Pierre Hadot, "Plotinus and Porphyry," in *Classical Mediterranean Spirituality: Egyptian, Greek, Roman*, ed. A.H. Armstrong (London: Routledge and Kegan Paul, 1986), p. 244.

epiphany of Light and vision (*epopteia*), derive from the philosophical interpretation of the Eleusinian and Ra-Osirian mysteries.

Ascension through the different levels of reality brings about a radical transformation of the being through the realization that the physical body and its constituents are a part of a much greater whole and that the human mind depends upon a superior divine Intellect, which illuminates it and permits it to think. The spiritual ascent is not a theoretical journey undertaken by reason, but (like the Sufi *mi'raj*) it is a movement in consciousness, active imagination, and spirit, which transforms one's being and brings an inner unification and union (*henosis*) with the divine. The supreme goal of human life is to be united to the Good who is above all things. As Stephen R.L. Clark maintains:

> Really, there is nothing that is truly ours that we can lose. Whatever seems to have been lost and divided from us, in this changing world, is There, where "all things are filled full of life, and, we may say, boiling with life" (*Enn.* VI.7.12.23-24).[39]

According to Plotinus, "our concern is not to be free of sin, but to be god" (*alla theon einai: Enn.* I.2.6.2-3). The soul must become "all things." However, "soul" is not a fixed entity, but rather a label for a variety of psychic and intellectual activities. It seems that Plotinus distinguished the concept of soul (*psuche*) and the egocentric consciousness, or self ("we," *hemeis*), which is lower than the "undescended" summit of the soul and higher that the subconscious processes. This moving "center of consciousness" is the subject both of "vulgar" ethical behavior and the "civic" virtues.[40] Soul is regarded as a continuum extending from the summit of the soul, which is constantly united to the divine Intellect (since

---

[39] Stephen R.L. Clark, "Plotinus: Body and Soul," in *The Cambridge Companion to Plotinus*, ed. Lloyd P. Gerson (Cambridge: Cambridge University Press, 1996), p. 291.

[40] John M. Dillon, "An Ethic for the Late Antique Sage," in *The Cambridge Companion to Plotinus*, ed. Lloyd P. Gerson (Cambridge: Cambridge University Press, 1996), p. 326.

"even our soul does not altogether come down, but there is always something of it in the intelligible": *Enn.* IV.8.8.1-3), through the empirical self, right down to the irrational image (*eidolon*) that is called *hemeis*, a fluctuating spotlight of consciousness.

The aspiration for self-realization, or self-knowledge, is the aspiration for one's true identity with the archetypal summit through the self's reverting upon itself. The incorporeal self cannot be known discursively. When consciousness returns to the stage of pure intellection and realizes its eternal unity with *Nous*, it is no longer soul: it has become Intellect. It is not clear whether Plotinus posits Forms of individual men (which, like all members of the noetic cosmos, at their highest must be intellects themselves), since an individual soul appears only when "the fluctuating focus of self" sinks below the level of Intellect and is somewhat "separated," though its eternal Form remains intact. In any case, as Plato Mamo has observed: "Having been established in the divine *Nous* we are no longer men."[41]

The journey to the noetic realm consists both in reflecting on the sensible world (viewed in its real symbolic and theophanic sense) and in turning within, toward the interior of the soul. For Plotinus, the role of beauty is to recall us to a knowledge of Forms, thus ascending to the true Beauty through the practice of virtues and purifications (*katharseis*). In this respect Plotinus follows Plato (*Symp.* 206d, *Phaed.* 69bc). All anagogic methods are employed in order to attain the spiritual separation of the soul and the body (the "death" conducted by the "initiation into the mysteries") and to live according to Intellect, thus contemplating both the beauties of the cosmos and the splendor of the noetic light which shines from within. Eventually, the soul attains to identification with *Nous* through the practice of concentration—not upon anything external, but upon its own immaterial self as the pure subject of awareness. If one wishes to understand this transformation in the

---

[41] Plato Mamo, "Is Plotinian Mysticism Monistic?" in *The Significance of Neoplatonism*, ed. R. Baine Harris (Norfolk: ISNS, 1976), p. 205.

terms of "mystical experience," it begins when the soul turns to its own interior and enters into direct touch with the light of the divine Intellect.

The model of imitation for the true "lover of wisdom" is the Soul of the World which is not disturbed by the body of the sensible cosmos that it governs. Therefore the sage (*sophos*) must act like the impassive universal Soul (which eternally contemplates the divine *Nous* and the Forms within *Nous* as the archetypes of the sensible realm) and unite the human intellect to the divine Intellect. J.M. Rist says:

> Plotinus is certainly confident that purification and dialectic will lead to their goal of union, since the universe has been providentially arranged to allow for this possibility and since man possesses a faculty capable of attaining this goal; but there is an element in the procedure that is outside the control of even the noblest philosopher. The One is present to those who look, but no man can be the judge of his own fitness to receive the vision, and hence, even with the aid of the highest aspect of *nous*, no man can attain union with the One by a quasi-magical or ritualist fulfillment of obligations. The One is ineffable and unknowable in terms of intellect. . . .[42]

Since there is within *Nous* a kind of unity derived from the One's presence, the awareness (*sunesis*) of the One arises not by intellection (*noesis*), as does awareness of the Forms, but by the mystical union (*henosis*) achieved through the "prime part of *nous*," tantamount to the "flower of the intellect" (*anthos nou*) of the *Chaldean Oracles*. Just as the Intellect is reached by becoming *noeideis* (*nous*-like), so the One is reached by becoming *henoeideis* (*hen*-like, i.e., like the One itself). Thus the way to the Good takes one beyond knowing. One must not chase after the Good, but "wait quietly till it appears" (*Enn.* V.5.8).4-5), like the descending grace, *Shaktipata*, in the Trika Shaivism of Kashmir. Plotinus says: "Shut your eyes, and change to and wake another way of seeing,

[42] John M. Rist, "Mysticism and Transcendence in Later Neoplatonism," in *Platonism and its Christian Heritage* (London: Variorum Reprints, 1985), p. 215.

which everyone has but few use" (*Enn.* I.6.8.24-27). The commentary provided by Deirdre Carabine is as follows:

> Since the One cannot know himself, it follows that the way of knowing is not appropriate as a means of attaining unity with the One. . . . Plotinus always speaks of the unity experienced at this level in terms of light and vision, although he emphasizes the fact that this "seeing" must be understood metaphorically, not in terms of having a real object present before the eyes. The true end of the soul is to "see" that light alone in itself, not through the medium of any other thing; this kind of vision excludes the possibility of the soul knowing that it is united with the One. The soul can no longer distinguish itself from the object of its intuition.[43]

The object and the act of vision have become identical, since "seeing and the seen coincide, and the sun is like the seeing and the seeing is like the sun" (*Enn.* V.3.8.16-17). The awakening in the presence of the Good is the result of the removal of multiplicity through negation, of putting away all "otherness" and reaching the ineffable union, since it is only by the One that we see the One. Thus "the two become one" (*ta duo hen ginetai*) through "simplification" (*haplosis*), contemplative vision (*theoria*), and union (*henosis*). This kind of "ecstasy" (when the ego is obliterated and one sees the formless), regarded as a return to the supreme Source, is a cosmic or rather divine event, "not a temporal event in the history of this person."[44] This is because it is not the soul or the empirical ego that "survives." Not only the ego, but the noetic self established in the divine Intellect is apparently lost in the supreme mystical union.

The eternal intelligible structure of *Nous* remains intact, though the normal self-awareness disappears when Intellect is immersed into the One's presence, being "senseless and in love" (*aphron*

---

[43] Deirdre Carabine, "A Thematic Investigation of the Neoplatonic Concepts of Vision and Unity," *Hermathena: A Trinity College Dublin Review*, no. CLVII, Winter 1994, p. 46.

[44] Plato Mamo, "Is Plotinian Mysticism Monistic?", p. 206.

kai eron). Therefore the "experience" of the Good (although the soul already has ceased to be itself and became one with its transcendent source) is modeled as loving union. This love incites the soul to assimilate itself to the pure object it loves. And since the One transcends both form (*eidos, morphe*) and intellection (*noesis*), whoever loves it must discard all form, image, and thought. Only by following this way, the soul (which lost its distinct individual "soulness") participates in the infinite desire of *Nous*, the divine Intellect, stricken with love for its ultimate Source, the One. Therefore the relation to the Good, as the transcendent Light of Lights, is established through the mystical love in which culminates the "erotic", i.e., philosophical, life. Strictly speaking, the divine Intellect is eternally united with the One and the soul shares this union when it is "annihilated" and realizes its ineffable roots in the Good.

Plotinus between East and West

Christian mysticism and negative theology, starting with the fourth century Cappadocian Fathers, came under strong Plotinian influence. Owing to the translation of Plotinus into Latin by Marius Victorinus, Plotinus (though sometimes viewed through Porphyrian eyes) became the main source of philosophical inspiration to such authors as Augustine (354-430). Plotinian philosophy proved to be extremely attractive. It may be regarded as an integral part of the Hellenic tradition of piety and religious reflection which, according to A.H. Armstrong and J.P. Kenney, issued in its own kind of "monotheism"—very different from the now widely recognized "classical Christian theism":

> Plotinus might, just conceivably, have accepted Christ as a theophany, and a great one, if he had been preached to him differently. But he could never have accepted him as the one and only theophany, excluding and devaluing all others.[45]

---

[45] A.H. Armstrong, "Plotinus and Christianity," in *Platonism in Late Antiquity*, ed. Stephen Gersh and Charles Kannengiesser (Notre Dame: University of Notre

J.P. Kenney argues that the "mystical monotheism" of Plotinus represents the coalescence of many disparate, theistic elements in Graeco-Roman religious thought. The One might therefore be said to have been "the culmination of Hellenic theism, the philosophical articulation of an increasingly significant strand in ancient theology."[46] The ineffable first Principle of Plotinus remained, as Kenney says, the only real deity throughout Neoplatonic theology, despite of any "polytheism" admitted at the level of religious observance:

> And because it remained rooted in Platonic, degree-of-reality theology, the modalistic aspects of Plotinian theology could never develop into monism, where only the One was real and all other beings were but its illusory epiphenomena. The theology of Plotinus should thus be understood not as monistic or pantheistic but as a special and distinctive sort of monotheism; Neoplatonism is not an advaitic archipelago into Western thought.[47]

Our task is not to contest terms and debate whether the Plotinian philosophy is "monotheistic," "monistic," or "pantheistic," because all of these terms are inventions of much later aggressive ideological quarrels and serve to impose a distinctively Western, Christian, or even "modern" perspective.

From the sixth until the fifteenth century (when Marsilio Ficino rendered the *Enneads* into Latin along with other Neoplatonic writings brought from Byzantium) the text of Plotinus was unknown in Western Europe, though still available in the Greek- and Arabic-speaking East. Franz Rosenthal argues that though Plotinus as a distinct person faded entirely among Muslims, his ideas became all the more acceptable for Islamic theology and mysticism:

Dame Press, 1992), pp. 127-128.

[46] John Peter Kenney, *Mystical Monotheism: A Study in Ancient Platonic Theology* (Hanover and London: Brown University Press, 1991), p. 155.

[47] Ibid., p. 156.

It has sometimes been claimed that Plotinus exercised the greatest single influence on the formation of Muslim civilization
as we have come to know it. This would seem to be a bit of
an exaggeration, but there can be no doubt that his work and
thought most profoundly affected Muslim intellectual and spiritual life. . . . As a result, Muslim medieval civilization became
imbued with an extraordinary measure of coherence and, at the
same time, manifoldness which gave it strength and vitality. If
the world of Islam was able to dominate intellectual life from
India to the Atlantic ocean for many centuries, this can justly be
ascribed to the fact that it had found in the work of Plotinus and
his spiritual descendants a powerhouse which made it possible
for it always to restore its creative impulses in a way which its
purely religious foundations, broad and inspiring though they
were, would have been unable to provide.[48]

The Islamic scholars (for example, al-Qifti, who wrote in the
first half of the thirteenth century) knew Plotinus as "a philosopher
resident in the land of the Greeks" (*bilad Yunan*). Presumably,
al-Shaykh al-Yunani, discussed by al-Shahrastani, is Plotinus.
However, Plotinus exercised his influence on the Islamic world
under the mask of Aristotle, and the Arabic version of the *Enneads*
paradoxically became known as the *Theology (Uthulujiya) of
Aristotle*. Some modern scholars argue that his *Theology* is a portion
of a compilation on philosophical theology prepared for al-Kindi
(d. 866) and his circle, also including selections from Proclus and
Alexander of Aphrodisias.[49] The *Theology of Aristotle* is actually a
collection of excerpts from *Enneads* IV-VI, along with connecting
material, unknown in Greek, and attributed to Porphyry. Its title
runs as follows:

---

[48] Franz Rosenthal, "Plotinus in Islam: The Power of Anonymity," *Atti del lon-
vegno internazionale sul tema: Plotino e il Neoplatonismo in Oriente e in Occidente*,
Accademia Nazionale dei Lincei, anno 371, Quaderno no. 198 (Rome, 1974), p.
437.

[49] John Walbridge, *The Leaven of the Ancients: Suhrawardi and the Heritage of the
Greeks* (Albany: SUNY Press, 2000), p. 133. See also F.W. Zimmermann, "The
Origins of the So-Called *Theology of Aristotle*," in *Pseudo-Aristotle in the Middle
Ages*, ed. J. Kraye et al (London: The Warburg Institute, 1986), pp. 110-240.

The book of Aristotle the Philosopher, called in Greek *Theologia*, being the discourse on the Divine Sovereignty (*rububiya*); the interpretation (*tafsir*) of Porphyry of Tyre, translated into Arabic by 'Abd al-Masih Ibn Na'ima of Emessa and corrected for Ahmad ibn al-Mu'tasim bi'llah by Abu Yusuf Ya'qub ibn Ishaq al-Kindi.

For this reason, Islamic philosophers and Sufis were convinced that Aristotle was also a mystic, even a kind of divine sage (*hakim muta'allih*). Shihab al-Din al-Suhrawardi, the Shaykh al-Ishraq (1153-1191), to whom the *Theology of Aristotle* was the most perfect example of the "divine philosophy" available, writes how he saw Aristotle, the author of the *Uthulujiya*, in a dream and asked if the Islamic Peripatetics were the real philosophers. Aristotle (i.e., Plotinus) answered negatively, arguing rather that the Sufis, such as Abu Yazid al-Bistami and Sahl al-Tustari were the real philosophers.[50] Thus Plotinus is indirectly recognized as a predecessor of the Sufis, who pass beyond theoretical knowledge (*'ilm suri*) to the knowledge of presence (*'ilm huduri, 'ilm shuhudi*).

Some contemporary scholars maintain that the philosophy of Plotinus serves as a vehicle which is able to bridge the so-called gap between East and West, though this artificial separation of East and West, much emphasized by the nineteenth century Orientalists, now seems rather anachronistic. L.J. Hatab observes that the thought of Plotinus presents a striking parallel to the forms of thought found in the *Upanishads*. For example, the four-fold structure of reality exposed in the *Mandukya Upanishad* (namely, the mantric syllable AUM which constitutes 1) the waking state of *viraj*, 2) the dream state of Hiranyagarbha, the World-Soul, 3) the dreamless state of Ishwara, and 4) the transcendent peace of Brahman) is analogous to the Plotinian Nature, Soul, Intellect, and the transcendent One:

[50] Seyyed Hossein Nasr, *The Intellectual Tradition in Persia*, ed. Mehdi Amin Razavi (Richmond: Curzon Press, 1996), p. 147.

Here the syllable AUM is seen as representing Brahman. This *Upanishad* views the levels of reality from the standpoint of the stages of consciousness leading to a realization of Brahman, and corresponds to Plotinus viewing a metaphysical structure in terms of spiritual attitudes, the inward ascension of the soul to the One.[51]

The *Enneads* are compared to the *Bhagavadgita* as well, because the path by which Plotinus leads his disciples and readers from ego-centered particularity to spiritual universality is "a path which leads on to something very like *moksha*, that union with the One or Good which lies beyond the true universe of *Nous.*"[52]

For R.K. Tripathi, the contemplative philosophy of Plotinus seems to be very close to the philosophy of Shankara (788-822). He compares the Plotinian ecstasy to what is called *samadhi* in Advaita Vedanta, arguing that both Plotinus and Shankara viewed philosophy as a way of life.[53] In certain respects, the Neoplatonic concept of *nous* corresponds to that of *atman-purusha-brahman.* While observing that *Brahman* appears as the object of one's knowledge (*jnana*) only when one is united with *Brahman,* and *Nous* appears as the object of one's *gnosis* only when the knower himself is united with *Nous,* A.H. Armstrong and R.R. Ravindra seek to show the striking parallels between ancient Indian thought and the *Enneads* of Plotinus:

> What is said of the man who has become *brahman* agrees almost exactly with what Plotinus says about the man who has become *nous.* And a man becomes *brahman* or *nous* because he always

[51] Lawrence J. Hatab, "Plotinus and the Upanishads," in *Neoplatonism and Indian Thought,* ed. R. Baine Harris (Norfolk: ISNS, 1982), p. 36.

[52] A.H. Armstrong and R.R. Ravindra, "*Buddhi* in the *Bhagavadgita* and *Psyche* in Plotinus," in *Neoplatonism and Indian Thought,* ed. R. Baine Harris (Norfolk: ISNS, 1982), pp. 64-65.

[53] R.K. Tripathi, "Advaita Vedanta and Neoplatonism," in *Neoplatonism and Indian Thought,* ed. R. Baine Harris (Norfolk: ISNS, 1982), p. 237.

was so. It is only that now he realizes it; this seeing or realizing is the same as becoming it.[54]

I.C. Sharma even equates the philosophical way to the One, described by Plotinus, with Buddhi-Yoga, maintaining that Yoga (the word derives from the root which means "to unite" or "to join"), as the means of the union of the soul with the One, and the state of that union itself, is analogous to the mystical path of Plotinus. Both lead to the Supreme Self, *Paramapurusha*, the Neoplatonic One.[55]

Owing to all these similarities (though more detailed comparison of Neoplatonic and Indian philosophies is beset with considerable difficulties), the debate is held for and against Eastern sources of Plotinus' philosophy. As A.M. Wolters aptly remarked, this is a debate for and against the "purity" of his philosophy, assuming (according to the ideological standards of the modern Western and so-called Europocentric mentality) that the Hellenic tradition stands for rationalism, objectivity, respectability, and clarity of thought, in contrast to "Eastern" impurity, superstition, mysticism, and irrationalism.[56] For those who regard the anti-traditional West as the apex of civilization, to admit "oriental influences" means not only to contaminate one's good name, but also to fall outside the line of "progress." These colonial attitudes continue to underline the theories of development claiming Western superiority even in respect of "mysticism" (which means to make Plotinus more prestigious through the "Westernization" of his philosophy),

[54] A.H. Armstrong and R.R. Ravindra, "*Buddhi* in the *Bhagavadgita* and *Psyche* in Plotinus," p. 81.

[55] I.C. Sharma, "The Plotinian One and the Concept of *Paramapurusa* in the *Bhagavadgita*," in *Neoplatonism and Indian Thought*, ed. R. Baine Harris (Norfolk: ISNS, 1982), p. 89.

[56] Albert M. Wolters, "A Survey of Modern Scholarly Opinion on Plotinus and Indian Thought," in *Neoplatonism and Indian Thought*, ed. R. Baine Harris (Norfolk: ISNS, 1982), p. 295.

though, in fact, all true mystical traditions are neglected, derided, or caricatured by the modernists.

Be that as it may, all discussions of "influences" and "sources" depend on a particular positivist view of history and on one's notion of historical causality. Certainly, the structural parallels between Plotinus and the *Upanishads* cannot prove any direct Indian influence, as E. Brehier and his uncritical followers (chiefly Indologists) maintain. H.R. Schwyzer, P. Henry, A.H. Armstrong, L.P. Gerson, J. Dillon, J. Trouillard, R.T. Wallis, and other eminent scholars (thus constituting the overwhelming academic consensus) argue that Plotinus must be understood strictly in terms of the Hellenic tradition, since his philosophy is a genuine Hellenic growth stemming from the creative interpretation of Plato, Aristotle, the Stoics, the Middle Platonists, and the Neopythagoreans. This position is well-founded and would seem to be true, especially bearing in mind that different traditions of the *philosophia perennis* are not necessarily a result of certain mechanical "influences" but rather depend on common archetypes. Frithjof Schuon expresses this attitude as follows:

> This question of knowing whether or not there is a historical connection between the "Eye of the Heart" of Plotinian doctrine, Augustinian doctrine, and Sufi doctrine ('*Ayn al-Qalb*) is doubtless insoluble and in any case unimportant from the standpoint at which we place ourselves; it suffices to know that this idea is fundamental and is met with almost everywhere.[57]

However, if it is clear that Neoplatonism (or simply Platonism) may be safely derived and deduced from Hellenic sources, we should not forget that the Platonic tradition itself is only a part (or the "modernized" and philosophically articulated version) of the ancient religious and mystical traditions which flourished as far as the Ramesside Egypt of the New Kingdom, Assyria, and Upanishadic India. As regards certain Augustinian and Sufi doc-

[57] Frithjof Schuon, *The Eye of the Heart* (Bloomington: World Wisdom Books, 1997), p. 6.

trines (mentioned by Schuon) we are almost certain that they are directly inherited from Plotinus or other Hellenic sources, at least in respect of their theoretical discourse, terms, and images. But, instead of asserting that "there is nothing Oriental about Neoplatonism," we ought to remember that so-called pre-Socratic thought is already a modified version of "Oriental" beliefs spread throughout the Achaemenid Empire, which extended from Ionia to Bactria and the Indus valley.

Now the crucial question may be asked: who, eventually, decided that ancient Greece belongs to the West, especially to the Christianized, Protestant, or Modern and Postmodern "West"? The early Greek and Upanishadic teachings stem from common or very similar backgrounds; therefore reciprocal influences are to be excepted. Thomas McEvilley discerns two massive transfers of ideas and methods of thinking: first from India into Greece in the pre-Socratic period and then from Greece back into India in the Hellenistic period, when the transmission of Hellenic logical and dialectical traditions shaped the formal structure and scientific concepts of Indian philosophical schools which had been proto-dialectical before this transmission. He says:

> Upanishadic influences on the pre-Socratics seem likely to have included monistic solutions to the problem of the One and the Many, the doctrine of the transformation of the elements into one another, at least the ethical aspect of the reincarnation doctrine associated with it, and elements or aspects of the doctrine of the cosmic cycle; at the same time Jain influences were entering Greece through the Orphic community.[58]

However, the formation of the Upanishadic tradition itself is inseparable from the much older Mesopotamian (or Sumero-Dravidian) and Egyptian influences—that widespread diffusion of Near Eastern cultural models which belong to the so-called Bronze Age synthesis, itself rooted in the Neolithic-Chalcolithic Age. Be

[58] Thomas McEvilley, *The Shape of Ancient Thought: Comparative Studies in Greek and Indian Philosophies* (New York: Alworth Press, 2002), p. 642.

that as it may, those historical, esoteric, or simply imagined routes of transmission are utterly irrelevant to the spiritual seeker who concentrates his spiritual eye upon "the only thing needful."

Remarks on MacKenna's Translation

Stephen MacKenna (1872-1935), the renowned translator of Plotinus into English, was not a Classical scholar, but a journalist without even a university degree. He was born in Liverpool as a son of an improvident Irish officer in the Indian Army. He visited Greece to fight the Turks and became European correspondent of the *New York World*. While staying in St. Petersburg (Russia) he discovered the *Enneads* of Plotinus and later devoted himself to their translation for two decades. Only in 1930 was MacKenna's life work over. Though he based his translation on the 1883 Teubner edition of Richard Volkmann and the 1935 Oxford edition of Friedrich Creuzer (which are very imperfect if compared with the modern Henry and Schwyzer edition), MacKenna's translation is truly inspiring and only on rare occasions incorrect. MacKenna had asserted that to translate Plotinus was "worth a life." The recent translation made by A.H. Armstrong[59] is truer to the original on the literal level, but sometimes lacks the stylistic qualities and beauty characteristic of the MacKenna's version.

In the MacKenna translation the first hypostasis of Plotinus is rendered as the One, or First Existent; the second hypostasis, Intellect, as the Divine Mind; and the third hypostasis, Soul, as the All-Soul.

The present selection from the *Enneads*, translated by Stephen MacKenna, is aimed not so much at the modern Classical scholar, but rather at those students of Plotinus who are spiritual seekers and who accept the metaphysical premises of *sophia perennis*, the

---

[59] Plotinus, *The Enneads*, trans. A.H. Armstrong, 7 volumes (Cambridge, Mass.: Heinemann, 1966-1988).

eternal wisdom, which has so many different "archetypal faces" and historical manifestations.

Algis Uždavinys

Plotinus

THE ENNEADS

Ennead I
Second Tractate

ON THE VIRTUES

This treatise belongs to the group of works written before the arrival of Porphyry. It is a commentary on Plato's *Theaetetus* (176a) and explains in what sense the virtues can make us godlike. Plotinus uses some ideas taken from Aristotle's *Nichomachean Ethics*, where two kinds of virtue, intellectual and moral, are discerned. Plotinus makes a distinction between the civic virtues (*politikai aretai*) and the purificatory virtues (*kathartikai aretai*). The civic virtues are described in Plato's *Republic* as the norms according to which one should act in this life, but they are not sufficient to attain likeness to God (*homoiosis theo: Theaet.* 176b) which is regarded as the end (*telos*) of life. The purificatory virtues help to free one from the body and are particularly discussed in Plato's *Phaedo*. According to John Dillon:

> It is clear that for Plotinus any action must be evaluated primarily from the perspective of its capacity to assimilate us to the divine realm. All earthly concerns, such as love for family or kin, not to mention care for the poor and oppressed, and all passions, such as pity or grief, must be shaken off (like clothes at an initiation ceremony) in the process of purification.[1]

Porphyry formalized the distinction between the civic and purificatory virtues, adding two other grades, namely, the theoretic virtues (of the soul which contemplates *nous* within itself) and the paradigmatic virtues (proper to *Nous*, the divine Intellect itself). Iamblichus elaborated this scheme further, thus making seven grades of virtue that resemble the seven steps of initiation in the mysteries leading to the supreme God, the ineffable One. In this elaborate hierarchy there are: 1) natural (*phusikai*), 2) ethical (*ethikai*), 3) civic (*politikai*), 4) purificatory (*kathartikai*), 5)

[1] John M. Dillon, "An Ethic for the Late Antique Sage," in *The Cambridge Companion to Plotinus*, ed. Lloyd P. Gerson (Cambridge: Cambridge University Press, 1996), p. 320.

theoretic (*theoretikai*), 6) paradigmatic (*paradeigmatikai*), and 7) hieratic (*hieratikai*) virtues.

1. Since Evil is here, "haunting this world by necessary law," and it is the Soul's design to escape from Evil, we must escape hence.

But what is this escape?

"In attaining Likeness to God," we read. And this is explained as "becoming just and holy, living by wisdom," the entire nature grounded in Virtue.

But does not Likeness by way of Virtue imply Likeness to some being that has Virtue? To what Divine Being, then, would our Likeness be? To the Being—must we not think?—in Which, above all, such excellence seems to inhere, that is to the Soul of the Cosmos and to the Principle ruling within it, the Principle endowed with a wisdom most wonderful. What could he more fitting than that we, living in this world, should become Like to its ruler?

But, at the beginning, we are met by the doubt whether even in this Divine-Being all the virtues find place—Moral-Balance (*Sophrosune*), for example; or Fortitude where there can be no danger since nothing is alien; where there can be nothing alluring whose lack could induce the desire of possession.

If, indeed, that aspiration towards the Intelligible which is in our nature exists also in this Ruling-Power, then we need not look elsewhere for the source of order and of the virtues in ourselves.

But does this Power possess the Virtues?

We cannot expect to find There what are called the Civic Virtues, the Prudence which belongs to the reasoning faculty; the Fortitude which conducts the emotional and passionate nature; the *Sophrosune* which consists in a certain pact, in a concord between the passionate faculty and the reason; or Rectitude which is the due application of all the other virtues as each in turn should command or obey.

Is Likeness, then, attained, perhaps, not by these virtues of the social order but by those greater qualities known by the same general name? And if so do the Civic Virtues give us no help at all?

It is against reason utterly to deny Likeness by these while admitting it by the greater: tradition at least recognizes certain men of the civic excellence as divine, and we must believe that these too had in some sort attained Likeness: on both levels there is virtue for us, though not the same virtue.

Now, if it be admitted that Likeness is possible, though by a varying use of different virtues and though the civic virtues do not suffice, there is no reason why we should not, by virtues peculiar to our state, attain Likeness to a model in which virtue has no place.

But is that conceivable?

When warmth comes in to make anything warm, must there needs be something to warm the source of the warmth?

If a fire is to warm something else, must there be a fire to warm that fire?

Against the first illustration it may be retorted that the source of the warmth does already contain warmth, not by an infusion but as an essential phase of its nature, so that, if the analogy is to hold, the argument would make Virtue something communicated to the Soul but an essential constituent of the Principle from which the Soul attaining Likeness absorbs it.

Against the illustration drawn from the fire, it may be urged that the analogy would make that Principle identical with virtue, whereas we hold it to be something higher.

The objection would be valid if what the Soul takes in were one and the same with the source, but in fact virtue is one thing, the source of virtue is quite another. The material house is not identical with the house conceived in the intellect, and yet stands in its likeness: the material house has distribution and order while the pure idea is not constituted by any such elements; distribution, order, symmetry are not parts of an idea.

So with us: it is from the Supreme that we derive order and distribution and harmony, which are virtues in this sphere: the

Existences There, having no need of harmony, order, or distribution, have nothing to do with virtue; and, none the less, it is by our
possession of virtue that we become like to Them.

Thus much to show that the principle that we attain Likeness
by virtue in no way involves the existence of virtue in the Supreme.
But we have not merely to make a formal demonstration: we must
persuade as well as demonstrate.

2. First, then, let us examine those good qualities by which we
hold Likeness comes, and seek to establish what is this thing which,
as we possess it, in transcription, is virtue, but as the Supreme possesses it, is in the nature of an exemplar or archetype and is not
virtue.

We must first distinguish two modes of Likeness.

There is the likeness demanding an identical nature in the
objects which, further, must draw their likeness from a common
principle: and there is the case in which B resembles A, but A is a
Primal, not concerned about B and not said to resemble B. In this
second case, likeness is understood in a distinct sense: we no longer
look for identity of nature, but on the contrary, for divergence,
since the likeness has come about by the mode of difference.

What, then, precisely is Virtue, collectively and in the particular? The clearer method will be to begin with the particular, for so
the common element by which all the forms hold the general name
will readily appear.

The Civic Virtues, on which we have touched above, are a
principle of order and beauty in us as long as we remain passing
our life here: they ennoble us by setting bound and measure to
our desires and to our entire sensibility, and dispelling false judgment—and this by sheer efficacy of the better, by the very setting
of the bounds, by the fact that the measured is lifted outside of the
sphere of the unmeasured and lawless.

And, further, these Civic Virtues—measured and ordered
themselves and acting as a principle of measure to the Soul which
is as Matter to their forming—are like to the measure reigning in
the over-world, and they carry a trace of that Highest Good in

the Supreme; for, while utter measurelessness is brute Matter and wholly outside of Likeness, any participation in Ideal-Form produces some corresponding degree of Likeness to the formless Being There. And participation goes by nearness: the Soul nearer than the body, therefore closer akin, participates more fully and shows a godlike presence, almost cheating us into the delusion that in the Soul we see God entire.

This is the way in which men of the Civic Virtues attain Likeness.

3. We come now to that other mode of Likeness which, we read, is the fruit of the loftier virtues: discussing this we shall penetrate more deeply into the essence of the Civic Virtue and be able to define the nature of the higher kind whose existence we shall establish beyond doubt.

To Plato, unmistakably, there are two distinct orders of virtue, and the civic does not suffice for Likeness: "Likeness to God," he says, "is a flight from this world's ways and things": in dealing with the qualities of good citizenship he does not use the simple term Virtue but adds the distinguishing word civic: and elsewhere he declares all the virtues without exception to be purifications.

But in what sense can we call the virtues purifications, and how does purification issue in Likeness?

As the Soul is evil by being interfused with the body and by coming to share the body's states and to think the body's thoughts, so it would be good, it would be possessed of virtue, if it threw off the body's moods and devoted itself to its own Act—the state of Intellection and Wisdom—never allowed the passions of the body to affect it—the virtue of *Sophrosune*—knew no fear at the parting from the body—the virtue of Fortitude—and if reason and the Intellectual-Principle ruled without opposition—in which state is Righteousness. Such a disposition in the Soul, become thus intellective and immune to passion, it would not be wrong to call Likeness to God; for the Divine, too, is pure and the Divine-Act is such that Likeness to it is Wisdom.

But would not this make virtue a state of the Divine also?

No: the Divine has no states; the state is in the Soul. The Act of Intellection in the Soul is not the same as in the Divine: of things in the Supreme, one (the Intellectual-Principle) has a different mode of intellection (from that of Soul), the other (the Absolute One) has none at all.

Then yet again, the one word, Intellection, covers two distinct Acts?

Rather there is primal Intellection and there is Intellection deriving from the Primal and of other scope.

As speech is the echo of the thought in the Soul, so thought in the Soul is an echo from elsewhere: that is to say, as the uttered thought is an image of the soul-thought, so the soul-thought images a thought above itself and is the interpreter of the higher sphere.

Virtue, in the same way, is a thing of the Soul: it does not belong to the Intellectual-Principle or to the Transcendence.

4. We come, so, to the question whether Purification is the whole of this human quality, virtue, or merely the forerunner upon which virtue follows? Does virtue imply the achieved state of purification or does the mere process suffice to it, Virtue being something of less perfection than the accomplished pureness which is almost the Term?

To have been purified is to have cleansed away everything alien: but Goodness is something more.

If before the impurity entered there was Goodness, the cleansing suffices; but even so, not the act of cleansing but the cleansed thing that emerges will be The Good. And it remains to establish what (in the case of the cleansed Soul) this emergent is.

It can scarcely prove to be The Good: The Absolute Good cannot be thought to have taken up its abode with Evil. We can think of it only as something of the nature of good but paying a double allegiance and unable to rest in the Authentic Good.

The Soul's true Good is in devotion to the Intellectual-Principle, its kin; evil to the Soul lies in frequenting strangers. There is no other way for it than to purify itself and so enter into relation with its own; the new phase begins by a new orientation.

52

After the Purification, then, there is still this orientation to be made? No: by the purification the true alignment stands accomplished.

The Soul's virtue, then, is this alignment? No: it is what the alignment brings about within.

And this is. . . ?

That it sees; that, like sight affected by the thing seen, the Soul admits the imprint, graven upon it and working within it, of the vision it has come to.

But was not the Soul possessed of all this always, or had it forgotten?

What it now sees, it certainly always possessed, but as lying away in the dark, not as acting within it: to dispel the darkness, and thus come to the knowledge of its inner content, it must thrust towards the light.

Besides, it possessed not the originals but images, pictures; and these it must bring into closer accord with the verities they represent. And, further, if the Intellectual-Principle is said to be a possession of the Soul, this is only in the sense that It is not alien and that the link becomes very close when the Soul's sight is turned towards It: otherwise, ever-present though It be, It remains foreign, just as our knowledge, if it does not determine action, is dead to us.

5. So we come to the scope of the purification: that understood, the nature of Likeness becomes clear. Likeness to what principle? Identity with what God? The question is substantially this: how far does purification dispel the two orders of passion— anger, desire, and the like, with grief and its kin—and in what degree the disengagement from the body is possible.

Disengagement means simply that the Soul withdraws to its own place.

It will hold itself above all passions and affections. Necessary pleasures and all the activity of the senses it will employ only for medicament and assuagement lest its work be impeded. Pain it may combat, but, failing the cure, it will bear meekly and ease it by refusing to assent to it. All passionate action it will check: the suppression will be complete if that be possible, but at worst the Soul will never itself take fire but will keep the involuntary and uncontrolled outside its own precincts and rare and weak at that. The Soul has nothing to dread, though no doubt the involuntary has some power here too: fear therefore must cease, except so far as it is purely monitory. What desire there may be can never be for the vile; even the food and drink necessary for restoration will lie outside the Soul's attention, and not less the sexual appetite: or if such desire there must be, it will turn upon the actual needs of the nature and be entirely under control; or if any uncontrolled motion takes place, it will reach no further than the imagination, be no more than a fleeting fancy.

The Soul itself will be inviolately free and will be working to set the irrational part of the nature above all attack, or if that may not be, then at least to preserve it from violent assault, so that any wound it takes may be slight and be healed at once by virtue of the Soul's presence; just as a man living next door to a Sage would profit by the neighborhood, either in becoming wise and good himself or, for sheer shame, never venturing any act which the nobler mind would disapprove.

There will be no battling in the Soul: the mere intervention of Reason is enough: the lower nature will stand in such awe of Reason that for any slightest movement it has made it will grieve, and censure its own weakness, in not having kept low and still in the presence of its lord.

6. In all this there is no sin—there is only matter of discipline— but our concern is not merely to be sinless but to be God.

As long as there is any such involuntary action, the nature is twofold, God and Demi-God, or rather God in association with a nature of a lower power: when all the involuntary is suppressed, there is God unmingled, a Divine Being of those that follow upon The First.

For, at this height, the man is the very being that came from the Supreme. The primal excellence restored, the essential man is There: entering this sphere, he has associated himself with a lower phase of his nature but even this he will lead up into likeness with his highest self, as far as it is capable, so that if possible it shall never be inclined to, and at the least never adopt, any course displeasing to its over-lord.

What form, then, does each virtue take in one so lofty?

Wisdom and understanding consist in the contemplation of all that exists in the Intellectual-Principle, and the Intellectual-Principle itself apprehends this all (not by contemplation but) as an immediate presence.

And each of these has two modes according as it exists in the Intellectual-Principle and in the Soul: in the Soul it is Virtue, in the Supreme not Virtue. In the Supreme, then, what is it?

Its proper Act and Its Essence.

That Act and Essence of the Supreme, manifested in a new form, constitute the virtue of this sphere. For the Ideal-Form of Justice or of any other virtue is not itself a virtue, but, so to speak, an exemplar, the source of what in the Soul becomes virtue: for virtue is dependent, seated in something not itself; the Ideal-Form is self-standing, independent.

But taking Rectitude to be the due ordering of faculty does it not always imply the existence of diverse parts?

No: there is a Rectitude of Diversity appropriate to what has parts, but there is another, not less Rectitude than the former though it resides in a Unity. And the authentic Absolute-Rectitude is the Act of a Unity upon itself, of a Unity in which there is no this and that and the other.

On this principle, the supreme Rectitude of the Soul is that it direct its Act towards the Intellectual-Principle: its Restraint (*Sophrosune*) is its inward bending towards the Intellectual-Principle; its Fortitude is its being impassive in the likeness of That towards Which its gaze is set, Whose nature comports an impassivity which the Soul acquires by virtue and must acquire if it is not to be at the mercy of every state arising in its less noble companion.

7. The virtues in the Soul run in a sequence correspondent to that existing in the over-world, that is among their exemplars in the Intellectual-Principle.

In the Supreme, Intellection constitutes Knowledge and Wisdom; self-concentration is *Sophrosune*; Its proper Act is Its Dutifulness; Its Immateriality, by which It remains inviolate within Itself, is the equivalent of Fortitude.

In the Soul, the direction of vision towards the Intellectual-Principle is Wisdom and Prudence, soul-virtues not appropriate to the Supreme where Thinker and Thought are identical. All the other virtues have similar correspondences.

And if the term of purification is the production of a pure being, then the purification of the Soul must produce all the virtues; if any are lacking, then not one of them is perfect.

And to possess the greater is potentially to possess the minor, though the minor need not carry the greater with them.

Thus we have indicated the dominant note in the life of a Sage; but whether his possession of the minor virtues be actual as well as potential, whether even the greater are in Act in him or yield to qualities higher still, must be decided afresh in each several case.

Take, for example, Contemplative-Wisdom. If other guides of conduct must be called in to meet a given need, can this virtue hold its ground even in mere potentiality?

And what happens when the virtues in their very nature differ in scope and province? Where, for example, *Sophrosune* would allow certain acts or emotions under due restraint and another virtue would cut them off altogether? And is it not clear that all may have to yield, once Contemplative-Wisdom comes into action?

The solution is in understanding the virtues and what each has to give: thus the man will learn to work with this or that as every several need demands. And as he reaches to loftier principles and other standards these in turn will define his conduct: for example, Restraint in its earlier form will no longer satisfy him; he will work for the final Disengagement; he will live, no longer, the human life of the good man—such as Civic Virtue commends—but, leaving this beneath him, will take up instead another life, that of the Gods.

For it is to the Gods, not to the good, that our Likeness must look: to model ourselves upon good men is to produce an image of an image: we have to fix our gaze above the image and attain Likeness to the Supreme Exemplar.

Ennead I
Third Tractate

ON DIALECTIC

This treatise is closely connected with the preceding one: if the goal of life (to become godlike) is established, the soul must be purified by separating itself from the body and ascending to the realm of *Nous*. This "separation" is analogous to the initiatic "death" practiced by the ancient Egyptian priests and later by the Sufis. Plotinus usually makes a distinction between the ascent to Intellect, in which the Forms are contemplated, and the final ascent to the One, which transcends the noetic cosmos. Dialectic is related to the former ascent, namely, the passing of the soul from sensible to intelligible reality on the upward path. Plotinus based his description on Plato's *Phaedrus* and *Symposium*. However, if the philosopher (*philosophos*), the musician (*mousikos*), and the lover (*erotikos*) are three different descriptions of the same kind of person in *Phaedrus* (248d), for Plotinus they are three distinct people. The philosopher goes up to the divine Intellect "by nature," but the musician and the lover must be led by schooling. Plotinus asserts the superiority of Platonic dialectic (as the science of wisdom which serves for the soul's ascent to the intelligible unity) to Aristotelian and Stoic logic.

1. What art is there, what method, what discipline to bring us there where we must go?

The Term at which we must arrive we may take as agreed: we have established elsewhere, by many considerations, that our journey is to the Good, to the Primal-Principle; and, indeed, the very reasoning which discovered the Term was itself something like an initiation.

But what order of beings will attain the Term?

Surely, as we read, those that have already seen all or most things, those who at their first birth have entered into the life-germ from which is to spring a metaphysician, a musician, or a born lover, the metaphysician taking to the path by instinct, the musician and the nature peculiarly susceptible to love needing outside guidance.

But how lies the course? Is it alike for all, or is there a distinct method for each class of temperament?

For all there are two stages of the path, as they are making upwards or have already gained the upper sphere.

The first degree is the conversion from the lower life; the second—held by those that have already made their way to the sphere of the Intelligibles, have set as it were a footprint there but must still advance within the realm—lasts until they reach the extreme hold of the place, the Term attained when the topmost peak of the Intellectual realm is won.

But this highest degree must bide its time: let us first try to speak of the initial process of conversion.

We must begin by distinguishing the three types. Let us take the musician first and indicate his temperamental equipment for the task.

The musician we may think of as being exceedingly quick to beauty, drawn in a very rapture to it: somewhat slow to stir of his own impulse, he answers at once to the outer stimulus: as the timid are sensitive to noise so he to tones and the beauty they convey; all that offends against unison or harmony in melodies or rhythms repels him; he longs for measure and shapely pattern.

This natural tendency must be made the starting-point to such a man; he must be drawn by the tone, rhythm, and design in things of sense: he must learn to distinguish the material forms from the Authentic-Existent which is the source of all these correspondences and of the entire reasoned scheme in the work of art: he must be led to the Beauty that manifests itself through these forms; he must be shown that what ravished him was no other than the Harmony of the Intellectual world and the Beauty in that sphere, not some one shape of beauty but the All-Beauty, the Absolute Beauty; and the truths of philosophy must be implanted in him to lead him to faith in that which, unknowing it, he possesses within himself. What these truths are we will show later.

2. The born lover, to whose degree the musician also may attain—and then either come to a stand or pass beyond—has a certain memory of beauty but, severed from it now, he no longer comprehends it: spellbound by visible loveliness he clings amazed about that. His lesson must be to fall down no longer in bewildered delight before some one embodied form; he must be led, under a system of mental discipline, to beauty everywhere and made to discern the One Principle underlying all, a Principle apart from the material forms, springing from another source, and elsewhere more truly present. The beauty, for example, in a noble course of life and in an admirably organized social system may be pointed out to him—a first training this in the loveliness of the immaterial—he must learn to recognize the beauty in the arts, sciences, virtues; then these severed and particular forms must be brought under the one principle by the explanation of their origin. From the virtues he is to be led to the Intellectual-Principle, to the Authentic-Existent; thence onward, he treads the upward way.

3. The metaphysician, equipped by that very character, winged already and not, like those others, in need of disengagement, stirring of himself towards the supernal but doubting of the way, needs only a guide. He must be shown, then, and instructed, a willing wayfarer by his very temperament, all but self-directed.

Mathematics, which as a student by nature he will take very easily, will be prescribed to train him to abstract thought and to faith in the unembodied; a moral being by native disposition, he must be led to make his virtue perfect; after the Mathematics he must be put through a course in Dialectic and made an adept in the science.

4. But this science, this Dialectic essential to all the three classes alike, what, in sum, is it?

It is the Method, or Discipline, that brings with it the power of pronouncing with final truth upon the nature and relation of things—what each is, how it differs from others, what common quality all have, to what Kind each belongs and in what rank each stands in its Kind and whether its Being is Real-Being, and how many Beings there are, and how many non-Beings to be distinguished from Beings.

Dialectic treats also of the Good and the not-Good, and of the particulars that fall under each, and of what is the Eternal and what the not-Eternal—and of these, it must be understood, not by seeming-knowledge ("sense-knowledge") but with authentic science.

All this accomplished, it gives up its touring of the realm of sense and settles down in the Intellectual Cosmos and there plies its own peculiar Act: it has abandoned all the realm of deceit and falsity, and pastures the Soul in the "Meadows of Truth": it employs the Platonic division to the discernment of the Ideal-Forms, of the Authentic-Existence, and of the First-Kinds (or Categories of Being): it establishes, in the light of Intellection, the affiliations of all that issues from the Firsts, until it has traversed the entire Intellectual Realm: then, by means of analysis, it takes the opposite path and returns once more to the First Principle.

Now it rests: instructed and satisfied as to the Being in that sphere, it is no longer busy about many things: it has arrived at Unity and it contemplates: it leaves to another science all that coil of premises and conclusions called the art of reasoning, much as it leaves the art of writing: some of the matter of logic, no doubt, it considers necessary—to clear the ground—but it makes itself the judge, here as in everything else; where it sees use, it uses; anything it finds superfluous, it leaves to whatever department of learning or practice may turn that matter to account.

5. But whence does this science derive its own initial laws?

The Intellectual-Principle furnishes standards, the most certain for any soul that is able to apply them. What else is necessary Dialectic puts together for itself, combining and dividing, until it has reached perfect Intellection. "For," we read, "it is the purest (perfection) of Intellection and Contemplative-Wisdom." And, being the noblest method and science that exists it must needs deal with Authentic-Existence, The Highest there is: as Contemplative-

Wisdom (or true-knowing) it deals with Being, as Intellection with what transcends Being.

What, then, is Philosophy?

Philosophy is the supremely precious.

Is Dialectic, then, the same as Philosophy?

It is the precious part of Philosophy. We must not think of it as the mere tool of the metaphysician: Dialectic does not consist of bare theories and rules: it deals with verities; Existences are, as it were, Matter to it, or at least it proceeds methodically towards Existences, and possesses itself, at the one step, of the notions and of the realities.

Untruth and sophism it knows, not directly, not of its own nature, but merely as something produced outside itself, something which it recognizes to be foreign to the verities laid up in itself; in the falsity presented to it, it perceives a clash with its own canon of truth. Dialectic, that is to say, has no knowledge of propositions—collections of words—but it knows the truth and, in that knowledge, knows what the schools call their propositions: it knows above all the operation of the Soul, and, by virtue of this knowing, it knows, too, what is affirmed and what is denied, whether the denial is of what was asserted or of something else, and whether propositions agree or differ; all that is submitted to it, it attacks with the directness of sense-perception and it leaves petty precisions of process to what other science may care for such exercises.

6. Philosophy has other provinces, but Dialectic is its precious part: in its study of the laws of the universe, Philosophy draws on Dialectic much as other studies and crafts use Arithmetic, though, of course, the alliance between Philosophy and Dialectic is closer.

And in morals, too, Philosophy uses Dialectic: by Dialectic it comes to contemplation, though it originates of itself the moral state or rather the discipline from which the moral state develops.

Our reasoning faculties employ the data of Dialectic almost as their proper possession, for their use of these data commonly involves Matter as well as Form.

And while the other virtues bring the reason to bear upon particular experiences and acts, the virtue of Wisdom (i.e. the virtue peculiarly induced by Dialectic) is a certain super-reasoning much closer to the Universal; for it deals with (such abstract ideas as) correspondence and sequence, the choice of time for action and inaction, the adoption of this course, the rejection of that other: Wisdom and Dialectic have the task of presenting all things as Universals and stripped of matter for treatment by the Understanding.

But can these inferior kinds of virtue exist without Dialectic and philosophy? Yes—but imperfectly, inadequately.

And is it possible to be a Sage, a Master in Dialectic, without these lower virtues?

It would not happen: the lower will spring either before or together with the higher. And it is likely that everyone normally possesses the natural virtues from which, when Wisdom steps in, the perfected virtue develops. After the natural virtues, then, Wisdom, and so the perfecting of the moral nature. Once the natural virtues exist, both orders, the natural and the higher, ripen side by side to their final excellence: or as the one advances it carries forward the other towards perfection.

But, ever, the natural virtue is imperfect in vision and in strength—and to both orders of virtue the essential matter is from what principles we derive them.

Ennead I
Sixth Tractate

ON BEAUTY

This treatise, which Porphyry identified as the earliest essay written by Plotinus, should be read with the later study *On the Intelligible Beauty* (V.8). Though the treatise is devoted to beauty (*kalon*), for Plotinus there is no independent sphere of aesthetics (as is the case of the modern Western attitude), and the theory of beauty is thus inseparable from the spiritual path and mysticism. All things in this world are beautiful only by their participation in the Forms, or noetic Archetypes. Plotinus' discussion is based on Plato's *Symposium* (206d), especially Diotima's speech, *Phaedrus* (the regrowing of the wings of the soul, 250e ff), and the Cave Simile of *Republic* VII. For Plotinus, to ascend to the intelligible Form is to reach the true divine Beauty. This is achieved through the practice of virtues, purifications (*katharseis*), and an assimilation to the intelligible world. According to Jean-Marc Narbonne:

> The soul is delighted in beauty because through the recognition of the imprint of that in which it participates and finds the source of its being, it comes to recognize itself. In noticing the Form which unifies and structures the diverse parts of a certain work; in perceiving the concept shaping otherwise insignificant matter, the soul discovers in nature or in the artifact the cohesive force of the Idea, the organizing principle which communicates symmetry, measure, and beauty to the object. And in its own self-recognition it is lightened, because it now can aspire to its own inner harmony and seek to re-ascend to that principle inside itself which regulates, unites, and appeases.[2]

1. Beauty addresses itself chiefly to sight; but there is a beauty for the hearing too, as in certain combinations of words and in all

---

[2] Jean-Marc Narbonne, "Action, Contemplation, and Interiority in the Thinking of Beauty in Plotinus," in *Neoplatonism and Western Aesthetics*, ed. Aphrodite Alexandrakis (Albany: SUNY Press, 2002), p. 5.

kinds of music, for melodies and cadences are beautiful; and minds that lift themselves above the realm of sense to a higher order are aware of beauty in the conduct of life, in actions, in character, in the pursuits of the intellect; and there is the beauty of the virtues. What loftier beauty there may be, yet, our argument will bring to light.

What, then, is it that gives comeliness to material forms and draws the ear to the sweetness perceived in sounds, and what is the secret of the beauty there is in all that derives from Soul?

Is there some One Principle from which all take their grace, or is there a beauty peculiar to the embodied and another for the bodiless? Finally, one or many, what would such a Principle be?

Consider that some things, material shapes for instance, are gracious not by anything inherent but by something communicated, while others are lovely of themselves, as, for example, Virtue.

The same bodies appear sometimes beautiful, sometimes not; so that there is a good deal between being body and being beautiful.

What, then, is this something that shows itself in certain material forms? This is the natural beginning of our inquiry.

What is it that attracts the eyes of those to whom a beautiful object is presented, and calls them, lures them, towards it, and fills them with joy at the sight? If we possess ourselves of this, we have at once a standpoint for the wider survey.

Almost everyone declares that the symmetry of parts towards each other and towards a whole, with, besides, a certain charm of color, constitutes the beauty recognized by the eye, that in visible things, as indeed in all else, universally, the beautiful thing is essentially symmetrical, patterned.

But think what this means.

Only a compound can be beautiful, never anything devoid of parts; and only a whole; the several parts will have beauty, not in themselves, but only as working together to give a comely total. Yet beauty in an aggregate demands beauty in details: it cannot be constructed out of ugliness; its law must run throughout.

All the loveliness of color and even the light of the sun, being devoid of parts and so not beautiful by symmetry, must be ruled out of the realm of beauty. And how comes gold to be a beautiful thing? And lightning by night, and the stars, why are these so fair?

In sounds also the simple must be proscribed, though often in a whole noble composition each several tone is delicious in itself.

Again since the one face, constant in symmetry, appears sometimes fair and sometimes not, can we doubt that beauty is something more than symmetry, that symmetry itself owes its beauty to a remoter principle?

Turn to what is attractive in methods of life or in the expression of thought; are we to call in symmetry here? What symmetry is to be found in noble conduct, or excellent laws, in any form of mental pursuit?

What symmetry can there be in points of abstract thought?

The symmetry of being accordant with each other? But there may be accordance or entire identity where there is nothing but ugliness: the proposition that honesty is merely a generous artlessness chimes in the most perfect harmony with the proposition that morality means weakness of will; the accordance is complete.

Then again, all the virtues are a beauty of the Soul, a beauty authentic beyond any of these others; but how does symmetry enter here? The Soul, it is true, is not a simple unity, but still its virtue cannot have the symmetry of size or of number: what standard of measurement could preside over the compromise or the coalescence of the Soul's faculties or purposes?

Finally, how by this theory would there be beauty in the Intellectual-Principle, essentially the solitary?

2. Let us, then, go back to the source, and indicate at once the Principle that bestows beauty on material things.

Undoubtedly this Principle exists; it is something that is perceived at the first glance, something which the Soul names as from an ancient knowledge and, recognizing, welcomes it, enters into unison with it.

But let the Soul fall in with the Ugly and at once it shrinks within itself, denies the thing, turns away from it, not accordant, resenting it.

Our interpretation is that the Soul—by the very truth of its nature, by its affiliation to the noblest Existents in the hierarchy of Being—when it sees anything of that kin, or any trace of that kinship, thrills with an immediate delight, takes its own to itself, and thus stirs anew to the sense of its nature and of all its affinity.

But, is there any such likeness between the loveliness of this world and the splendors in the Supreme? Such a likeness in the particulars would make the two orders alike: but what is there in common between beauty here and beauty There?

We hold that all the loveliness of this world comes by communion in Ideal-Form.

All shapelessness whose kind admits of pattern and form, as long as it remains outside of Reason and Idea, is ugly by that very isolation from the Divine-Thought. And this is the Absolute Ugly: an ugly thing is something that has not been entirely mastered by pattern, that is by Reason, the Matter not yielding at all points and in all respects to Ideal-Form.

But where the Ideal-Form has entered, it has grouped and co-ordinated what from a diversity of parts was to become a unity: it has rallied confusion into co-operation: it has made the sum one harmonious coherence: for the Idea is a unity and what it moulds must come to unity as far as multiplicity may.

And on what has thus been compacted to unity, Beauty enthrones itself, giving itself to the parts as to the sum: when it lights on some natural unity, a thing of like parts, then it gives itself to that whole. Thus, for an illustration, there is the beauty, conferred by craftsmanship, of all a house with all its parts, and the beauty which some natural quality may give to a single stone.

This, then, is how the material thing becomes beautiful – by communicating in the thought (Reason, *Logos*) that flows from the Divine.

3. And the Soul includes a faculty peculiarly addressed to Beauty—one incomparably sure in the appreciation of its own, when Soul entire is enlisted to support its judgment.

Or perhaps the Soul itself acts immediately, affirming the Beautiful where it finds something accordant with the Ideal-Form within itself, using this Idea as a canon of accuracy in its decision.

But what accordance is there between the material and that which antedates all Matter?

On what principle does the architect, when he finds the house standing before him correspondent with his inner ideal of a house, pronounce it beautiful? Is it not that the house before him, the stones apart, is the inner idea stamped upon the mass of exterior matter, the indivisible exhibited in diversity?

So with the perceptive faculty: discerning in certain objects the Ideal-Form which has bound and controlled shapeless matter, opposed in nature to Idea, seeing further stamped upon the common shapes some shape excellent above the common, it gathers into unity what still remains fragmentary, catches it up and carries it within, no longer a thing of parts, and presents it to the Ideal-Principle as something concordant and congenial, a natural friend: the joy here is like that of a good man who discerns in a youth the early signs of a virtue consonant with the achieved perfection within his own soul.

The beauty of color is also the outcome of a unification: it derives from shape, from the conquest of the darkness inherent in Matter by the pouring-in of light, the unembodied, which is a Rational-Principle and an Ideal-Form.

Hence it is that Fire itself is splendid beyond all material bodies, holding the rank of Ideal-Principle to the other elements, making ever upwards, the subtlest and sprightliest of all bodies, as very near to the unembodied; itself alone admitting no other, all the others penetrated by it: for they take warmth but this is never cold; it has color primally; they receive the Form of color from it: hence the splendor of its light, the splendor that belongs to the Idea. And all that has resisted and is but uncertainly held by its light remains outside of beauty, as not having absorbed the plenitude of the Form of color.

And harmonies unheard in sound create the harmonies we hear and wake the Soul to the consciousness of beauty, showing it the one essence in another kind: for the measures of our sensible music are not arbitrary but are determined by the Principle whose labor is to dominate Matter and bring pattern into being.

Thus far of the beauties of the realm of sense, images and shadow-pictures, fugitives that have entered into Matter—to adorn, and to ravish, where they are seen.

4. But there are earlier and loftier beauties than these. In the sense-bound life we are no longer granted to know them, but the Soul, taking no help from the organs, sees and proclaims them. To the vision of these we must mount, leaving sense to its own low place.

As it is not for those to speak of the graceful forms of the material world who have never seen them or known their grace—men born blind, let us suppose—in the same way those must be silent upon the beauty of noble conduct and of learning and all that order who have never cared for such things, nor may those tell of the splendor of virtue who have never known the face of Justice and of Moral-Wisdom beautiful beyond the beauty of Evening and of Dawn.

Such vision is for those only who see with the Soul's sight—and at the vision, they will rejoice, and awe will fall upon them and a trouble deeper than all the rest could ever stir, for now they are moving in the realm of Truth.

This is the spirit that Beauty must ever induce, wonderment and a delicious trouble, longing and love and a trembling that is all delight. For the unseen all this may be felt as for the seen; and this the Souls feel for it, every Soul in some degree, but those the more deeply that are the more truly apt to this higher love—just as all take delight in the beauty of the body but all are not stung as sharply, and those only that feel the keener wound are known as Lovers.

5. These Lovers, then, lovers of the beauty outside of sense, must be made to declare themselves.

What do you feel in presence of the grace you discern in actions, in manners, in sound morality, in all the works and fruits of virtue, in the beauty of Souls? When you see that you yourselves are beautiful within, what do you feel? What is this Dionysiac exultation that thrills through your being, this straining upwards of all your Soul, this longing to break away from the body and live sunken within the veritable self?

These are no other than the emotions of Souls under the spell of love.

But what is it that awakens all this passion? No shape, no color, no grandeur of mass: all is for a Soul, something whose beauty rests upon no color, for the moral wisdom the Soul enshrines and all the other hueless splendor of the virtues. It is that you find in yourself, or admire in another, loftiness of spirit; righteousness of life; disciplined purity; courage of the majestic face; gravity, modesty that goes fearless and tranquil and passionless; and, shining down upon all, the light of godlike Intellection.

All these noble qualities are to be reverenced and loved, no doubt, but what entitles them to be called beautiful?

They exist: they manifest themselves to us: anyone that sees them must admit that they have reality of Being; and is not Real-Being really beautiful?

But we have not yet shown by what property in them they have wrought the Soul to loveliness: what is this grace, this splendor as of Light, resting upon all the virtues?

Let us take the contrary, the ugliness of the Soul, and set that against its beauty: to understand, at once, what this ugliness is and how it comes to appear in the Soul will certainly open our way before us.

Let us then suppose an ugly Soul, dissolute, unrighteous: teeming with all the lusts; torn by internal discord; beset by the fears of its cowardice and the envies of its pettiness; thinking, in the little thought it has, only of the perishable and the base; perverse in all its impulses; the friend of unclean pleasures; living the life of abandonment to bodily sensation and delighting in its deformity.

What must we think but that all this shame is something that has gathered about the Soul, some foreign bane outraging it, soiling it, so that, encumbered with all manner of turpitude, it has no longer a clean activity or a clean sensation, but commands only a life smoldering dully under the crust of evil; that, sunk in manifold death, it no longer sees what a Soul should see, may no longer rest in its own being, dragged ever as it is towards the outer, the lower, the dark?

An unclean thing, I dare to say; flickering hither and thither at the call of objects of sense, deeply infected with the taint of body, occupied always in Matter, and absorbing Matter into itself, in its commerce with the Ignoble it has trafficked away for an alien nature its own essential Idea.

If a man has been immersed in filth or daubed with mud, his native comeliness disappears and all that is seen is the foul stuff besmearing him: his ugly condition is due to alien matter that has encrusted him, and if he is to win back his grace it must be his business to scour and purify himself and make himself what he was.

So, we may justly say, a Soul becomes ugly—by something foisted upon it, by sinking itself into the alien, by a fall, a descent into body, into Matter. The dishonor of the Soul is in its ceasing to be clean and apart. Gold is degraded when it is mixed with earthy particles; if these be worked out, the gold is left and is beautiful, isolated from all that is foreign, gold with gold alone. And so the Soul; let it be but cleared of the desires that come by its too intimate converse with the body, emancipated from all the passions, purged of all that embodiment has thrust upon it, withdrawn, a solitary, to itself again—in that moment the ugliness that came only from the alien is stripped away.

6. For, as the ancient teaching was, moral-discipline and courage and every virtue, not even excepting Wisdom itself, all is purification.

Hence the Mysteries with good reason adumbrate the immersion of the unpurified in filth, even in the Nether-World, since the unclean loves filth for its very filthiness, and swine foul of body find their joy in foulness.

What else is *Sophrosune*, rightly so-called, but to take no part in the pleasures of the body, to break away from them as unclean and unworthy of the clean? So too, Courage is but being fearless of the death which is but the parting of the Soul from the body, an event which no one can dread whose delight is to be his unmingled self. And Magnanimity is but disregard for the lure of things here. And Wisdom is but the Act of the Intellectual-Principle withdrawn from the lower places and leading the Soul to the Above.

The Soul thus cleansed is all Idea and Reason, wholly free of body, intellective, entirely of that divine order from which the wellspring of Beauty rises and all the race of Beauty.

Hence the Soul heightened to the Intellectual-Principle is beautiful to all its power. For Intellection and all that proceeds from Intellection are the Soul's beauty, a graciousness native to it and not foreign, for only with these is it truly Soul. And it is just to say that in the Soul's becoming a good and beautiful thing is its becoming like to God, for from the Divine comes all the Beauty and all the Good in beings.

We may even say that Beauty *is* the Authentic-Existents and Ugliness is the Principle contrary to Existence: and the Ugly is also the primal evil; therefore its contrary is at once good and beautiful, or is Good and Beauty: and hence the one method will discover to us the Beauty-Good and the Ugliness-Evil.

And Beauty, this Beauty which is also The Good, must be posed as The First: directly deriving from this First is the Intellectual-Principle which is pre-eminently the manifestation of Beauty; through the Intellectual-Principle Soul is beautiful. The beauty in things of a lower order—actions and pursuits for instance—comes by operation of the shaping Soul which is also the author of the beauty found in the world of sense. For the Soul, a divine thing, a fragment as it were of the Primal Beauty, makes beautiful to the fullness of their capacity all things whatsoever that it grasps and moulds.

7. Therefore we must ascend again towards the Good, the desired of every Soul. Anyone that has seen This, knows what I intend when I say that it is beautiful. Even the desire of it is to be desired as a Good. To attain it is for those that will take the upward path, who will set all their forces towards it, who will divest themselves of all that we have put on in our descent: so, to those that approach the Holy Celebrations of the Mysteries, there are appointed purifications and the laying aside of the garments worn before, and the entry in nakedness—until, passing, on the upward way, all that is other than the God, each in the solitude of himself shall behold that solitary-dwelling Existence, the Apart, the Unmingled, the Pure, that from Which all things depend, for Which all look and live and act and know, the Source of Life and of Intellection and of Being.

And one that shall know this vision—with what passion of love shall he not be seized, with what pang of desire, what longing to be molten into one with This, what wondering delight! If he that has never seen this Being must hunger for It as for all his welfare, he that has known must love and reverence It as the very Beauty; he will be flooded with awe and gladness, stricken by a salutary terror; he loves with a veritable love, with sharp desire; all other loves than this he must despise, and disdain, all that once seemed fair.

This, indeed, is the mood even of those who, having witnessed the manifestation of Gods or Supernals, can never again feel the old delight in the comeliness of material forms: what then are we to think of one that contemplates Absolute Beauty in Its essential integrity, no accumulation of flesh and matter, no dweller on earth or in the heavens—so perfect Its purity—far above all such things in that they are non-essential, composite, not primal but descending from This?

Beholding this Being—the Choragus of all Existence, the Self-Intent that ever gives forth and never takes—resting, rapt, in the vision and possession of so lofty a loveliness, growing to Its likeness, what Beauty can the Soul yet lack? For This, the Beauty supreme, the absolute, and the primal, fashions Its lovers to Beauty and makes them also worthy of love.

And for This, the sternest and the uttermost combat is set before the Souls; all our labor is for This, lest we be left without part in this noblest vision, which to attain is to be blessed in the blissful sight, which to fail of is to fail utterly.

For not he that has failed of the joy that is in color or in visible forms, not he that has failed of power or of honors or of kingdom has failed, but only he that has failed of only This, for Whose winning he should renounce kingdoms and command over earth and ocean and sky, if only, spurning the world of sense from beneath his feet, and straining to This, he may see.

8. But what must we do? How lies the path? How come to vision of the inaccessible Beauty, dwelling as if in consecrated precincts, apart from the common ways where all may see, even the profane?

He that has the strength, let him arise and withdraw into himself, foregoing all that is known by the eyes, turning away for ever from the material beauty that once made his joy. When he perceives those shapes of grace that show in body, let him not pursue: he must know them for copies, vestiges, shadows, and hasten away towards That they tell of. For if anyone follow what is like a beautiful shape playing over water—is there not a myth telling in symbol of such a dupe, how he sank into the depths of the current and was swept away to nothingness? So too, one that is held by material beauty and will not break free shall be precipitated, not in body but in Soul, down to the dark depths loathed of the Intellective-Being, where, blind even in the Lower-World, he shall have commerce only with shadows, there as here.

"Let us flee then to the beloved Fatherland": this is the soundest counsel. But what is this flight? How are we to gain the open sea? For Odysseus is surely a parable to us when he commands the flight from the sorceries of Circe or Calypso—not content to linger for all the pleasure offered to his eyes and all the delight of sense filling his days.

The Fatherland to us is There whence we have come, and There is The Father.

What then is our course, what the manner of our flight? This is not a journey for the feet; the feet bring us only from land to land; nor need you think of coach or ship to carry you away; all this order of things you must set aside and refuse to see: you must close the eyes and call instead upon another vision which is to be waked within you, a vision, the birth-right of all, which few turn to use.

9. And this inner vision, what is its operation?

Newly awakened it is all too feeble to bear the ultimate splendor. Therefore the Soul must be trained—to the habit of remarking, first, all noble pursuits, then the works of beauty produced not by the labor of the arts but by the virtue of men known for their goodness: lastly, you must search the souls of those that have shaped these beautiful forms.

But how are you to see into a virtuous Soul and know its loveliness?

Withdraw into yourself and look. And if you do not find yourself beautiful yet, act as does the creator of a statue that is to be made beautiful: he cuts away here, he smoothes there, he makes this line lighter, this other purer, until a lovely face has grown upon his work. So do you also: cut away all that is excessive, straighten all that is crooked, bring light to all that is overcast, labor to make all one glow of beauty and never cease chiseling your statue, until there shall shine out on you from it the godlike splendor of virtue, until you shall see the perfect goodness surely established in the stainless shrine.

When you know that you have become this perfect work, when you are self-gathered in the purity of your being, nothing now remaining that can shatter that inner unity, nothing from without clinging to the authentic man, when you find yourself wholly true to your essential nature, wholly that only veritable Light which is not measured by space, not narrowed to any circumscribed form nor again diffused as a thing void of term, but ever unmeasurable as something greater than all measure and more than all quantity—when you perceive that you have grown to this, you are now become very vision: now call up all your confidence, strike forward yet a step—you need a guide no longer—strain, and see.

This is the only eye that sees the mighty Beauty. If the eye that adventures the vision be dimmed by vice, impure, or weak, and unable in its cowardly blenching to see the uttermost brightness, then it sees nothing even though another point to what lies plain to sight before it. To any vision must be brought an eye adapted to what is to be seen, and having some likeness to it. Never did eye see the sun unless it had first become sunlike, and never can the Soul have vision of the First Beauty unless itself be beautiful.

Therefore, first let each become godlike and each beautiful who cares to see God and Beauty. So, mounting, the Soul will come first to the Intellectual-Principle and survey all the beautiful Ideas in the Supreme and will avow that this is Beauty, that the Ideas are Beauty. For by their efficacy comes all Beauty else, by the offspring and essence of the Intellectual-Being. What is beyond the Intellectual-Principle we affirm to be the nature of Good radiating Beauty before it. So that, treating the Intellectual-Cosmos as one, the first is the Beautiful: if we make distinction there, the Realm of Ideas constitutes the Beauty of the Intellectual Sphere; and The Good, which lies beyond, is the Fountain at once and Principle of Beauty: the Primal Good and the Primal Beauty have the one dwelling-place and, thus, always, Beauty's seat is There.

Ennead II
Ninth Tractate: 6-9

AGAINST THE GNOSTICS

This treatise is only the concluding section of a single long text which Porphyry divided into four parts and put into different *Enneads*, the other three being III.8, V.8, and V.5. The title *Against the Gnostics* is given by Porphyry himself. The alternative title is *Against those who Say that the Maker of the Universe is Evil and the Universe is Evil*. Plotinus regarded the teachings of the Gnostics (who belonged to the religious trend of thought designated as "Gnosticism" both by later Christian and modern writers) as untraditional, irrational, and immoral. Plotinus considers absurd the Gnostic claim of the possibility of being good while yet despising all human virtues and hating the whole world and its numerous gods. The Gnostics also despise and revile the Platonic teaching, which stands in accord with the much older paradigms of ancient civilizations. In this sense, Gnosticism is a kind of revolution, or spiritual revolt, which takes on truly cosmic dimensions. Thus, in his anti-Gnostic polemic, Plotinus provides a defense of Hellenism and Hellenic philosophy, which by that time was threatened by the irrational and hubristic claims of both Gnosticism and Christianity. As Christos Evangeliou says:

> The Gnostic cosmology should be rejected, according to Plotinus, not only because it is fanciful and strange but also for the reason that its hubristic and blasphemous doctrines would have deleterious effects on the morals of the people. He was well aware of the vulnerability of human beings to the Gnostic revolutionary and immoral teaching, especially when that sort of teaching is followed by talk like this: "You yourself are to be nobler than all else, nobler than men, nobler than even gods".[3]

---

[3] Christos Evangeliou, "Plotinus' Anti-Gnostic Polemic and Porphyry's 'Against the Christians,'" in *Neoplatonism and Gnosticism*, ed. R.T. Wallis (Albany: SUNY Press, 1992), p. 119.

Plotinus thinks that the Gnostics are worse than the Epicureans, who denied Providence, and he seeks to defend traditional values, asserting that the sensible cosmos as a whole is the best possible copy of the noetic cosmos, therefore it is beautiful:

> For Plotinus, even man's life on earth can become beautiful if it is guided by reason and crowned with virtue and true wisdom. For him, as for Socrates, the first and highest duty of man is to fulfill Apollo's command: "Know thyself". The true Platonists, no less than the Gnostics, are convinced that their real abode is elsewhere. The basic difference between the two is their attitude towards this life.[4]

6. And, what are we to think of the new forms of being they introduce—their "Exiles" and "Impressions" and "Repentings"?

If all comes to states of the Soul—"Repentance" when it has undergone a change of purpose; "Impressions" when it contemplates not the Authentic Existences but their simulacra—there is nothing here but a jargon invented to make a case for their school: all this terminology is piled up only to conceal their debt to the ancient Greek philosophy which taught, clearly and without bombast, the ascent from the cave and the gradual advance of souls to a truer and truer vision.

For, in sum, a part of their doctrine comes from Plato; all the novelties through which they seek to establish a philosophy of their own have been picked up outside of the truth.

From Plato come their punishments, their rivers of the underworld, and the changing from body to body; as for the plurality they assert in the Intellectual Realm—the Authentic Existent, the Intellectual-Principle, the Second Creator, and the Soul—all this is taken over from the *Timaeus*, where we read:

"As many Ideal-Forms as the Divine Mind beheld dwelling within the Veritably Living Being, so many the Maker resolved should be contained in this All."

---

[4] Ibid., p. 121.

Misunderstanding their text, they conceived one Mind passively including within itself all that has being, another mind, a distinct existence, having vision, and a third planning the Universe—though often they substitute Soul for this planning Mind as the creating Principle—and they think that this third being is the Creator according to Plato.

They are in fact quite outside of the truth in their identification of the Creator.

In every way they misrepresent Plato's theory as to the method of creation as in many other respects they dishonor his teaching: they, we are to understand, have penetrated the Intellectual Nature, while Plato and all those other illustrious teachers have failed.

They hope to get the credit of minute and exact identification by setting up a plurality of intellectual Essences; but in reality this multiplication lowers the Intellectual Nature to the level of the Sense-Kind: their true course is to seek to reduce number to the least possible in the Supreme, simply referring all things to the second Hypostasis—which is all that exists as it is Primal Intellect and Reality and is the only thing that is good except only for the First Nature—and to recognize Soul as the third Principle, accounting for the difference among souls merely by diversity of experience and character. Instead of insulting those venerable teachers they should receive their doctrine with the respect due to the older thought and honor all that noble system—an immortal Soul, an Intellectual and Intelligible Realm, the Supreme God, the Soul's need of emancipation from all intercourse with the body, the fact of separation from it, the escape from the world of process to the world of essential-being. These doctrines, all emphatically asserted by Plato, they do well to adopt: where they differ, they are at full liberty to speak their minds, but not to procure assent for their own theories by flaying and flouting the Greeks: where they have a divergent theory to maintain they must establish it by its own merits, declaring their own opinions with courtesy and with philosophical method and stating the controverted opinion fairly; they must point their minds towards the truth and not hunt fame by insult, reviling and seeking in their own persons to replace men honored by the fine intelligences of ages past.

As a matter of fact the ancient doctrine of the Divine Essences was far the sounder and more instructed, and must be accepted by all not caught in the delusions that beset humanity: it is easy also to identify what has been conveyed in these later times from the ancients with incongruous novelties—how for example, where they must set up a contradictory doctrine, they introduce a medley of generation and destruction, how they cavil at the Universe, how they make the Soul blamable for the association with body, how they revile the Administrator of this All, how they ascribe to the Creator, identified with the Soul, the character and experiences appropriate to partial beings.

7. That this world has neither beginning nor end but exists for ever as long as the Supreme stands is certainly no novel teaching. And before this school rose it had been urged that commerce with the body is no gain to a soul.

But to treat the human Soul as a fair presentment of the Soul of the Universe is like picking out potters and blacksmiths and making them warrant for discrediting an entire well-ordered city.

We must recognize how different is the governance exercised by the All-Soul; the relation is not the same: it is not in fetters. Among the very great number of differences it should not have been overlooked that the We (the human Soul) lies under fetter; and this in a second limitation, for the Body-Kind, already fettered within the All-Soul, imprisons all that it grasps.

But the Soul of the Universe cannot be in bond to what itself has bound: it is sovereign and therefore immune of the lower things, over which we on the contrary are not masters. That in it which is directed to the Divine and Transcendent is ever unmingled, knows no encumbering; that in it which imparts life to the body admits nothing bodily to itself. It is the general fact that an inset (as the Body) necessarily shares the conditions of its containing principle (as the Soul), and does not communicate its own conditions where that principle has an independent life: thus a graft will die if the stock dies, but the stock will live on by its proper life though the graft wither. The fire within your own self may be quenched, but the thing, fire, will exist still; and if fire itself were annihilated that would make no difference to the Soul, the Soul in the Supreme, but only to the plan of the material world; and if the other elements sufficed to maintain a Cosmos, the Soul in the Supreme would be unconcerned.

The constitution of the All is very different from that of the single, separate forms of life: there, the established rule commanding to permanence is sovereign; here things are like deserters kept to their own place and duty by a double bond; there is no outlet from the All, and therefore no need of restraining or of driving errants back to bounds: all remains where from the beginning the Soul's nature appointed.

The natural movement within the plan will be injurious to anything whose natural tendency it opposes: one group will sweep bravely onward with the great total to which it is adapted; the others, not able to comply with the larger order, are destroyed. A great choral is moving to its concerted plan; midway in the march, a tortoise is intercepted; unable to get away from the choral line it is trampled under foot; but if it could only range itself within the greater movement it too would suffer nothing.

8. To ask why the Soul has created the Cosmos, is to ask why there is a Soul and why a Creator creates. The question, also, implies a beginning in the eternal and, further, represents creation as the act of a changeful Being who turns from this to that.

Those that so think must be instructed—if they would but bear with correction— in the nature of the Supernals, and brought to desist from that blasphemy of majestic powers which comes so easily to them, where all should be reverent scruple.

Even in the administration of the Universe there is no ground for such attack, for it affords manifest proof of the greatness of the Intellectual Kind.

This All that has emerged into life is no amorphous structure—like those lesser forms within it which are born night and day out of the lavishness of its vitality—the Universe is a life organized, effective, complex, all-comprehensive, displaying an unfathomable wisdom. How, then, can anyone deny that it is a clear image, beautifully formed, of the Intellectual Divinities? No doubt it is copy, not original; but that is its very nature; it cannot be at once symbol and reality. But to say that it is an inadequate copy is false; nothing has been left out which a beautiful representation within the physical order could include.

Such a reproduction there must necessarily be—though not by deliberation and contrivance—for the Intellectual could not be the last of things, but must have a double Act, one within itself and one outgoing; there must, then, be something later than the Divine; for only the thing with which all power ends fails to pass downwards something of itself. In the Supreme there flourishes marvelous vigor and therefore it produces.

Since there is no Universe nobler than this, is it not clear what this must be? A representation carrying down the features of the Intellectual Realm is necessary; there is no other Cosmos than this; therefore this is such a representation.

This earth of ours is full of varied life-forms and of immortal being; to the very heavens it is crowded. And the stars, those of the upper and the under spheres, moving in their ordered path, fellow travelers with the universe, how can they be less than gods? Surely they must be morally good: what could prevent them? All that occasions vice here below is unknown there—no evil of body, perturbed and perturbing.

Knowledge, too; in their unbroken peace, what hinders from the intellectual grasp of the God-Head and the Intellectual Gods? What can be imagined to give us a wisdom higher than belongs to the Supernals? Could anyone, not fallen to utter folly, bear with such an idea?

Admitting that human souls have descended under constraint of the All-Soul, are we to think the constrained the nobler? Among souls, what commands must be higher than what obeys. And if the coming was unconstrained, why find fault with a world you have chosen and can quit if you dislike it?

And further, if the order of this Universe is such that we are able, within it, to practice wisdom and to live our earthly course by the Supernal does not that prove it a dependency of the Divine?

9. Wealth and poverty, and all inequalities of that order are made ground of complaint. But this is to ignore that the Sage demands no equality in such matters: he cannot think that to own many things is to be richer or that the powerful have the better of the simple; he leaves all such preoccupations to another kind of man. He has learned that life on earth has two distinct forms, the way of the Sage and the way of the mass, the Sage intent upon the sublimest, upon the realm above, while those of the more strictly human type fall, again, under two classes, the one reminiscent of virtue and therefore not without touch with good, the other mere populace, serving to provide necessaries to the better sort.

But what of murder? What of the feebleness that brings men under slavery to the passions?

Is it any wonder that there should be failing and error, not in the highest, the intellectual, Principle but in souls that are like undeveloped children? And is not life justified even so if it is a training ground with its victors and its vanquished?

You are wronged; need that trouble an immortal? You are put to death; you have attained your desire. And from the moment your citizenship of the world becomes irksome you are not bound to it.

Our adversaries do not deny that even here there is a system of law and penalty: and surely we cannot in justice blame a dominion which awards to every one his due, where virtue has its honor, and vice comes to its fitting shame, in which there are not merely representations of the gods, but the gods themselves, watchers from above, and—as we read—easily rebutting human reproaches, since they lead all things in order from a beginning to an end, allotting to each human being, as life follows life, a fortune shaped to all that has preceded—the destiny which, to those that do not penetrate it, becomes the matter of boorish insolence upon things divine.

A man's one task is to strive towards making himself perfect—though not in the idea—really fatal to perfection—that to be
perfect is possible to himself alone.

We must recognize that other men have attained the heights
of goodness; we must admit the goodness of the celestial spirits,
and above all of the gods—those whose presence is here but their
contemplation in the Supreme, and loftiest of them, the lord of this
All, the most blessed Soul. Rising still higher, we hymn the divinities of the Intellectual Sphere, and, above all these, the mighty
King of that dominion, whose majesty is made patent in the very
multitude of the gods.

It is not by crushing the divine into a unity but by displaying
its exuberance—as the Supreme himself has displayed it—that we
show knowledge of the might of God, who, abidingly what He is,
yet creates that multitude, all dependent on Him, existing by Him
and from Him.

This Universe, too, exists by Him and looks to Him—the
Universe as a whole and every god within it—and tells of Him to
men, all alike revealing the plan and will of the Supreme.

These, in the nature of things, cannot be what He is, but that
does not justify you in contempt of them, in pushing yourself forward as not inferior to them.

The more perfect the man, the more compliant he is, even
towards his fellows; we must temper our importance, not thrusting
insolently beyond what our nature warrants; we must allow other
beings, also, their place in the presence of the Godhead; we may
not set ourselves alone next after the First in a dream-flight which
deprives us of our power of attaining identity with the Godhead in
the measure possible to the human Soul, that is to say, to the point
of likeness to which the Intellectual-Principle leads us; to exalt ourselves above the Intellectual-Principle is to fall from it.

Yet imbeciles are found to accept such teaching at the mere
sound of the words "You yourself are to be nobler than all else,
nobler than men, nobler than even gods." Human audacity is very
great: a man once modest, restrained, and simple hears, "You, yourself, are the child of God; those men whom you used to venerate,

those beings whose worship they inherit from antiquity, none of these are His children; you without lifting hand are nobler than the very heavens"; others take up the cry: the issue will be much as if in a crowd all equally ignorant of figures, one man were told that he stands a thousand cubic feet; he will naturally accept his thousand cubits even though the others present are said to measure only five cubits; he will merely tell himself that the thousand indicates a considerable figure.

Another point: (you hold that) God has care for you; how then can He be indifferent to the entire Universe in which you exist?

We may be told that He is too much occupied to look upon the Universe, and that it would not be right for Him to do so; yet when He looks down and upon these people, is He not looking outside Himself and upon the Universe in which they exist? If He cannot look outside Himself so as to survey the Cosmos, then neither does He look upon them.

But they have no need of Him?

The Universe has need of Him, and He knows its ordering and its indwellers and how far they belong to it and how far to the Supreme, and which of the men upon it are friends of God, mildly acquiescing with the cosmic dispensation when in the total course of things some pain must be brought to them—for we are to look not to the single will of any man but to the universe entire, regarding every one according to worth but not stopping for such things where all that may is hastening onward.

Not one only kind of being is bent upon this quest, which brings bliss to whatsoever achieves, and earns for the others a future destiny in accord with their power. No man, therefore, may flatter himself that he alone is competent; a pretension is not a possession; many boast though fully conscious of their lack and many imagine themselves to possess what was never theirs and even to be alone in possessing what they alone of men never had.

Ennead III
Second Tractate: 4-9

ON PROVIDENCE (I)

This treatise is the first part of a long work on Providence (the second part of it is *Enn.* III.3). A great number of Hellenic philosophers, especially Stoics and Platonists, had written on Providence (*pronoia*) before Plotinus. However, A.H. Armstrong regards "this austere, honest, and profound work" as "the finest of all Greek contributions to theodicy."[5] The Peripatetic Alexander of Aphrodisias, whose doctrine of the identity of the Intellect with its intelligible objects was a major influence on Plotinus' noetics, viewed God as knowing and approving the general features of the cosmic order. Since God's Providence is neither deliberately contrived by Him nor merely an incidental consequence of His self-contemplation, He cannot know all the world's indefinite details, because the indefinite and contingent are not possible objects of knowledge.

Plotinus partly follows this tradition. However, he speaks of *logos*, a rational forming principle, of the entire universe. This *logos* is not a distinct hypostasis, but a directive pattern, derived from Intellect through Soul, which keeps the material universe in the best possible order. Therefore the cosmos, governed by *pronoia*, is good as a whole: everything in it is good and seeks the Good, each in its proper degree. Disorder and violence result from failure to attain the good and lead to deserved punishment. Human beings (standing midway between gods and beasts) cannot expect the gods to help them if they do not do what is necessary for their own well-being. According to John Dillon:

> Plotinus is not suggesting, of course, toleration of any form of antinomianism, or disregard for the norms of decent society, such as commended itself to certain contemporary Gnostic sects. Any such suggestion would have appalled him. He would, of course, observe the vulgar decencies; it is just that they would be subsumed into something higher. One feels of Plotinus that he would

[5] A.H. Armstrong, "Introductory Notes," in Plotinus, *The Enneads*, vol. III (Cambridge, Mass.: Harvard University Press, 1967), p. 38.

have gladly helped an old lady across the road—but he might very well fail to notice her at all. And if she were squashed by a passing wagon, he would remain quite unmoved.[6]

In Neoplatonism the doctrine of Providence is related to another doctrine of pre-existing and the remaining of all things in the higher causes. Therefore Proclus not only says that the higher causes contain their lower effects, but that they know these effects beforehand, that is they foreknow (*pro-noein*). According to L.J. Rosan, this foreknowledge is also a kind of love, i.e., the "providential love" (*eros pronoetikos*) by which the higher causes benevolently fore-know and even care for their effects.[7]

However, Providence leaves room for human initiative, therefore men get what they deserve at the hands of the wicked through their own slackness and folly. As Georges Leroux says:

> In the Plotinian conception of human freedom, therefore, what strikes us most is the strength of the metaphysical premises. In a manner quite different from that of Aristotle, who appeared to be exclusively interested by the problems of choice and contingency, Plotinus conceives of liberty as the true property of virtuous life. By stressing this theme, he appropriates the great heritage of the Platonic tradition centered on the divine origin of the soul and the ideal of resemblance to God.[8]

4. That water extinguishes fire and fire consumes other things should not astonish us. The thing destroyed derived its being from outside itself: this is no case of a self-originating substance being annihilated by an external; it rose on the ruin of something else, and thus in its own ruin it suffers nothing strange; and for every fire quenched, another is kindled.

---

[6] John M. Dillon, "An Ethic for the Late Antique Sage," in *The Cambridge Companion to Plotinus*, ed. Lloyd P. Gerson (Cambridge: Cambridge University Press, 1996), p. 324.

[7] Laurence J. Rosan, "Proclus and the Tejobindu Upanishad," in *Neoplatonism and Indian Thought*, ed. Baine Harris (Norfolk: ISNS, 1982), p. 49.

[8] Georges Leroux, "Human Freedom in the Thought of Plotinus," in *The Cambridge Companion to Plotinus*, p. 311.

In the immaterial heaven every member is unchangeably itself for ever; in the heavens of our universe, while the whole has life eternally and so too all the nobler and lordlier components, the souls pass from body to body entering into varied forms—and, when it may, a soul will rise outside of the realm of birth and dwell with the one Soul of all. For the embodied lives by virtue of a Form or Idea: individual or partial things exist by virtue of Universals; from these priors they derive their life and maintenance, for life here is a thing of change; only in that prior realm is it unmoving. From that unchangingness change had to emerge and from that self-cloistered Life its derivative, this which breathes and stirs, the respiration of the still life of the divine.

The conflict and destruction that reign among living beings are inevitable, since things here are derived, brought into existence because the Divine Reason which contains all of them in the upper Heavens—how could they come here unless they were There?—must outflow over the whole extent of Matter.

Similarly, the very wronging of man by man may be derived from an effort towards the Good; foiled, in their weakness, of their true desire, they turn against each other: still, when they do wrong, they pay the penalty—that of having hurt their souls by their evil conduct and of degradation to a lower place—for nothing can ever escape what stands decreed in the law of the Universe.

This is not to accept the idea, sometimes urged, that order is an outcome of disorder and law of lawlessness, as if evil were a necessary preliminary to their existence or their manifestation: on the contrary order is the original and enters this sphere as imposed from without: it is because order, law, and reason exist that there can be disorder; breach of law and unreason exist because Reason exists—not that these better things are directly the causes of the bad but simply that what ought to absorb the Best is prevented by its own nature, or by some accident, or by foreign interference. An entity which must look outside itself for a law may be foiled of its purpose by either an internal or an external cause; there will be some flaw in its own nature, or it will be hurt by some alien influence, for often harm follows, unintended, upon the action of others in the pursuit of quite unrelated aims. Such living beings, on the other hand, as have freedom of motion under their own will sometimes take the right turn, sometimes the wrong.

Why the wrong course is followed is scarcely worth inquiring: a slight deviation at the beginning develops with every advance into a continuously wider and graver error—especially since there is the attached body with its inevitable concomitant of desire—and the first step, the hasty movement not previously considered and not immediately corrected, ends by establishing a set habit where there was at first only a fall.

Punishment naturally follows: there is no injustice in a man suffering what belongs to the condition in which he is; nor can we ask to be happy when our actions have not earned us happiness; the good, only, are happy; divine beings are happy only because they are good.

5. Now, once Happiness is possible at all to souls in this Universe, if some fail of it, the blame must fall not upon the place but upon the feebleness insufficient to the staunch combat in the one arena where the rewards of excellence are offered. Men are not born divine; what wonder that they do not enjoy a divine life. And poverty and sickness mean nothing to the good, while to the evil they bring benefit: where there is body there must be ill health.

Besides, these accidents are not without their service in the co-ordination and completion of the Universal system.

One thing perishes, and the Cosmic Reason—whose control nothing anywhere eludes—employs that ending to the beginning of something new; and, so, when the body suffers and the Soul, under the affliction, loses power, all that has been bound under illness and evil is brought into a new set of relations, into another class or order. Some of these troubles are helpful to the very sufferers—poverty and sickness, for example—and as for vice, even this brings something to the general service: it acts as a lesson in right-doing, and, in many ways even, produces good; thus, by setting men face to face with the ways and consequences of iniquity, it calls them from lethargy, stirs the deeper mind, and sets the understanding to work; by the contrast of the evil under which wrong-doers labor it displays the worth of the right. Not that evil exists for this purpose; but, as we have indicated, once the wrong has come to be, the Reason of the Cosmos employs it to good ends; and, precisely, the proof of the mightiest power is to be able to use the ignoble nobly and, given formlessness, to make it the material of unknown forms.

The principle is that evil by definition is a falling short in good, and good cannot be at full strength in this Sphere where it is lodged in the alien: the good here is in something else, in something distinct from the Good, and this something else constitutes the falling short, for it is not good. And this is why "evil is ineradicable": there is, first, the fact that in relation to this principle of Good, thing will always stand less than thing, and, besides, all things come into being through it, and are what they are by standing away from it.

6. As for the disregard of desert—the good afflicted, the unworthy thriving—it is a sound explanation no doubt that to the good nothing is evil and to the evil nothing can be good: still the question remains why should what essentially offends our nature fall to the good while the wicked enjoy all it demands? How can such an allotment be approved?

No doubt since pleasant conditions add nothing to true happiness and the unpleasant do not lessen the evil in the wicked, the conditions matter little: as well complain that a good man happens to be ugly and a bad man handsome.

Still, under such a dispensation, there would surely be a propriety, a reasonableness, a regard to merit which, as things are, do not appear, though this would certainly be in keeping with the noblest Providence: even though external conditions do not affect a man's hold upon good or evil, none the less it would seem utterly unfitting that the bad should be the masters, be sovereign in the state, while honorable men are slaves: a wicked ruler may commit the most lawless acts; and in war the worst men have a free hand and perpetrate every kind of crime against their prisoners.

We are forced to ask how such things can be, under a Providence. Certainly a maker must consider his work as a whole, but none the less he should see to the due ordering of all the parts, especially when these parts have Soul, that is, are Living and Reasoning Beings: the Providence must reach to all the details; its functioning must consist in neglecting no point.

Holding, therefore, as we do, despite all, that the Universe lies under an Intellectual Principle whose power has touched every existent, we cannot be absolved from the attempt to show in what ways the details of this sphere is just.

7. A preliminary observation: in looking for excellence in this thing of mixture, the Cosmos, we cannot require all that is implied in the excellence of the unmingled; it is folly to ask for Firsts in the Secondary, and since this Universe contains body, we must allow for some bodily influence upon the total and be thankful if the mingled existent lack nothing of what its nature allowed it to receive from the Divine Reason.

Thus, supposing we were inquiring for the finest type of the human being as known here, we would certainly not demand that he prove identical with Man as in the Divine Intellect; we would think it enough in the Creator to have so brought this thing of flesh and nerve and bone under Reason as to give grace to these corporeal elements and to have made it possible for Reason to bloom on the surface of Matter.

Our progress towards the object of our investigation must begin from this principle of gradation which will open to us the wonder of the Providence and of the power by which our universe holds its being.

We begin with evil acts entirely dependent upon the souls which perpetrate them—the harm, for example, which perverted souls do to the good and to each other. Unless the fore-planning power alone is to be charged with the vice in such souls, we have no ground of accusation, no claim to redress: "the blame lies on the Soul exercising its choice." Even a soul, we have seen, must have its individual movement; it is not abstract Spirit; the first step towards animal life has been taken and the conduct will naturally be in keeping with that character.

It is not because the world existed that souls are here: before the world was, they had it in them to be of the world, to concern themselves with it, to presuppose it, to administer it: it was in their nature to produce it—by whatever method, whether by giving forth some emanation while they themselves remained above, or by an actual descent, or in both ways together, some presiding from above, others descending; for we are not at the moment concerned about the mode of creation but are simply urging that, however the world was produced, no blame falls on Providence for what exists within it.

There remains the other phase of the question—the distribution of evil to the opposite classes of men: the good go bare while the wicked are rich: all that human need demands, the least deserving have in abundance; it is they that rule, peoples and states are at their disposal. Would not all this imply that the divine power does not reach to earth?

That it does is sufficiently established by the fact that Reason rules in the lower things: animals and plants have their share in Reason, Soul, and Life. Perhaps, then, it reaches to earth but is not master over all?

We answer that the universe is one living organism: as well maintain that while human head and face are the work of nature and of the ruling reason-principle, the rest of the frame is due to other agencies—accident or sheer necessity—and owes its inferiority to this origin, or to the incompetence of unaided Nature. And even granting that those less noble members are not in themselves admirable it would still be neither pious nor even reverent to censure the entire structure.

8. Thus we come to our inquiry as to the degree of excellence found in things of this Sphere, and how far they belong to an ordered system or in what degree they are, at least, not evil.

Now in every living being the upper parts—head, face—are the most beautiful, the mid and lower members inferior. In the

Universe the middle and lower members are human beings; above
them, the Heavens and the Gods that dwell there; these Gods with
the entire circling expanse of the heavens constitute the greater
part of the Cosmos: the earth is but a central point, and stands
in relation to only one among the stars. Yet human wrongdoing is
made a matter of wonder; we are evidently asked to take humanity
as the choice member of the Universe, nothing wiser existent!

But humanity, in reality, is poised midway between the gods
and the beasts, and inclines now to the one order, now to the other;
some men grow like to the divine, others to the brute, the greater
number stand neutral. But those that are corrupted to the point of
approximating to irrational animals and wild beasts pull the mid-
folk about and inflict wrong upon them; the victims are no doubt
better than the wrongdoers, but are at the mercy of their inferiors
in the field in which they themselves are inferior, where, that is,
they cannot be classed among the good since they have not trained
themselves in self-defense.

A gang of lads, morally neglected, and in that respect inferior
to the intermediate class, but in good physical training, attack and
throw another set, trained neither physically or morally, and make
off with their food and their dainty clothes. What more is called
for than a laugh?

And surely even the lawgiver would be right in allowing the
second group to suffer this treatment, the penalty of their sloth and
self-indulgence: the gymnasium lies there before them, and they, in
laziness and luxury and listlessness, have allowed themselves to fall
like fat-loaded sheep, a prey to the wolves.

But the evildoers also have their punishment: first they pay in
that very wolfishness, in the disaster to their human quality: and
next there is laid up for them the due of their kind; living ill here,
they will not get off by death; on every precedent through all the
line there waits its sequent, reasonable and natural—worse to the
bad, better to the good.

This at once brings us outside the gymnasium with its fun for
boys; they must grow up, both kinds, amid their childishness and
both one day stand girt and armed. Then there is a finer spectacle

than is ever seen by those that train in the ring. But at this stage some have not armed themselves—and the duly armed win the day.

Not even a God would have the right to deal a blow for the unwarlike: the law decrees that to come safe out of battle is for fighting men, not for those that pray. The harvest comes home not for praying but for tilling; healthy days are not for those that neglect their health: we have no right to complain of the ignoble getting the richer harvest if they are the only workers in the fields, or the best.

Again: it is childish, while we carry on all the affairs of our life to our own taste and not as the Gods would have us, to expect them to keep all well for us in spite of a life that is lived without regard to the conditions which the Gods have prescribed for our well-being. Yet death would be better for us than to go on living lives condemned by the laws of the Universe. If things took the contrary course, if all the modes of folly and wickedness brought no trouble in life—then indeed we might complain of the indifference of a Providence leaving the victory to evil.

Bad men rule by the feebleness of the ruled: and this is just; the triumph of weaklings would not be just.

9. It would not be just, because Providence cannot be a something reducing us to nothingness: to think of Providence as everything, with no other thing in existence, is to annihilate Providence itself, since it could have no field of action; nothing would exist except the Divine. As things are, the Divine, of course, exists, but has reached forth to something other—not to reduce that to nothingness but to preside over it; thus in the case of Man, for instance, the Divine presides as the Providence, preserving the character of human nature, that is the character of a being under the providential law, which, again, implies subjection to what that law may enjoin.

And that law enjoins that those who have made themselves good shall know the best of life, here and later, the bad the reverse. But the law does not warrant the wicked in expecting that their prayers should bring others to sacrifice themselves for their sakes; or that the gods should lay aside the divine life in order to direct their daily concerns; or that good men, who have chosen a path nobler than all earthly rule, should become their rulers. The perverse have never made a single effort to bring the good into authority, so intent are they upon securing power for themselves; they are all spite against anyone that becomes good of his own motion, though if good men were placed in authority the total of goodness would be increased.

In sum: Man has come into existence, a living being but not a member of the noblest order; he occupies by choice an intermediate rank; still, in that place in which he exists, Providence does not allow him to be reduced to nothing; on the contrary he is ever being led upwards by all those varied devices which the Divine employs in its labor to increase the dominance of moral value. The human race, therefore, is not deprived by Providence of its rational being; it retains its share, though necessarily limited, in wisdom, intelligence, executive power, and right-doing, the right-doing, at least, of individuals to each other—and even in wronging others people think they are doing right and only paying what is due.

Man is, therefore, a noble creation, as perfect as the scheme allows; a part, no doubt, in the fabric of the All, he yet holds a lot higher than that of all the other living things of earth.

Now, no one of any intelligence complains of these others, man's inferiors, which serve to the adornment of the world; it would be feeble indeed to complain of animals biting man, as if we were to pass our days asleep. No: the animal, too, exists of necessity, and is serviceable in many ways, some obvious and many progressively discovered—so that not one lives without profit even to humanity. It is ridiculous, also, to complain that many of them are dangerous—there are dangerous men abroad as well—and if they distrust us, and in their distrust attack, is that anything to wonder at?

Ennead III
Fifth Tractate

ON LOVE

This treatise is based on Plato's *Phaedrus* and *Symposium*; it concerns the allegorical interpretation of myth. Zeus and Aphrodite are viewed by Plotinus as Intellect and Soul. Love (*eros*) is represented both by the higher heavenly Aphrodite (a goddess) and the lower Aphrodite (a daimon, equated to the universal Soul). Plenty is interpreted as an intelligible reality, Poverty—as intelligible matter which is indefinite and giving unbounded desire. They are parents of love. Therefore *eros* has an intermediate and double nature, leading either upwards, or downwards. As daimon, *eros* is adapted to every form of the soul: not only to the individual soul, but also to the World Soul. The transformation and ascent of the soul is motivated by *eros*, since being a mean, *eros* mediates between the desired and the desiring. It is the "eye of longing" tending toward a vision of true Being, because *eros* derives its being from seeing. According to Werner Beierwaltes:

> As the moving element in the ascent of the human soul, *eros* has essentially two points of reference: the intellect, which as reflective unity and formedness is identical with the beautiful, and the One, which as superabundance or "flower" of the beautiful, and precisely because of its elevation above what is beautiful in the actual sense, is to be understood as its ground and origin. Both however are divine: the One as the God-himself, illustrated by the metaphor of the "king," the intellect as the most intensive manifestation of this God-One; "second God". Consequently the *eros* of the soul that assimilates itself to the intellect and tends toward the One is related in different ways to "God" or to manifestation of the divine itself. The goal of the abstraction, purification, self-clarification, concentration of vision, and associated increase in the soul's self-consciousness is the union with the One itself.... Again and again Plotinus compares the erotic movement toward the intellect and toward the One with the experience of lovers: they wish to see the beloved, to become like him, and to become one with him. The transformation of the soul into intel-

lect and thus into truly intelligible beauty is the starting point for an *eros* that proceeds toward the One or the Good itself and has actually moved the soul from the beginning. Because of its object this *eros* is "limitless," infinite.[9]

1. What is Love? A God, a Celestial Spirit, a state of mind? Or is it, perhaps, sometimes to be thought of as a God or Spirit and sometimes merely as an experience? And what is it essentially in each of these respects?

These important questions make it desirable to review prevailing opinions on the matter, the philosophical treatment it has received and, especially, the theories of the great Plato who has many passages dealing with Love, from a point of view entirely his own.

Plato does not treat of it as simply a state observed in souls; he also makes it a Spirit-being; so that we read of the birth of Eros, under definite circumstances and by a certain parentage.

Now everyone recognizes that the emotional state for which we make this "Love" responsible rises in souls aspiring to be knit in the closest union with some beautiful object, and that this aspiration takes two forms, that of the good whose devotion is for beauty itself, and that other which seeks its consummation in some vile act. But this generally admitted distinction opens a new question: we need a philosophical investigation into the origin of the two phases.

It is sound, I think, to find the primal source of Love in a tendency of the Soul towards pure beauty, in a recognition, in a kinship, in an unreasoned consciousness of friendly relation. The vile and ugly is in clash, at once, with Nature and with God: Nature produces by looking to the Good, for it looks towards Order—which has its being in the consistent total of the good, while the unordered is ugly, a member of the system of evil—and besides,

[9] Werner Beierwaltes, "The Love of Beauty and the Love of God," in *Classical Mediterranean Spirituality: Egyptian, Greek, Roman*, ed. A.H. Armstrong (London: Routledge & Kegan Paul, 1986), p. 304.

Nature itself, clearly, springs from the divine realm, from Good and Beauty; and when anything brings delight and the sense of kinship, its very image attracts.

Reject this explanation, and no one can tell how the mental state rises and what are its causes: it is the explanation of even copulative love, which is the will to beget in beauty; Nature seeks to produce the beautiful and therefore by all reason cannot desire to procreate in the ugly.

Those that desire earthly procreation are satisfied with the beauty found on earth, the beauty of image and of body; it is because they are strangers to the Archetype, the source of even the attraction they feel towards what is lovely here. There are souls to whom earthly beauty is a leading to the memory of that in the higher realm and these love the earthly as an image; those that have not attained to this memory do not understand what is happening within them, and take the image for the reality. Once there is perfect self-control, it is no fault to enjoy the beauty of earth; where appreciation degenerates into carnality, there is sin.

Pure Love seeks the beauty alone, whether there is Reminiscence or not; but there are those that feel, also, a desire of such immortality as lies within mortal reach; and these are seeking Beauty in their demand for perpetuity, the desire of the eternal; Nature teaches them to sow the seed and to beget in beauty, to sow towards eternity, but in beauty through their own kinship with the beautiful. And indeed the eternal is of the one stock with the beautiful, the Eternal-Nature is the first shaping of beauty and makes beautiful all that rises from it.

The less the desire for procreation, the greater is the contentment with beauty alone, yet procreation aims at the engendering of beauty; it is the expression of a lack; the subject is conscious of insufficiency and, wishing to produce beauty, feels that the way is to beget in a beautiful form. Where the procreative desire is lawless or against the purposes of nature, the first inspiration has been natural, but they have diverged from the way, they have slipped and fallen, and they grovel; they neither understand whither Love sought to lead them nor have they any instinct to production; they have not mastered the right use of the images of beauty; they do not know what the Authentic Beauty is.

Those that love beauty of person without carnal desire love for beauty's sake; those that have—for women, of course—the copulative love, have the further purpose of self-perpetuation: as long as they are led by these motives, both are on the right path, though the first have taken the nobler way. But, even in the right, there is the difference that the one set, worshipping the beauty of earth, look no further, while the others, those of recollection, venerate also the beauty of the other world while they, still, have no contempt for this in which they recognize, as it were, a last outgrowth, an attention of the higher. These, in sum, are innocent frequenters of beauty, not to be confused with the class to whom it becomes an occasion of fall into the ugly—for the aspiration towards a good degenerates into an evil often.

So much for love, the state.

Now we have to consider Love, the God.

2. The existence of such a being is no demand of the ordinary man, merely; it is supported by Theologians (Orphic teachers) and, over and over again, by Plato to whom Eros is child of Aphrodite, minister of beautiful children, inciter of human souls towards the supernal beauty or quickener of an already existing impulse thither. All this requires philosophical examination. A cardinal passage is that in The Banquet where we are told Eros was not a child of Aphrodite but born on the day of Aphrodite's birth, Penia, Poverty, being the mother, and Poros, Possession, the father.

The matter seems to demand some discussion of Aphrodite since in any case Eros is described as being either her son or in some association with her. Who then is Aphrodite, and in what sense is Love either her child or born with her or in some way both her child and her birth-fellow?

To us Aphrodite is twofold; there is the heavenly Aphrodite, daughter of Ouranos or Heaven: and there is the other the daughter of Zeus and Dione, this is the Aphrodite who presides over earthly unions; the higher was not born of a mother and has no part in marriages, for in Heaven there is no marrying.

The Heavenly Aphrodite, daughter of Kronos (Saturn)—who is no other than the Intellectual Principle—must be the Soul at its divinest: unmingled as the immediate emanation of the unmingled; remaining ever Above, as neither desirous nor capable of descending to this sphere, never having developed the downward tendency, a divine Hypostasis essentially aloof, so unreservedly an Authentic Being as to have no part with Matter—and therefore mythically "the unmothered"—justly called not Celestial Spirit but God, as knowing no admixture, gathered cleanly within itself.

Any nature springing directly from the Intellectual Principle must be itself also a clean thing: it will derive a resistance of its own from its nearness to the Highest, for all its tendency, no less than its fixity, centers upon its author whose power is certainly sufficient to maintain it Above.

Soul then could never fall from its sphere; it is closer held to the divine Mind than the very sun could hold the light it gives forth to radiate about it, an outpouring from itself held firmly to it, still.

But following upon Kronos—or, if you will, upon Heaven (Ouranos), the father of Kronos—the Soul directs its Act towards him and holds closely to him and in that love brings forth the Eros through whom it continues to look towards him. This Act of the Soul has produced an Hypostasis, a Real-Being; and the mother and this Hypostasis—her offspring, noble Love—gaze together upon Divine Mind. Love, thus, is ever intent upon that other loveliness, and exists to be the medium between desire and that object of desire. It is the eye of the desirer; by its power what loves is enabled to see the loved thing. But it is first; before it becomes the vehicle of vision, it is itself filled with the sight; it is first, therefore, and not even in the same order—for desire attains to vision only through the efficacy of Love, while Love, in its own Act, harvests the spectacle of beauty playing immediately above it.

3. That Love is a Hypostasis (a "Person"), a Real-Being sprung from a Real-Being—lower than the parent but authentically existent—is beyond doubt.

For the parent-Soul was a Real-Being sprung directly from the Act of the Hypostasis that ranks before it: it had life; it was a constituent in the Real-Being of all that authentically is—in the Real-Being which looks, rapt, towards the very Highest. That was the first object of its vision; it looked towards it as towards its good, and it rejoiced in the looking; and the quality of what it saw was such that the contemplation could not be void of effect; in virtue of that rapture, of its position in regard to its object, of the intensity of its gaze, the Soul conceived and brought forth an offspring worthy of itself and of the vision. Thus; there is a strenuous activity of contemplation in the Soul; there is an emanation towards it from the object contemplated; and Eros is born, the Love which is an eye filled with its vision, a seeing that bears its image with it; Eros taking its name, probably, from the fact that its essential being is due to this (*horasis*) this seeing. Of course Love, as an emotion, will take its name from Love, the Person, since a Real-Being cannot but be prior to what lacks this reality. The mental state will be designated as Love, like the Hypostasis, though it is no more than a particular act directed towards a particular object; but it must not be confused with the Absolute Love, the Divine Being. The Eros that belongs to the supernal Soul must be of one temper with it; it must itself look aloft as being of the household of that Soul, dependent upon that Soul, its very offspring; and therefore caring for nothing but the contemplation of the Gods.

Once that Soul which is the primal source of light to the heavens is recognized as an Hypostasis standing distinct and aloof, it must be admitted that Love too is distinct and aloof. To describe the Soul as "celestial" is not to question its separateness (or immateriality); our own best we conceive as inside ourselves and yet something apart. So, we must think of this Love—as essentially resident where the unmingling Soul inhabits.

But besides this purest Soul, there must be also a Soul of the All: at once there is another Love—the eye with which this second

Soul looks upwards—like the supernal Eros engendered by force of desire. This Aphrodite, the secondary Soul, is of this Universe—not Soul unmingled alone, not Soul the Absolute—giving birth, there-fore, to the Love concerned with the universal life; no, this is the Love presiding over marriages; but it, also, has its touch of the upward desire; and, in the degree of that striving, it stirs and leads upwards the souls of the young and every soul with which it is incorporated in so far as there is a natural tendency to remembrance of the divine. For every soul is striving towards The Good, even the mingling Soul and that of particular beings, for each holds directly from the divine Soul, and is its offspring.

4. Does each individual Soul, then, contain within itself such a Love in essence and substantial reality?

Since not only the pure All-Soul but also that of the Universe contains such a Love, it would be difficult to explain why our per-sonal Soul should not. It must be so, even, with all that has life.

This indwelling love is no other than the Spirit which, as we are told, walks with every being, the affection dominant in each several nature. It implants the characteristic desire; the particular Soul, strained towards its own natural objects, brings forth its own Eros, the guiding spirit realizing its worth and the quality of its Being.

As the All-Soul contains the Universal Love, so must the single Soul be allowed its own single Love: and as closely as the single Soul holds to the All-Soul, never cut off but embraced within it, the two together constituting one principle of life, so the single separate Love holds to the All-Love. Similarly, the individual Love keeps with the individual Soul as that other, the great Love, goes with the All-Soul; and the Love within the All permeates it throughout so that the one Love becomes many, showing itself where it chooses at any moment of the Universe, taking definite shape in these its partial phases and revealing itself at its will.

In the same way we must conceive many Aphrodites in the All, Spirits entering it together with Love, all emanating from an Aphrodite of the All, a train of particular Aphrodites dependent upon the first, and each with the particular Love in attendance: this

multiplicity cannot be denied, if Soul be the mother of Love, and
Aphrodite mean Soul, and Love be an act of a Soul seeking good.

This Love, then, leader of particular souls to The Good, is twofold: the Love in the loftier Soul would be a god ever linking the
Soul to the divine; the Love in the mingling Soul will be a celestial
spirit.

5. But what is the nature of this Spirit—of the Celestials
(Daimones) in general?

The Spirit-Kind is treated in the Symposium where, with
much about the others, we learn of Eros—Love—born to Penia—
Poverty—and Poros—Possession—who is son of Metis—Resource—
at Aphrodite's birth feast.

But (the passage has been misunderstood for) to take Plato as
meaning, by Eros, this Universe—and not simply the Love native
within it—involves much that is self-contradictory.

For one thing, the universe is described as a blissful god and as
self-sufficing, while this "Love" is confessedly neither divine nor
self-sufficing but in ceaseless need.

Again, this Cosmos is a compound of body and soul; but
Aphrodite to Plato is the Soul itself, therefore Aphrodite would
necessarily be a constituent part of Eros, (not mother but) dominant member! A man is the man's Soul; if the world is, similarly,
the world's Soul, then Aphrodite, the Soul, is identical with Love,
the Cosmos! And why should this one spirit, Love, be the Universe
to the exclusion of all the others, which certainly are sprung from
the same Essential-Being? Our only escape would be to make the
Cosmos a complex of Celestials.

Love, again, is called the Dispenser of beautiful children: does
this apply to the Universe? Love is represented as homeless, bed-
less, and bare-footed: would not that be a shabby description of the
Cosmos and quite out of the truth?

6. What then, in sum, is to be thought of Love and of his
"birth" as we are told of it?

Clearly we have to establish the significance, here, of Poverty and Possession, and show in what way the parentage is appropriate: we have also to bring these two into line with the other Celestials, since one spirit nature, one spirit essence, must characterize all unless they are to have merely a name in common.

We must, therefore, lay down the grounds on which we distinguish the Gods from the Celestials—that is, when we emphasize the separate nature of the two orders and are not, as often in practice, including these Spirits under the common name of Gods.

It is our teaching and conviction that the Gods are immune to all passion, while we attribute experience and emotion to the Celestials which, though eternal Beings and directly next to the Gods, are already a step towards ourselves and stand between the divine and the human.

But by what process (of degeneration) was the immunity lost? What in their nature led them downwards to the inferior?

And other questions present themselves.

Does the Intellectual Realm include no member of this spirit order, not even one? And does the Cosmos contain only these spirits, God being confined to the Intellectual? Or are there Gods in the sub-celestial too, the Cosmos itself being a God, the third, as is commonly said, and the Powers down to the Moon being all Gods as well?

It is best not to use the word "Celestial" of any Being of that Realm; the word "God" may be applied to the Essential-Celestial— the auto-daimon, if he exists—and even to the Visible Powers of the Universe of Sense down to the Moon; Gods, these too, visible, secondary, sequent upon the Gods of the Intellectual Realm, consonant with Them, held about Them, as the radiance about the star.

What, then, are these spirits?

A Celestial is the representative generated by each Soul when it enters the Cosmos.

And why, by a Soul entering the Cosmos?

Because Soul pure of the Cosmos generates not a Celestial Spirit but a God; hence it is that we have spoken of Love, offspring of Aphrodite the Pure Soul, as a God.

But, first, what prevents every one of the Celestials from being an Eros, a Love? And why are they not untouched by Matter like the Gods?

On the first question: every Celestial born in the striving of the Soul towards the good and beautiful is an Eros; and all the souls within the Cosmos do engender this Celestial; but other Spirit-Beings, equally born from the Soul of the All, but by other faculties of that Soul, have other functions: they are for the direct service of the All, and administer particular things to the purpose of the Universe entire. The Soul of the All must be adequate to all that is and therefore must bring into being spirit powers serviceable not merely in one function but to its entire charge.

But what participation can the Celestial have in Matter, and in what Matter?

Certainly none in bodily Matter; that would make them simply living things of the order of sense. And if, even, they are to invest themselves in bodies of air or of fire, their nature must have already been altered before they could have any contact with the corporeal. The Pure does not mix, unmediated, with body—though many think that the Celestial-Kind, of its very essence, comports a body aerial or of fire.

But (since this is not so) why should one order of Celestial descend to body and another not? The difference implies the existence of some cause or medium working upon such as thus descend. What would constitute such a medium?

We are forced to assume that there is a Matter of the Intellectual Order, and that Beings partaking of it are thereby enabled to enter into the lower Matter, the corporeal.

7. This is the significance of Plato's account of the birth of Love.

The drunkenness of the father Poros or Possession is caused by Nectar, "wine yet not existing"; Love is born before the realm of sense has come into being: Penia (Poverty) had participation in the Intellectual before the lower image of that divine Realm had appeared; she dwelt in that Sphere, but as a mingled being consisting partly of Form but partly also of that indetermination which belongs to the Soul before she attains the Good and when all her knowledge of Reality is a fore-intimation veiled by the indeterminate and unordered: in this state (of fore-feeling and desiring The Good) Poverty brings forth the Hypostasis, Love.

This, then, is a union of Reason with something that is not Reason but a mere indeterminate striving in a being not yet illuminated: the offspring Love, therefore, is not perfect, not self-sufficient, but unfinished, bearing the signs of its parentage, the undirected striving and the self-sufficient Reason. This offspring is a Reason-Principle but not purely so; for it includes within itself an aspiration ill-defined, unreasoned, unlimited—it can never be sated as long as it contains within itself that element of the Indeterminate. Love, then, clings to the Soul, from which it sprang as from the principle of its Being, but it is lessened by including an element of the Reason-Principle which did not remain self-concentrated but blended with the indeterminate, not, it is true, by immediate contact but through its emanation. Love, therefore, is like a goad; it is without resource in itself; even winning its end, it is poor again.

It cannot be satisfied because a thing of mixture never can be so: true satisfaction is only for what has its plenitude in its own being; where craving is due to an inborn deficiency, there may be satisfaction at some given moment but it does not last. Love, then, has on the one side the powerlessness of its native inadequacy, on the other the resource inherited from the Reason-Kind.

Such must be the nature and such the origin of the entire Spirit Order: each—like its fellow, Love—has its appointed sphere, is powerful there, and wholly devoted to it, and, like Love, none is ever complete of itself but always straining towards some good which it sees in things of the partial sphere.

We understand, now, why good men have no other Love—no other Eros of life— than that for the Absolute and Authentic Good, and never follow the random attractions known to those ranged under the lower Spirit Kind.

Each human being is set under his own Spirit-Guides, but this is mere blank possession when they ignore their own and live by some other spirit adopted by them as more closely attuned to the operative part of the Soul in them. Those that go after evil are natures that have merged all the Love-Principles within them in the evil desires springing in their hearts and allowed the right reason, which belongs to our kind, to fall under the spell of false ideas from another source.

All the natural Loves, all that serve the ends of Nature, are good; in a lesser Soul, inferior in rank and in scope; in the greater Soul, superior; but all belong to the order of Being. Those forms of Love that do not serve the purposes of Nature are merely accidents attending on perversion: in no sense are they Real-Beings or even manifestations of any Reality; for they are no true issue of Soul; they are merely accompaniments of a spiritual flaw which the Soul automatically exhibits in the total of disposition and conduct.

In a word; all that is truly good in a Soul acting to the purposes of nature and within its appointed order, all this is Real-Being: anything else is alien, no act of the Soul, but merely something that happens to it: a parallel may be found in false mentation, notions behind which there is no reality as there is in the case of authentic ideas, the eternal, the strictly defined, in which there is at once an act of true knowing, a truly knowable object and authentic existence—and this not merely in the Absolute, but also in the particular being that is occupied by the authentically knowable and by the Intellectual-Principle manifest in every several form. In each particular human being we must admit the existence of the authentic Intellective Act and of the authentically knowable object—though not as wholly merged into our being, since we are not these in the absolute and not exclusively these.

It follows that Love, like our intellectual activities, is concerned with absolute things: if we sometimes are for the partial, that affection is not direct but accidental, like our knowledge that a given triangular figure is made up of two right angles because the absolute triangle is so.

8. But what are we to understand by this Zeus with the garden into which, we are told, Poros or Wealth entered? And what is the garden?

We have seen that the Aphrodite of the Myth is the Soul and that Poros, Wealth, is the Reason-Principle of the Universe: we have still to explain Zeus and his garden.

We cannot take Zeus to be the Soul, which we have agreed is represented by Aphrodite.

Plato, who must be our guide in this question, speaks in the Phaedrus of this God, Zeus, as the Great Leader—though elsewhere he seems to rank him as one of three—but in the Philebus he speaks more plainly when he says that there is in Zeus not only a royal Soul, but also a royal Intellect.

As a mighty Intellect and Soul, he must be a principle of Cause; he must be the highest for several reasons but especially because to be King and Leader is to be the chief cause: Zeus then is the Intellectual Principle. Aphrodite, his daughter, issue of him, dwelling with him, will be Soul, her very name Aphrodite (= the *habra*, delicate) indicating the beauty and gleam and innocence and delicate grace of the Soul.

And if we take the male gods to represent the Intellectual Powers and the female gods to be their souls—to every Intellectual Principle its companion Soul—we are forced, thus also, to make Aphrodite the Soul of Zeus; and the identification is confirmed by Priests and Theologians who consider Aphrodite and Hera one and the same and call Aphrodite's star ("Venus") the star of Hera.

9. This Poros, Possession, then, is the Reason-Principle of all that exists in the Intellectual Realm and in the supreme Intellect; but being more diffused, kneaded out as it were, it must touch Soul, be in Soul (as the next lower principle).

For, all that lies gathered in the Intellect is native to it: nothing enters from without; but "Poros intoxicated" is some Power deriving satisfaction outside itself: what, then, can we understand by this member of the Supreme filled with Nectar but a Reason-Principle falling from a loftier essence to a lower? This means that the

Reason-Principle upon "the birth of Aphrodite" left the Intellectual for the Soul, breaking into the garden of Zeus.

A garden is a place of beauty and a glory of wealth: all the loveliness that Zeus maintains takes its splendor from the Reason-Principle within him; for all this beauty is the radiation of the Divine Intellect upon the Divine Soul, which it has penetrated. What could the Garden of Zeus indicate but the images of his Being and the splendors of his glory? And what could these divine splendors and beauties be but the Reason-Principles streaming from him?

These Reason-Principles—this Poros who is the lavishness, the abundance of Beauty—are at one and are made manifest; this is the Nectar-drunkenness. For the Nectar of the gods can be no other than what the god-nature receives from outside itself, and that whose place is after the divine Mind (namely, Soul) receives a Reason-Principle.

The Intellectual Principle possesses itself to satiety, but there is no "drunken" abandonment in this possession which brings nothing alien to it. But the Reason-Principle—as its offspring, a later hypostasis—is already a separate Being and established in another Realm, and so is said to lie in the garden of this Zeus who is divine Mind; and this lying in the garden takes place at the moment when, in our way of speaking, Aphrodite enters the realm of Being.

"Our way of speaking"—for myths, if they are to serve their purpose, must necessarily import time-distinctions into their subject and will often present as separate, Powers which exist in unity but differ in rank and faculty; and does not philosophy itself relate the births of the unbegotten and discriminate where all is one substance? The truth is conveyed in the only manner possible; it is left to our good sense to bring all together again.

On this principle we have, here, Soul (successively) dwelling with the divine Intelligence, breaking away from it, and yet again being filled to satiety with Reason-Principles—the beautiful abounding in all plenty, so that every splendor become manifest in it with the images of whatever is lovely—Soul which, taken as one all, is Aphrodite, while in it may be distinguished the Reason-

Principles summed under the names of Plenty and Possession, produced by the downflow of the Nectar of the over realm. The splendors contained in Soul are thought of as the garden of Zeus with reference to their existing within Life; and Poros sleeps in this garden in the sense of being sated and heavy with its produce. Life is eternally manifest, an eternal existent among the existences, and the banqueting of the gods means no more than that they have their Being in that vital blessedness. And Love—"born at the banquet of the gods"—has of necessity been eternally in existence, for it springs from the intention of the Soul towards its Best, towards the Good; as long as Soul has been, Love has been.

Still this Love is of mixed quality. On the one hand there is in it the lack which keeps it craving: on the other, it is not entirely destitute; the deficient seeks more of what it has, and certainly nothing absolutely void of good would ever go seeking the Good.

It is said then to spring from Poverty and Possession in the sense that Lack and Aspiration and the Memory of the Reason-Principles, all present together in the Soul, produce that Act towards The Good which is Love. Its Mother is Poverty, since striving is for the needy; and this Poverty is Matter, for Matter is the wholly poor: the very ambition towards the Good is a sign of existing indetermination; there is a lack of shape and of Reason in that which must aspire towards the Good, and the greater degree of indetermination implies the lower depth of materiality. To the thing aspiring the Good is an Ideal-Principle distinct and unchanging, and aspiration prepares that which would receive the Good to offer itself as Matter to the incoming power.

Thus Love is, at once, in some degree a thing of Matter and at the same time a Celestial sprung of the Soul's unsatisfied longing for The Good.

Ennead III
Sixth Tractate: 4-5; 7; 19

ON THE IMPASSIVITY OF THE UNEMBODIED

This treatise is devoted to the problem of incorporeality. Plotinus asserts the impassibility and independence of incorporeal soul, insisting that it is always active. He excludes from philosophy ways of speaking and thinking about incorporeal things as subject to impressions, modifications, or contaminations.[10] Matter as such is utterly powerless and is the medium in which images of true Being exist. Henri Oosthout says:

> However, the distinction between "soul" (*psuche*) and "body" (*soma*) is by no means sharply drawn. In fact, "soul" and "body" tend to have more of a relative meaning with respect to each other. "Soul" is, in a narrow sense, identified with the most characteristic function of a living creature. But in a general sense, the notion of soul covers a broad range of qualities, from highly organized and complex functions, such as thinking and perception, to the most elementary properties, such as shape and color, which, in ordinary language, one would call "material" rather than "psychical." Accordingly, functions and properties that do not belong to the soul proper are called properties of the "body," or they are described as activities of the soul that operate through bodily organs. . . . When one tries to determine what "body" means in its strictest sense—what properties a body can have that should not be ascribed to the activity of the soul—then one is left with almost nothing. "Bodies" that are completely without a "soul," and that do not partake in any *energeia* whatsoever, are reduced to sheer indeterminacy.[11]

[10] A.H. Armstrong, "Introductory Notes," in Plotinus, *The Enneads*, vol. III (Cambridge, Mass.: Harvard University Press, 1967), p. 206.

[11] Henry Oosthout, *Modes of Knowledge and the Transcendental: An Introduction to Plotinus Ennead 5.3 [49] with a Commentary and Translation* (Amsterdam: B.R. Gruner, 1991), p. 48.

To regard bodies as real is a dream from which one should wake up. Therefore philosophical purification consists in waking up the soul from its various dreams, freeing it from affection and from ghostly mental pictures, in order to turn to the realm of Intellect.

4. We have, however, still to examine what is called the affective phase of the Soul. This has, no doubt, been touched upon above where we dealt with the nature of the various passions as grouped about the initiative phase of the Soul and the desiring faculty: but more is required; we must begin by forming a clear idea of what is meant by this affective faculty of the Soul.

In general terms it means the center about which we recognize the affections to be grouped; and by affections we mean those states upon which follow pleasure and pain.

Now among these affections we must distinguish. Some are pivoted upon judgments; thus, a man judging his death to be at hand may feel fear; foreseeing some fortunate turn of events, he is happy: the opinion lies in one sphere; the affection is stirred in another. Sometimes the affections take the lead and automatically bring in the notion which thus becomes present to the appropriate faculty: but as we have explained, an act of opinion does not introduce any change into the Soul or Mind: what happens is that from the notion of some impending evil is produced the quite separate thing, fear, and this fear, in turn, becomes known in that part of the Mind which is said under such circumstances to harbor fear.

But what is the action of this fear upon the Mind?

The general answer is that it sets up trouble and confusion before an evil anticipated. It should, however, be quite clear that the Soul or Mind is the seat of all imaginative representation—both the higher representation which is not so much a judgment as a vague notion unattended by discrimination, something resembling the action by which, as is believed, the "Nature" of common speech produces, unconsciously, the objects of the partial sphere. It is equally certain that in all that follows upon the mental act or state, the disturbance, confined to the body, belongs to the sense-order; trembling, pallor, inability to speak, have obviously nothing to do with the spiritual portion of the being. The Soul, in fact, would have to be described as corporeal if it were the seat of such symptoms: besides, in that case the trouble would not even reach the body since the only transmitting principle, oppressed by sensation, jarred out of itself, would be inhibited.

None the less, there is an affective phase of the Soul or Mind and this is not corporeal; it can be, only, some kind of Ideal-form.

Now Matter is the one field of the desiring faculty, as of the principles of nutrition, growth, and engendering, which are root and spring to desire and to every other affection known to this Ideal-form. No Ideal-form can be the victim of disturbance or be in any way affected: it remains in tranquility; only the Matter associated with it can be affected by any state or experience induced by the movement which its mere presence suffices to set up. Thus the vegetal principle induces vegetal life but it does not, itself, pass through the process of vegetation; it gives growth but it does not grow; in no movement which it originates is it moved with the motion it induces; it is in perfect repose, or, at least, its movement, really its act, is utterly different from what it causes elsewhere.

The nature of an Ideal-form is to be, of itself, an activity; it operates by its mere presence: it is as if Melody itself plucked the strings. The affective phase of the Soul or Mind will be the operative cause of all affection; it originates the movement either under the stimulus of some sense-presentment or independently—and it is a question to be examined whether the judgment leading to the movement operates from above or not—but the affective phase itself remains unmoved like Melody dictating music. The causes originating the movement may be likened to the musician; what is moved is like the strings of his instrument, and, once more, the Melodic Principle itself is not affected, but only the strings, though, however much the musician desired it, he could not pluck the strings except under dictation from the principle of Melody.

5. But why have we to call in Philosophy to make the Soul immune if it is thus (like the Melodic Principle of our illustration) immune from the beginning?

Because representations attack it at what we call the affective phase and cause a resulting experience, a disturbance, to which disturbance is joined the image of threatened evil: this amounts to an affection and Reason seeks to extinguish it, to ban it as destructive to the well-being of the Soul which by the mere absence of such a condition is immune, the one possible cause of affection not being present.

Take it that some such affections have engendered appearances presented before the Soul or Mind from without but taken (for practical purposes) to be actual experiences within it—then Philosophy's task is like that of a man who wishes to throw off the shapes presented in dreams, and to this end recalls to waking condition the mind that is breeding them.

But what can be meant by the purification of a Soul that has never been stained and by the separation of the Soul from a body to which it is essentially a stranger?

The purification of the Soul is simply to allow it to be alone; it is pure when it keeps no company; when it looks to nothing without itself; when it entertains no alien thoughts—be the mode or origin of such notions or affections what they may, a subject on which we have already touched—when it no longer sees in the world of image, much less elaborates images into veritable affections. Is it not a true purification to turn away towards the exact contrary of earthly things?

Separation, in the same way, is the condition of a soul no longer entering into the body to lie at its mercy; it is to stand as a light, set in the midst of trouble but unperturbed through all.

In the particular case of the affective phase of the Soul, purification is its awakening from the baseless visions which beset it, the refusal to see them; its separation consists in limiting its descent towards the lower and accepting no picture thence, and of course in the banning of all that it ignores when the pneuma (finer-body or spirit) on which it is poised is not turbid from gluttony and surfeit of impure flesh, but is a vehicle so slender that the Soul may ride upon it in tranquility.

7. We are thus brought back to the nature of that underlying matter and the things believed to be based upon it; investigation will show us that Matter has no reality and is not capable of being affected.

Matter must be bodiless—for body is a later production, a compound made by Matter in conjunction with some other entity. Thus it is included among incorporeal things in the sense that body is something that is neither Real-Being nor Matter.

Matter is not Soul; it is not Intellect, is not Life, is no Ideal-Principle, no Reason-Principle; it is no limit or bound, for it is mere indetermination; it is not a power, for what does it produce?

It lives on the farther side of all these categories and so has no title to the name of Being. It will be more plausibly called a non-being, and this not in the sense that movement and station are Not-Being (i.e. as merely different from Being) but in the sense of veritable Not-Being, so that it is no more than the image and phantasm of Mass, a bare aspiration towards substantial existence; it is stationary but not in the sense of having position, it is in itself invisible, eluding all effort to observe it, present where no one can look, unseen for all our gazing, ceaselessly presenting contraries in the things based upon it; it is large and small, more and less, deficient and excessive; a phantasm unabiding and yet unable to withdraw—not even strong enough to withdraw, so utterly has it failed to accept strength from the Intellectual Principle, so absolute its lack of all Being.

Its every utterance, therefore, is a lie; it pretends to be great and it is little, to be more and it is less; and the Existence with which it masks itself is no Existence, but a passing trick making trickery of all that seems to be present in it, phantasms within a phantasm; it is like a mirror showing things as in itself when they are really elsewhere, filled in appearance but actually empty, containing nothing, pretending everything. Into it and out of it move mimicries of the Authentic Existents, images playing upon an image devoid of Form, visible against it by its very formlessness; they seem to modify it but in reality effect nothing, for they are ghostly and feeble, have no thrust and meet none in Matter either; they pass through it leaving no cleavage, as through water; or they might be compared to shapes projected so as to make some appearance upon what we can know only as the Void.

Further: if visible objects were of the rank of the originals from which they have entered into Matter we might believe Matter to be really affected by them, for we might credit them with some share of the power inherent in their senders: but the objects of our experiences are of very different virtue than the realities they represent, and we deduce that the seeming modification of matter by visible things is unreal since the visible thing itself is unreal, having at no point any similarity with its source and cause. Feeble, in itself, a false thing and projected upon a falsity, like an image in dream or against water or on a mirror, it can but leave Matter unaffected; and even this is saying too little, for water and mirror do give back a faithful image of what presents itself before them.

19. The Ideal Principles entering into Matter as to a Mother affect it neither for better nor for worse.

Their action is not upon Matter but upon each other; these powers conflict with their opponent principles, not with their substrata—unless the substrata are taken as comprised with the entrant forms—Heat (the Principle) annuls Cold, and Blackness annuls Whiteness; or, the opponents blend to form an intermediate quality. Only that is affected which enters into combinations: being affected is losing something of self-identity.

In beings of soul and body, the affection occurs in the body, modified according to the qualities and powers presiding at the act of change: in all such dissolution of constituent parts, in the new combinations, in all variation from the original structure, the affection is bodily, the Soul or Mind having no more than an accompanying knowledge of the more drastic changes, or perhaps not even that. (Body is modified: Mind knows) but the Matter concerned remains unaffected; heat enters, cold leaves it, and it is unchanged because neither Principle is associated with it as friend or enemy.

So the appellation "Recipient and Nurse" is the better description: Matter is the mother only in the sense indicated; it has no begetting power. But probably the term Mother is used by those who think of a Mother as Matter to the offspring, as a container only, giving nothing to them, the entire bodily frame of the child being formed out of food. But if the mother does give anything to the offspring she does so not in her quality as Matter but as being an Ideal-Form; for only the Idea is generative; the contrary Kind is sterile.

This, I think, is why the doctors of old, teaching through symbols and mystic representations, exhibit the ancient Hermes with the generative organ always in active posture; this is to convey that the generator of things of sense is the Intellectual Reason-Principle: the sterility of Matter, eternally unmoved, is indicated by the eunuchs surrounding it in its representation as the All-Mother.

This too exalting title is conferred upon it in order to indicate that it is the source of things in the sense of being their underlie: it is an approximate name chosen for a general conception; there is no intention of suggesting a complete parallel with motherhood to those not satisfied with a surface impression but needing a precisely true presentment; by a remote symbolism, the nearest they could find, they indicate that Matter is sterile, not female to full effect, female in receptivity only, not in pregnancy: this they accomplish by exhibiting Matter as approached by what is neither female nor effectively male, but castrated of that impregnating power which belongs only to the unchangeably masculine.

Ennead III
Eighth Tractate

ON NATURE, CONTEMPLATION, AND THE ONE

This treatise is devoted to the doctrine of contemplation (*theoria*) which constitutes the very heart of the Plotinian philosophy. All life is essentially contemplation and derives from contemplation which is also the goal of action. At the level of Intellect the perfect identity of contemplation and the object of contemplation is observed. At the level of Nature contemplation is weakest and dream-like. According to A.H. Armstrong:

> There is of course no mirroring or imaging in the self-contemplation of Nous as self-contemplation. . . . What is mirrored or imaged is this archetypal contemplation which in the intelligible world is the First, the Origin of all reality, the transcendent One or Good: so that Nous and Psuche are in their contemplation true images of God: and all human souls which take part in that and the material cosmos and all things in it which spring from it are not only the products of that ultimate self-diffusive goodness but have, in their various ways and degrees, the form of good and so are images and signs of God. But this ultimate and archetypal contemplative image or mirroring is an image in a very strange sense indeed, because it is an image of the unimageable, of that which no image and likeness can be made. . . .
>
> At every stage of this great cosmos of reflections (this word is used here with deliberate ambiguity) down to the dreaming of Nature the mirror does not just passively receive the reflection, but, because it only reflects in this sense because it is reflecting in another, that is, contemplating, it plays its part in creating the mirror-image and gives it the character appropriate to its level: that is, because it is that reflection or image which it creates in contemplation, it can be said to bring itself into that being which is none the less given from above. And it is because the mirror is active in contemplation in this way that the image is true and living. It is only in the last and strangest mirror, the mirror which does not exist, the darkness of matter, that there is no contem-

plative activity, and so the image is false and dead. . . . But at the highest level, that of the imaging of the unimageable, where the reflection is the world of real being, the intelligible cosmos which is Divine Intellect, creative contemplation is at its most intense and productive.[12]

1. Supposing we played a little before entering upon our serious concern and maintained that all things are striving after Contemplation, looking to Vision as their one end—and this, not merely beings endowed with reason but even the unreasoning animals, the Principle that rules in growing things, and the Earth that produces these—and that all achieve their purpose in the measure possible to their kind, each attaining Vision and possessing itself of the End in its own way and degree, some things in entire reality, others in mimicry and in image—we would scarcely find anyone to endure so strange a thesis. But in a discussion entirely among ourselves there is no risk in a light handling of our own ideas.

Well—in the play of this very moment am I engaged in the act of Contemplation?

Yes; I and all that enter this play are in Contemplation: our play aims at Vision; and there is every reason to believe that child or man, in sport or earnest, is playing or working only towards Vision, that every act is an effort towards Vision; the compulsory act, which tends rather to bring the Vision down to outward things, and the act thought of as voluntary, less concerned with the outer, originate alike in the effort towards Vision.

The case of Man will be treated later on: let us speak, first, of the earth and of the trees and vegetation in general, asking ourselves what is the nature of Contemplation in them, how we relate to any Contemplative activity the labor and productiveness of the earth, how Nature, held to be devoid of reason and even of conscious representation, can either harbor Contemplation or produce by means of the Contemplation which it does not possess.

[12] A.H. Armstrong, "Platonic Mirrors," *Eranos 1987, Jahrbuch*, vol. 56 (Insel Verlag Frankfurt am Main, 1989), pp. 167, 168-169.

2. There is, obviously, no question here of hands or feet, of any implement borrowed or inherent: Nature needs simply the Matter which it is to work upon and bring under Form; its productivity cannot depend upon mechanical operation. What driving or hoisting goes to produce all that variety of color and pattern?

The wax-workers, whose methods have been cited as parallel to the creative act of Nature, are unable to make colors; all they can do is to impose upon their handicraft colors taken from elsewhere. None the less there is a parallel which demands attention: in the case of workers in such arts there must be something locked up within themselves, an efficacy not going out from them and yet guiding their hands in all their creation; and this observation should have indicated a similar phenomenon in Nature; it should be clear that this indwelling efficacy, which makes without hands, must exist in Nature, no less than in the craftsman—but, there, as a thing completely inbound. Nature need possess no outgoing force as against that remaining within, the only moved thing is Matter; there can be no moved phase in this Nature-Principle; any such moved phase could not be the primal mover; this Nature-Principle is no such moved entity; it is the unmoved Principle operating in the Cosmos.

We may be answered that the Reason-Principle is, no doubt, unmoved, but that the Nature-Principle, another being, operates by motion.

But, if Nature entire is in question here, it is identical with the Reason-Principle; and any part of it that is unmoved is the Reason-Principle. The Nature-Principle must be an Ideal-Form, not a compound of Form and Matter; there is no need for it to possess (such a changeable element as) Matter, hot and cold: the Matter that underlies it, on which it exercises its creative act, brings all that with it, or, natively without quality, becomes hot and cold, and all the rest, when brought under Reason: Matter, to become fire, demands the approach not of fire but of a Reason-Principle.

This is no slight evidence that in the animal and vegetable realms the Reason-Principles are the makers and that Nature is a Reason-Principle producing a second Reason-Principle, its offspring, which, in turn, while itself, still, remaining intact, communicates something to the underlie, Matter.

The Reason-Principle presiding over visible Shape is the very ultimate of its order, a dead thing unable to produce further: that which produces in the created realm is the living Reason-Principle—brother, no doubt, to that which gives mere shape, but having life-giving power.

3. But if this Reason-Principle (Nature) is in act—and produces by the process indicated—how can it have any part in Contemplation?

To begin with, since in all its production it is stationary and intact, a Reason-Principle self-indwelling, it is in its own nature a Contemplative act. All doing must be guided by an Idea, and will therefore be distinct from that Idea: the Reason-Principle then, as accompanying and guiding the work, will be distinct from the work; not being action but Reason-Principle it is, necessarily, Contemplation. Taking the Reason-Principle, the Logos, in all its phases, the lowest and last springs from a mental act (in the higher Logos) and is itself a contemplation, though only in the sense of being contemplated (i.e. of being object and not subject), but above it stands the total Logos with its two distinguishable phases, first, that identified not as Nature but as All-Soul and, next, that operating in Nature and being itself the Nature-Principle.

And does this Reason-Principle, Nature, spring from a contemplation?

Wholly and solely.

From self-contemplation, then? Or what are we to think? It derives from a Contemplation and some contemplating Being; how are we to suppose it to have Contemplation itself?

The Contemplation springing from the reasoning faculty—that, I mean, of planning its own content—it does not possess.

But why not, since it is a phase of Life, a Reason-Principle, and a creative Power?

Because to plan for a thing is to lack it: Nature does not lack; it creates because it possesses. Its creative act is simply its possession of its own characteristic Essence; now its Essence, since it is a Reason-Principle, is to be at once an act of contemplation and an object of contemplation. In other words, the Nature-Principle produces by virtue of being an act of contemplation, an object of contemplation, and a Reason-Principle; on this triple character depends its creative efficacy.

Thus the act of production is seen to be in Nature an act of contemplation, for creation is the outcome of a contemplation which never becomes anything else, which never does anything else, but creates by simply being a contemplation.

4. And Nature, asked why it brings forth its works, might answer if it cared to listen and to speak: "It would have been more becoming to put no question but to learn in silence just as I myself am silent and make no habit of talking. And what is your lesson? This; that whatsoever comes into being is my vision, seen in my silence, the vision that belongs to my character who, sprung from vision, am vision-loving and create vision by the vision-seeing faculty within me. The mathematicians from their vision draw their figures: but I draw nothing: I gaze and the figures of the material world take being as if they fell from my contemplation. As with my Mother (the All-Soul) and the Beings that begot me so it is with me: they are born of a Contemplation and my birth is from them, not by their Act but by their Being; they are the loftier Reason-Principles, they contemplate themselves and I am born."

Now what does this tell us?

It tells: that what we know as Nature is a Soul, offspring of a yet earlier Soul of more powerful life; that it possesses, therefore, in its repose, a vision within itself; that it has no tendency upward nor even downward but is at peace, steadfast, in its own Essence, that, in this immutability accompanied by what may be called Self-Consciousness, it possesses—within the measure of its possibility—a knowledge of the realm of subsequent things perceived in virtue of that understanding and consciousness; and, achieving thus a resplendent and delicious spectacle, has no further aim.

Of course, while it may be convenient to speak of "understanding" or "perception" in the Nature-Principle, this is not in the full sense applicable to other beings; we are applying to sleep a word borrowed from the wake.

For the Vision on which Nature broods, inactive, is a self-intuition, a spectacle laid before it by virtue of its unaccompanied self-concentration and by the fact that in itself it belongs to the order of intuition. It is a Vision silent but somewhat blurred, for there exists another, a clearer, of which Nature is the image: hence all that Nature produces is weak; the weaker act of intuition produces the weaker object.

In the same way, human beings, when weak on the side of contemplation, find in action their trace of vision and of reason: their spiritual feebleness unfits them for contemplation; they are left with a void, because they cannot adequately seize the vision; yet they long for it; they are hurried into action as their way to the vision which they cannot attain by intellection. They act from the desire of seeing their action, and of making it visible and sensible to others when the result shall prove fairly well equal to the plan. Everywhere, doing and making will be found to be either an attenuation or a complement of vision—attenuation if the doer was aiming only at the thing done; complement if he is to possess something nobler to gaze upon than the mere work produced.

Given the power to contemplate the Authentic, who would run, of choice, after its image?

The relation of action to contemplation is indicated in the way duller children, inapt to study and speculation, take to crafts and manual labor.

5. This discussion of Nature has shown us how the origin of things is a Contemplation: we may now take the matter up to the higher Soul; we find that the Contemplation pursued by this, its instinct towards knowing and inquiring, the birth pangs set up by the knowledge it attains, its teeming fullness, have caused it—in itself all one object of Vision—to produce another Vision (that of the Cosmos): it is just as a given science, complete in itself,

becomes the source and cause of what might be called a minor science in the student who attains to some partial knowledge of all its divisions. But the visible objects and the objects of intellectual contemplation of this later creation are dim and helpless by the side of the content of the Soul.

The primal phase of the Soul—inhabitant of the Supreme and, by its participation in the Supreme, filled and illuminated—remains unchangeably There; but in virtue of that first participation, that of the primal participant, a secondary phase also participates in the Supreme, and this secondary goes forth ceaselessly as Life streaming from Life; for energy runs through the Universe and there is no extremity at which it dwindles out. But, travel as far as it may, it never draws that first part of itself from the place whence the outgoing began: for if it abandoned its prior (the Intellectual-Principle), it would no longer be everywhere (its continuous Being would be broken and) it would be present at the end, only, of its course.

None the less that which goes forth cannot be equal to that which remains.

In sum, then:

The Soul is to extend throughout the Universe, no spot void of its energy: but, a prior is always different from its secondary, and energy is a secondary, rising as it must from contemplation or act; act, however, is not at this stage existent since it depends upon contemplation: therefore the Soul while its phases differ must, in all of them, remain a contemplation, and what seems to be an act done under contemplation must be in reality that weakened contemplation of which we have spoken: the engendered must respect the Kind, but in weaker form, dwindled in the descent.

All goes softly since nothing here demands the parade of thought or act upon external things: it is a Soul in vision and, by this vision, creating its own subsequent—this Principle (of Nature), itself also contemplative but in the feebler degree since it lies further away and cannot reproduce the quality or experiences of its prior—a Vision creates the Vision.

(Such creative contemplation is not inexplicable) for no limit exists either to contemplation or to its possible objects, and this explains how the Soul's creation is everywhere: where can this thing fail to be, which is one identical thing in every soul? Vision is not cabined within the bournes of magnitude.

This, of course, does not mean that the Soul is present at the same strength in each and every place and thing—any more than that it is at the same strength in each of its own phases.

The Charioteer (the Leading Principle of the Soul, in the Phaedrus Myth) gives the two horses (its two dissonant faculties) what he has seen and they, taking that gift, showed that they were hungry for what made that vision; there was something lacking to them: if in their desire they acted, their action aimed at what they craved for—and that was vision, and an object of vision.

6. Action, thus, is set towards contemplation and an object of contemplation, so that even those whose life is in doing have seeing as their object; what they have not been able to achieve by the direct path, they hope to come at by the circuit.

Further: suppose they succeed; they desired a certain thing to come about, not in order to be unaware of it but to know it, to see it present before the mind: their success is the laying up of a vision. We act for the sake of some good; this means not for something to remain outside ourselves, not in order that we may possess nothing but that we may hold the good of the action. And hold it, where? Where but in the mind?

Thus once more, action is brought back to contemplation: for (mind or) Soul is a Reason-Principle and anything that one lays up in the Soul can be no other than a Reason-Principle, a silent thing, the more certainly such a principle as the impression made is the deeper.

This vision achieved, the acting instinct pauses; the mind is satisfied and seeks nothing further; the contemplation, in one so conditioned, remains absorbed within as having acquired certainty to rest upon. The brighter the certainty, the more tranquil is the contemplation as having acquired the more perfect unity; and—for now we come to the serious treatment of the subject—

125

In proportion to the truth with which the knowing faculty knows, it comes to identification with the object of its knowledge.

As long as duality persists, the two lie apart, parallel as it were to each other; there is a pair in which the two elements remain strange to one another, as when Ideal-Principles laid up in the mind or Soul remain idle.

Hence the Idea must not be left to lie outside but must be made one identical thing with the Soul of the novice so that he finds it really his own.

The Soul, once domiciled within that Idea and brought to likeness with it, becomes productive, active; what it always held by its primary nature it now grasps with knowledge and applies in deed, so becoming, as it were, a new thing and, informed as it now is by the purely intellectual, it sees (in its outgoing act) as a stranger looking upon a strange world. It was, no doubt, essentially a Reason-Principle, even an Intellectual Principle; but its function is to see a (lower) realm which these do not see.

For, it is not a complete thing: it has a lack; it is incomplete in regard to its Prior; yet it, also, has a tranquil vision of what it produces. What it has once brought into being it produces no more, for all its productiveness is determined by this lack: it produces for the purpose of Contemplation, in the desire of knowing all its content: when there is question of practical things it adapts its content to the outside order.

The Soul has a greater content than Nature has and therefore it is more tranquil; it is more nearly complete and therefore more contemplative. It is, however, not perfect, and is all the more eager to penetrate the object of contemplation, and it seeks the vision that comes by observation. It leaves its native realm and busies itself elsewhere; then it returns, and it possesses its vision by means of that phase of itself from which it had parted. The self-indwelling Soul inclines less to such experiences.

The Sage, then, has gone through a process of reasoning when he expounds his act to others; but in relation to himself he is Vision: such a man is already set, not merely in regard to exterior things but also within himself, towards what is one and at rest: all his faculty and life are inward-bent.

7. Certain Principles, then, we may take to be established—some self-evident, others brought out by our treatment above:

All the forms of Authentic Existence spring from vision and are a vision. Everything that springs from these Authentic Existences in their vision is an object of vision—manifest to sensation or to true knowledge or to surface-awareness. All act aims at this knowing; all impulse is towards knowledge, all that springs from vision exists to produce Ideal-Form, that is a fresh object of vision, so that universally, as images of their engendering principles, they all produce objects of vision, Ideal-Forms. In the engendering of these existences, imitations of the Authentic, it is made manifest that the creating powers operate not for the sake of creation and action but in order to produce an object of vision. This same vision is the ultimate purpose of all the acts of the mind and, even further downward, of all sensation, since sensation also is an effort towards knowledge; lower still, Nature, producing similarly its subsequent principle, brings into being the vision and Idea that we know in it. It is certain, also, that as the Firsts exist in vision all other things must be straining towards the same condition; the starting-point is, universally, the goal.

When living things reproduce their kind, it is that the Reason-Principles within stir them; the procreative act is the expression of a contemplation, a travail towards the creation of many forms, many objects of contemplation, so that the universe may be filled full with Reason-Principles and that contemplation may be, as nearly as possible, endless: to bring anything into being is to produce an Idea-Form and that again is to enrich the universe with contemplation: all the failures, alike in being and in doing, are but the swerving of visionaries from the object of vision: in the end the sorriest craftsman is still a maker of forms, ungracefully. So Love, too, is vision with the pursuit of Ideal-Form.

8. From this basis we proceed:

In the advancing stages of Contemplation rising from that in Nature, to that in the Soul and thence again to that in the Intellectual-Principle itself, the object contemplated becomes progressively a more and more intimate possession of the Contemplating Beings, more and more one thing with them; and in the advanced Soul the objects of knowledge, well on the way towards the Intellectual-Principle, are close to identity with their container.

Hence we may conclude that, in the Intellectual-Principle itself, there is complete identity of Knower and Known, and this not by way of domiciliation, as in the case of even the highest soul, but by Essence, by the fact that, there, no distinction exists between Being and Knowing; we cannot stop at a principle containing separate parts; there must always be a yet higher, a principle above all such diversity.

The Supreme must be an entity in which the two are one; it will, therefore, be a Seeing that lives, not an object of vision like things existing in something other than themselves: what exists in an outside element owes its life to that element; it is not self-living.

If, therefore, the pure object of Intellection or Contemplation is to have life, it must be Life Absolute and distinct from the vegetative or sensitive life or any other life determined by Soul.

In a certain sense no doubt all lives are thoughts—but qualified as thought vegetative, thought sensitive, and thought psychic.

What, then, makes them thoughts?

The fact that they are Reason-Principles. Every life is some form of thought, but of a dwindling clearness like the degrees of life itself. The first and clearest Life and the first Intelligence are one Being. The First Life, then, is an Intellection and the next form of Life is the next Intellection and the last form of Life is the last form of Intellection. Thus every Life is of this order; it is an Intellection.

But while men may recognize grades in life they reject grades in thought; to them there are thoughts (full and perfect) and anything else is no thought. This is simply because they do not seek to establish what Life is.

The essential is to observe that, here again, all reasoning shows that whatever exists is a bye-work of visioning: if, then, the truest Life is such by virtue of an Intellection and is identical with the truest Intellection, then the truest Intellection is a living being; Contemplation and its object constitute a living thing, a Life, two inextricably one.

The duality, thus, is a unity; but how is this unity also a plurality?

The explanation is that in a unity there can be no seeing (a pure unity has no room for vision and an object); and in its Contemplation the One is not acting as a Unity; if it were, the Intellectual-Principle cannot exist. The Highest began as a unity but did not remain as it began; all unknown to itself, it became manifold; it grew, as it were, pregnant: desiring universal possession, it flung itself outward, though it were better had it never known the desire by which a Secondary came into being: it is like a Circle (in the Idea) which in projection becomes a figure, a surface, a circumference, a center, a system of radii, of upper and lower segments. The Whence is the better; the Whither is less good: the Whither is not of the quality of the Whence-and-Whither, and the Whence-and-Whither is not of the quality of the Whence alone.

The Intellectual-Principle on the other hand was never merely the Principle of an inviolable unity; it was a universal as well and, being so, was the Intellectual-Principle of all things. Being, thus, all things and the Principle of all, it must be such that every part of it is universal, is all things: otherwise, it contains a part which is not Intellectual-Principle: it will be a juxtaposition of non-Intellectuals, a huddled heap waiting to be made over from the mass of things into the Intellectual-Principle!

We conclude that this Being is limitless and that in all the out-flow from it there is no lessening, either in its emanation, since this also is the entire universe, nor in itself, the starting point, since it is no assemblage of parts (to be diminished by any outgo).

9. Clearly a Being of this nature is not the primal existent; there must exist that which transcends it, that Being (the Absolute), to which all our discussion has been leading.

In the first place, Plurality is later than Unity. The Intellectual-Principle is a number (= the expression of a plurality); and number derives from unity: the source of a number such as this must be the authentically One. Further, it is the sum of an Intellectual-Being with the object of its Intellection, so that it is a duality; and, given this duality, we must find what exists before it.

What is this?

The Intellectual-Principle taken separately, perhaps?

No: an Intellect is always inseparable from an intelligible object; eliminate the intelligible, and the Intellectual-Principle disappears with it. If, then, what we are seeking cannot be the Intellectual-Principle but must be something that rejects the duality there present, then the Prior demanded by that duality must be something on the further side of the Intellectual-Principle.

But might it not be the Intelligible object itself?

No: for the Intelligible makes an equally inseparable duality with the Intellectual-Principle.

If, then, neither the Intellectual-Principle nor the Intelligible Object can be the First Existent, what is?

Our answer can only be:

The source of both.

What will This be; under what character can we picture It?

(We will be told that) It must be either Intellective or without Intellection: if Intellective it is the Intellectual-Principle; if not, it will be without even knowledge of itself—and then, what is there so august about it?

If we define it as The Good and the wholly simplex, we will, no doubt, be telling the truth, but we will not be giving any certain and lucid account of it as long as we have in mind no entity in which to lodge the conception by which we define it.

Yet: our knowledge of everything else comes by way of our intelligence; our power is that of knowing the intelligible by means of the intelligence: but this Entity transcends all of the intellectual nature; by what direct intuition, then, can it be brought within our grasp?

To this question the answer is that we can know it only in the degree of human faculty: we indicate it by virtue of what in ourselves is like it.

For in us, also, there is something of that Being; nay, nothing, ripe for that participation, can be void of it.

Wherever you be, you have only to range over against this omnipresent Being that in you which is capable of drawing from It, and you have your share in it: imagine a voice sounding over a vast waste of land, and not only over the emptiness alone but over human beings; wherever you be in that great space you have but to listen and you take the voice entire—entire though yet with a difference.

And what do we take when we thus point the Intelligence?

The Intellectual-Principle in us must mount to its origins: essentially a thing facing two ways, it must deliver itself over to those powers within it which tend upward; if it seeks the vision of that Being, it must become something more than Intellect.

For the Intellectual-Principle is the earliest form of Life: it is the Activity presiding over the outflowing of the universal Order—the outflow, that is, of the first moment, not that of the continuous process.

In its character as Life, as emanation, as containing all things in their precise forms and not merely in the agglomerate mass—for this would be to contain them (against its specific character) imperfectly and inarticulately—it must of necessity derive from some other Being, from one that does not emanate but is the Principle of Emanation, of Life, of Intellect, and of the Universe.

For the Universe is not a Principle and Source: it springs from a source, and that source cannot be the All or anything belonging to the All since it is to generate the All, and must be not a plurality but the Source of plurality since universally a begetting power is less complex than the begotten. Thus the Being that has engendered the Intellectual-Principle must be more simplex than the Intellectual-Principle.

We may be told that this engendering Principle is the One-and-All.

But, at that, it must be either each separate entity from among all or it will be all things in the one mass.

Now if it were the massed total of all, it must be of later origin than any of the things of which it is the sum; if it precedes the total, it differs from the things that make up the total and they from it: if it and the total of things constitute a co-existence, it is not a Source. But what we are probing for must be a Source; it must exist before all, that all may be fashioned as sequel to it.

As for the notion that it may be each separate entity of the All, this would make a self-Identity into a what you like, where you like, indifferently, and would, besides, abolish all distinction in things themselves.

Once more we see that this can be no thing among things but must be prior to all things.

10. And what will such a Principle essentially be?

The potentiality of the Universe: the potentiality whose non-existence would mean the non-existence of all the Universe and even of the Intellectual-Principle which is the primal Life and all Life.

This Principle on the thither side of Life is the cause of Life— for that Manifestation of Life which is the Universe of things is not the First Activity; it is itself poured forth, so to speak, like water from a spring.

Imagine a spring that has no source outside itself; it gives itself to all the rivers, yet is never exhausted by what they take, but remains always integrally as it was; the rides that proceed from it are at one within it before they run their several ways, yet all, in some sense, know beforehand down what channels they will pour their streams.

Or: think of the Life coursing throughout some mighty tree while yet it is the stationary Principle of the whole, in no sense scattered over all that extent but, as it were, vested in the root: it is the giver of the entire and manifold life of the tree, but remains unmoved itself, not manifold but the Principle of that manifold life.

And this surprises no one: though it is in fact astonishing how all that varied vitality springs from the unvarying, and how that very manifoldness could not be unless before the multiplicity there were something all singleness; for, the Principle is not broken into parts to make the total; on the contrary, such partition would destroy both; nothing would come into being if its cause, thus broken up, changed character.

Thus we are always brought back to The One.

Every particular thing has a One of its own to which it may be traced; the All has its One, its Prior but not yet the Absolute One; through this we reach that Absolute One, where all such reference comes to an end.

Now when we reach a One—the stationary Principle—in the tree, in the animal, in Soul, in the All—we have in every case the most powerful, the precious element: when we come to the One in the Authentically Existent Beings—their Principle and source and potentiality—shall we lose confidence and suspect it of being—nothing?

Certainly this Absolute is none of the things of which it is the source—its nature is that nothing can be affirmed of it—not existence, not essence, not life—since it is That which transcends all these. But possess yourself of it by the very elimination of Being and you hold a marvel. Thrusting forward to This, attaining, and resting in yourself, seek to grasp it more and more—understanding it by that intuitive thrust alone, but knowing its greatness by the Beings that follow upon it and exist by its power.

11. Another approach:

The Intellectual-Principle is a Seeing, and a Seeing which itself sees; therefore it is a potentiality which has become effective.

This implies the distinction of Matter and Form in it—as there must be in all actual seeing—the Matter in this case being the Intelligibles which the Intellectual-Principle contains and sees. All actual seeing implies duality; before the seeing takes place there is the pure unity (of the power of seeing). That unity (of principle) acquires duality (in the act of seeing), and the duality is (always to be traced back to) a unity.

Now as our sight requires the world of sense for its satisfaction and realization, so the vision in the Intellectual-Principle demands, for its completion, The Good.

It cannot be, itself, The Good, since then it would not need to see or to perform any other Act; for The Good is the center of all else, and it is by means of The Good that every thing has Act, while The Good is in need of nothing and therefore possesses nothing beyond itself.

Once you have uttered "The Good," add no further thought: by any addition, and in proportion to that addition, you introduce a deficiency.

Do not even say that it has Intellection; you would be dividing it; it would become a duality, Intellect and The Good. The Good has no need of the Intellectual-Principle which, on the contrary, needs it, and attaining it, is shaped into Goodness and becomes perfect by it: the Form thus received, sprung from The Good, brings it to likeness with The Good.

Thus the traces of The Good discerned upon it must be taken as indication of the nature of that Archetype: we form a conception of its true character from its image playing upon the Intellectual-Principle. This image of itself it has communicated to the Intellect that contemplates it: thus all the striving is on the side of the Intellect, which is the eternal striver and eternally the attainer. The Being beyond neither strives, since it feels no lack, nor attains, since it has no striving. And this marks it off from the Intellectual-Principle, to which characteristically belongs the striving, the concentrated strain towards its Form.

Yet: The Intellectual-Principle; beautiful; the most beautiful of all; lying lapped in pure light and in clear radiance; circumscribing the Nature of the Authentic Existents; the original of which this beautiful world is a shadow and an image; tranquil in the fullness of glory since in it there is nothing devoid of intellect, nothing dark or out of rule; a living thing in a life of blessedness: this, too, must overwhelm with awe any that has seen it, and penetrated it, to become a unit of its Being.

But: as one that looks up to the heavens and sees the splendor of the stars thinks of the Maker and searches, so whoever has contemplated the Intellectual Universe and known it and wondered for it must search after its Maker too. What Being has raised so noble a fabric? And how? Who has begotten such a child, this Intellectual-Principle, this lovely abundance so abundantly endowed?

The Source of all this cannot be an Intellect; nor can it be an abundant power: it must have been before Intellect and abundance were; these are later and things of lack; abundance had to be made abundant and Intellection needed to know.

These are very near to the un-needing, to that which has no need of knowing, they have abundance and intellection authentically, as being the first to possess. But, there is That before them which neither needs nor possesses anything, since, needing or possessing anything else, it would not be what it is—The Good.

Ennead IV
Third Tractate: 15-17; 24-25; 27; 32

PROBLEMS OF THE SOUL (I)

This treatise is the first major part of a greater work devoted to the main difficulties and problems in the Platonic teaching of soul. The second part of this work, divided by Porphyry, constitutes *Enn.* IV.4. The Neoplatonic concept of *psuche* is partly inherited from early Hellenic thought, but in Homeric poems *psuche* is still understood as (1) a phantom (*phasma*), created by a god in the semblance of a living person, (2) the dream image (*oneiros*), considered to be a sleep apparition of a ghostly double, (3) a shadow-like image (*eidolon*) of the dead. Due to the Egyptian concept of *ba*, i.e. the winged "soul" separated from the body, inherited by the Orphics and Pythagoreans, the *psuche*, instead of being viewed as an *eidolon* of the body, became the immortal soul that constitutes one's real being. To put it into Egyptian terms, the human *ba*, separated from the body, realizes its divine essence and is turned into *akh*, the light of divine Intellect. In Pythagoreanism and Platonism, the mortal body became a simple appearance, and the main task of this "Egyptianized" philosophy was purification and separation of the soul, recollection (*anamnesis*), and emancipation of one's soul in this life as it will be after death. According to Pythagorean and Orphic belief, the *psuche* is a spiritual being fallen from a higher noetic realm into the cycle of birth and death. The soul must thus eventually return to its original state through the exercise of virtue, contemplation, spiritual hermeneutics, philosophical *askesis*, and hieratic rites.

In Plotinus, *psuche* is the principle of life. Hence, the universe is a single ensouled living body. The individual souls are not parts or products of the World-Soul, but the World-Soul and individual souls derive from the divine hypostasis Soul. Therefore the World-Soul is not our mother but rather our elder sister. The soul is the principle of all emotions and thinks discursively, but at its highest it is an eternal inhabitant of the noetic cosmos and shares the activity and life of Intellect. At this level it thinks intuitively, not discursively. It should be observed that a *nous* in the individual *psuche* is distinct from the hypostasis *Nous*, but is illuminated by it. Since everything in the universe is regarded as a living organism, the life of Soul is a continuum, reaching from living minerals and plants to living gods. All souls (*psuchai*) are in a sense one, though differentiated in their unity and at different ontological levels. As A.H. Armstrong and R.R. Ravindra have pointed out, the limits of universal Soul are no narrower than the limits of all existence.[13] Man has all levels of Soul within him and, through the participation of the highest part of his soul in the eternal life of Intellect, he has the eternal noetic world within him as well.

15. The souls peering forth from the Intellectual Realm descend first to the heavens and there put on a body; this becomes at once the medium by which as they reach out more and more towards magnitude (physical extension) they proceed to bodies progressively more earthy. Some even plunge from heaven to the very lowest of corporeal forms; others pass, stage by stage, too feeble to lift towards the higher the burden they carry, weighed downwards by their heaviness and forgetfulness.

As for the differences among them, these are due to variation in the bodies entered, or to the accidents of life, or to upbringing, or to inherent peculiarities of temperament, or to all these influences together, or to specific combinations of them.

Then again some have fallen unreservedly into the power of the destiny ruling here: some yielding betimes are betimes too their own: there are those who, while they accept what must be borne, have the strength of self-mastery in all that is left to their own act; they have given themselves to another dispensation: they live by the code of the aggregate of beings, the code which is woven out of the Reason-Principles and all the other causes ruling in the Cosmos, out of soul-movements and out of laws springing in the Supreme; a code, therefore, consonant with those higher existences, founded upon them, linking their sequents back to them, keeping unshakably true all that is capable of holding itself set towards the divine nature, and leading round by all appropriate means whatsoever is less natively apt.

[13] A.H. Armstrong and R.R. Ravindra, "*Buddhi* in the *Bhagavadgita* and Psyche in Plotinus," in *Neoplatonism and Indian Thought*, ed. Baine Harris (Norfolk: ISNS, 1982), p. 75.

In fine all diversity of condition in the lower spheres is determined by the descendent beings themselves.

16. The punishment justly overtaking the wicked must therefore be ascribed to the cosmic order which leads all in accordance with the right.

But what of chastisements, poverty, illness, falling upon the good outside of all justice? These events, we will be told, are equally interwoven into the world order and fall under prediction, and must consequently have a cause in the general reason: are they therefore to be charged to past misdoing?

No: such misfortunes do not answer to reasons established in the nature of things; they are not laid up in the master-facts of the universe, but were merely accidental sequents: a house falls, and anyone that chances to be underneath is killed, no matter what sort of man he be: two squadrons of cavalry are moving in perfect order—or one if you like—but anything getting in the way is wounded or trampled down. Or we may reason that the undeserved stroke can be no evil to the sufferer in view of the beneficent interweaving of the All; or again, no doubt, that nothing is unjust that finds justification in a past history.

We may not think of some things being fitted into a system with others abandoned to the capricious; if things must happen by cause, by natural sequences, under one Reason-Principle and a single set scheme, we must admit that the minor equally with the major is fitted into that order and pattern.

Wrongdoing from man to man is wrong in the doer and must be imputed, but, as belonging to the established order of the universe, is not a wrong even as regards the innocent sufferer; it is a thing that had to be, and, if the sufferer is good, the issue is to his gain. For we cannot think that this ordered combination proceeds without God and justice; we must take it to be precise in the distribution of due, while, yet, the reasons of things elude us, and to our ignorance the scheme presents matter of censure.

17. Various considerations explain why the souls going forth from the Intellectual proceed first to the heavenly regions. The heavens, as the noblest portion of sensible space, would border with the least exalted of the Intellectual, and will, therefore, be first ensouled, first to participate as most apt; while what is of earth is at the very extremity of progression, least endowed towards participation, remotest from the unembodied.

All the souls, then, shine down upon the heavens and spend there the main of themselves and the best; only their lower phases illuminate the lower realms; and those souls which descend deepest show their light furthest down—not themselves the better for the depth to which they have penetrated.

There is, we may put it, something that is center; about it, a circle of light shed from it; round center and first circle alike, another circle, light from light; outside that again, not another circle of light but one which, lacking light of its own, must borrow.

The last we may figure to ourselves as a revolving circle, or rather a sphere, of a nature to receive light from that third realm, its next higher, in proportion to the light which that itself receives. Thus all begins with the great light, shining self-centered; in accordance with the reigning plan (that of emanation) this gives forth its brilliance; the later (divine) existents (souls) add their radiation—some of them remaining above, while there are some that are drawn further downward, attracted by the splendor of the object they illuminate. These last find that their charges need more and more care; the steersman of a storm-tossed ship is so intent on saving it that he forgets his own interest and never thinks that he is recurrently in peril of being dragged down with the vessel; similarly the souls are intent upon contriving for their charges and finally come to be pulled down by them; they are fettered in bonds of sorcery, gripped and held by their concern for the realm of Nature.

If every living being were of the character of the All—perfect, self-sufficing, in peril from no outside influence—the Soul now spoken of as indwelling would not occupy the body; it would infuse life while clinging, entire, within the Supreme.

24. Now comes the question of the Soul leaving the body: where does it go?

It cannot remain in this world where there is no natural recipient for it; and it cannot remain attached to anything not of a character to hold it; it can be held here when only it is less than wise, containing within itself something of that which lures it.

If it does contain any such alien element it gives itself, with increasing attachment, to the sphere to which that element naturally belongs and tends.

The space open to the Soul's resort is vast and diverse; the difference will come by the double force of the individual condition and of the justice reigning in things. No one can ever escape the suffering entailed by ill deeds done: the divine law is ineluctable, carrying bound up, as one with it, the fore-ordained execution of its doom. The sufferer, all unaware, is swept onward towards his due, hurried always by the restless driving of his errors, until at last wearied out by that against which he struggled, he falls into his fit place and, by self-chosen movement, is brought to the lot he never chose. And the law decrees, also, the intensity and the duration of the suffering while it carries with it, too, the lifting of chastisement and the faculty of rising from those places of pain—all by power of the harmony that maintains the universal scheme.

Souls, body-bound, are apt to body-punishment; clear souls no longer drawing to themselves at any point any vestige of body are, by their very being, outside the bodily sphere; body-free, containing nothing of body—there where Essence is, and Being, and the Divine within the Divinity, among Those, within That, such a soul must be.

If you still ask Where, you must ask where those Beings are—and in your seeking, seek otherwise than with the sight, and not as one seeking for body.

25. Now comes the question, equally calling for an answer, whether those souls that have quitted the places of earth retain memory of their lives—all souls or some, of all things, or of some

things, and, again, for ever or merely for some period not very long after their withdrawal.

A true investigation of this matter requires us to establish first what a remembering principle must be—I do not mean what memory is, but in what order of beings it can occur. The nature of memory has been indicated, labored even, elsewhere; we still must try to understand more clearly what characteristics are present where memory exists.

Now a memory has to do with something brought into ken from without, something learned or something experienced; the Memory-Principle, therefore, cannot belong to such things as are immune from experience and from time.

No memory, therefore, can be ascribed to any divine being, or to the Authentic-Existent or the Intellectual-Principle: these are intangibly immune; time does not approach them; they possess eternity centered around Being; they know nothing of past and sequent; all is an unbroken state of identity, not receptive of change. Now a being rooted in unchanging identity cannot entertain memory, since it has not and never had a state differing from any previous state, or any new intellection following upon a former one, so as to be aware of contrast between a present perception and one remembered from before.

But what prevents such a being (from possessing memory in the sense of) perceiving, without variation in itself, such outside changes as, for example, the cosmic periods?

Simply the fact that following the changes of the revolving Cosmos it would have perception of earlier and later: intuition and memory are distinct.

We cannot hold its self-intellections to be acts of memory; this is no question of something entering from without, to be grasped and held in fear of an escape; if its intellections could slip away from it (as a memory might) its very Essence (as the Hypostasis of inherent Intellection) would be in peril.

For the same reason memory, in the current sense, cannot be attributed to the Soul in connexion with the ideas inherent in its essence: these it holds not as a memory but as a possession, though, by its very entrance into this sphere, they are no longer the mainstay of its Act.

The Soul-action which is to be observed seems to have induced the Ancients to ascribe memory, and "Recollection" (the Platonic Anamnesis), to souls bringing into outward manifestation the ideas they contain: we see at once that the memory here indicated is another kind; it is a memory outside of time. . . .

26. . . . Memory, in point of fact, is impeded by the body: even as things are, addition often brings forgetfulness; with thinning and clearing away, memory will often revive. The Soul is a stability; the shifting and fleeting things which body is can be a cause only of its forgetting, not of its remembering—Lethe stream may be understood in this sense—and memory is a fact of the Soul.

27. But of what soul—of that which we envisage as the more divine, by which we are human beings, or that other which springs from the All?

Memory must be admitted in both of these, personal memories and shared memories; and when the two souls are together, the memories also are as one; when they stand apart, assuming that both exist and endure, each soon forgets the other's affairs, retaining for a longer time its own. Thus it is that the Shade of Heracles in the lower regions—this "Shade," as I take it, being the characteristically human part—remembers all the action and experience of the life, since that career was mainly of the hero's personal shaping; the other souls (soul-phases) going to constitute the joint-being could, for all their different standing, have nothing to recount but the events of that same life, doings which they knew from the time of their association: perhaps they would add also some moral judgment.

What the Heracles standing outside the Shade spoke of we are not told: what can we think that other, the freed and isolated, soul would recount?

The soul which still drags a burden will tell of all the man did and felt; but upon death there will appear, as time passes, memories of the lives lived before, some of the events of the most recent life being dismissed as trivial. As it grows away from the body, it will revive things forgotten in the corporeal state, and if it passes in and out of one body after another, it will tell over the events of the discarded life, it will treat as present that which it has just left, and it will remember much from the former existence. But with lapse of time it will come to forgetfulness of many things that were mere accretion.

Then, free and alone at last, what will it have to remember?

The answer to that question depends on our discovering in what faculty of the Soul memory resides.

32. But the memory of friends, children, wife? Country too, and all that the better sort of man may reasonably remember?

All these, the one (the lower man) retains with emotion, the authentic man passively: for the experience, certainly, was first felt in that lower phase from which, however, the best of such impressions pass over to the graver soul in the degree in which the two are in communication.

The lower soul must be always striving to attain to memory of the activities of the higher: this will be especially so when it is itself of a fine quality, for there will always be some that are better from the beginning and bettered here by the guidance of the higher.

The loftier, on the contrary, must desire to come to a happy forgetfulness of all that has reached it through the lower: for one reason, there is always the possibility that the excellence of the higher goes with a baseness in the lower, which is only kept down by sheer force. In any case the more urgent the intention towards the Supreme, the more extensive will be the Soul's forgetfulness, unless indeed when the entire living has, even here, been such that memory has nothing but the noblest to deal with: in this world itself, all is best when human interests have been held aloof; so, therefore, it must be with the memory of them. In this sense we may truly say that the good soul is the forgetful. It flees multiplicity; it seeks to escape the unbounded by drawing all to unity, for only thus is it free from entanglement, light-footed, self-conducted.

Thus it is that even in this world the soul which has the desire of the other is putting away, amid its actual life, all that is foreign to that order. While it is in the heavenly regions it puts away more again. Little of what is gathered here is taken with it to the Intellectual Realm.

The Heracles of the heavenly regions would still tell of his feats: but there is the other man to whom all of that is trivial; he has been translated to a holier Place; he has won his way to the Intellectual Realm; he is more than Heracles, proven in the combats in which the combatants are the wise.

Ennead IV
Fourth Tractate: 5; 7-9; 32-33; 38; 40-41; 45

PROBLEMS OF THE SOUL (II)

This treatise is simply the continuation of *Enn.* IV.3, thus constituting a single work, artificially divided by Porphyry.

5. But this power which determines memory, is it also the principle by which the Supreme becomes effective in us?

At any time when we have not been in direct vision of that sphere, memory is the source of its activity within us; when we have possessed that vision, its presence is due to the principle by which we enjoyed it: this principle awakens where it wakens; and it alone has vision in that order; for this is no matter to be brought to us by way of analogy, or by the syllogistic reasoning whose grounds lie elsewhere; the power which we possess of discoursing upon the Intellectual Beings, so far as such discourse is here possible, is vested in that principle which alone is capable of their contemplation. That we must awaken, so to speak, and thus attain the vision of the Supreme, as one, standing on some lofty height and lifting his eyes, sees what to those that have not mounted with him is invisible.

Memory, by this account, commences after the Soul has left the highest spheres; it is first known in the celestial period.

A soul that has descended from the Intellectual region to the celestial and there comes to rest, may very well be understood to recognize many other souls known in its former state—supposing that, as we have said, it retains recollection of much that it knew here. This recognition would be natural if the bodies with which those souls are vested in the celestial must reproduce the former appearance; supposing the spherical form (of the stars inhabited by souls in the mid-realm) means a change of appearance, recognition would go by character, by the distinctive quality of personality:

this is not fantastic; conditions changing need not mean a change of character. If the souls have mutual conversation, this too would mean recognition.

But those whose descent from the Intellectual is complete, how is it with them?

They will recall their memories, of the same things, but with less force than those still in the celestial, since they have had other experiences to remember, and the lapse of time will have utterly obliterated much of what was formerly present to them.

But what way of remembering the Supreme is left if the souls have turned to the sense-known Cosmos, and are to fall into this sphere of process?

They need not fall to the ultimate depth: their downward movement may be checked at some one moment of the way; and as long as they have not touched the lowest of the region of process (the point at which non-being begins) there is nothing to prevent them rising once more.

7. In other words, they have seen God and they do not remember?

Ah, no: it is that they see God still and always, and that as long as they see, they cannot tell themselves they have had the vision; such reminiscence is for souls that have lost it.

Well, but can they not tell themselves that yesterday, or last year, they moved round the earth, that they lived yesterday or at any given moment in their lives?

Their living is eternal, and eternity is an unchanging unity. To identify a yesterday or a last year in their movement would be like isolating the movement of one of the feet, and finding a this or a that and an entire series in what is a single act. The movement of the celestial beings is one movement: it is our measuring that presents us with many movements, and with distinct days determined by intervening nights: There all is one day; series has no place; no yesterday, no last year.

Still: the space traversed is different; there are the various sections of the Zodiac: why, then, should not the Soul say, "I have traversed that section and now I am in this other?" If, also, it looks down over the concerns of men, must it not see the changes that befall them, that they are not as they were, and, by that observation, that the beings and the things concerned were otherwise formerly? And does not that mean memory?

8. But, we need not record in memory all we see; mere incidental concomitants need not occupy the imagination; when things vividly present to intuition, or knowledge, happen to occur in concrete form, it is not necessary—unless for purposes of a strictly practical administration—to pass over that direct acquaintance, and fasten upon the partial sense-preparation, which is already known in the larger knowledge.

I will take this point by point:

First: it is not essential that everything seen should be laid up in the mind; for when the object is of no importance, or of no personal concern, the sensitive faculty, stimulated by the differences in the objects present to vision, acts without accompaniment of the will, and is alone in entertaining the impression. The Soul does not take into its deeper recesses such differences as do not meet any of its needs, or serve any of its purposes. Above all, when the Soul's act is directed towards another order, it must utterly reject the memory of such things, things over and done with now, and not even taken into knowledge when they were present.

On the second point: circumstances, purely accidental, need not be present to the imaging faculty, and if they do so appear they need not be retained or even observed, and in fact the impression of any such circumstance does not entail awareness. Thus in local movement, if there is no particular importance to us in the fact that we pass through first this and then that portion of air, or that we proceed from some particular point, we do not take notice, or even know it as we walk. Similarly, if it were of no importance to us to accomplish any given journey, mere movement in the air being the main concern, we would not trouble to ask at what particular point of place we were, or what distance we had traversed; if we have to observe only the act of movement and not its duration, nothing to do which obliges us to think of time, the minutes are not recorded in our minds.

And finally, it is of common knowledge that, when the understanding is possessed of the entire act undertaken and has no reason to foresee any departure from the normal, it will no longer observe the detail; in a process unfailingly repeated without variation, attention to the unvarying detail is idleness.

So it is with the stars. They pass from point to point, but they move on their own affairs and not for the sake of traversing the space they actually cover; the vision of the things that appear on the way, the journey by, nothing of this is their concern; their passing this or that is of accident not of essence, and their intention is to greater objects: moreover each of them journeys, unchangeably, the same unchanging way; and again, there is no question to them of the time they spend in any given section of the journey, even supposing time-division to be possible in the case. All this granted, nothing makes it necessary that they should have any memory of places or times traversed. Besides, this life of the ensouled stars is one identical thing (since they are one in the All-Soul) so that their very spatial movement is pivoted upon identity and resolves itself into a movement not spatial but vital, the movement of a single living being whose act is directed to itself, a being which to anything outside is at rest, but is in movement by dint of the inner life it possesses, the eternal life. Or we may take the comparison of the movement of the heavenly bodies to a choral dance; if we think of it as a dance which comes to rest at some given period, the entire dance, accomplished from beginning to end, will be perfect while at each partial stage it was imperfect: but if the dance is a thing of eternity, it is in eternal perfection. And if it is in eternal perfection, it has no points of time and place at which it will achieve perfection; it will, therefore, have no concern about attaining to any such points: it will, therefore, make no measurements of time or place; it will have, therefore, no memory of time and place.

If the stars live a blessed life in their vision of the life inherent in their souls, and if, by force of their souls' tendency to become one, and by the light they cast from themselves upon the entire heavens, they are like the strings of a lyre which, being struck in tune, sing a melody in some natural scale: if this is the way the heavens, as one, are moved, and the component parts in their relation to the whole—the sidereal system moving as one, and each part in its own way, to the same purpose, though each too hold its own place—then our doctrine is all the more surely established; the life of the heavenly bodies is the more clearly an unbroken unity.

9. But Zeus—ordering all, governor, guardian, and disposer, possessor for ever of the kingly soul and the kingly intellect, bringing all into being by his providence, and presiding over all things as they come, administering all under plan and system, unfolding the periods of the Cosmos, many of which stand already accomplished—would it not seem inevitable that, in this multiplicity of concern, Zeus should have memory of all the periods, their number, and their differing qualities? Contriving the future, coordinating, calculating for what is to be, must he not surely be the chief of all in remembering, as he is chief in producing?

Even this matter of Zeus' memory of the cosmic periods is difficult; it is a question of their being numbered, and of his knowledge of their number. A determined number would mean that the All had a beginning in time (which is not so); if the periods are unlimited, Zeus cannot know the number of his works.

The answer is that he will know himself to be a unity existing in virtue of one life for ever and in this sense unlimited; and his knowledge of the unity will not be as of something seen from outside but as of something embraced in true knowledge, for this unlimited is an eternal indweller within himself—or, to be more accurate, eternally follows upon him—and is seen by an indwelling knowledge; Zeus knows his own unlimited life, and, in that knowledge, knows the activity that flows from him to the Cosmos; but he knows it in its unity not in its process.

32. If we can trace neither to material agencies (blind elements) nor to any deliberate intention the influences from without which

reach to us and to the other forms of life and to the terrestrial in general, what cause satisfactory to reason remains?

The secret is: firstly, that this All is one universally comprehensive living being, encircling all the living beings within it, and having a soul, one soul, which extends to all its members in the degree of participant membership held by each; secondly, that every separate thing is an integral part of this All by belonging to the total material fabric—unrestrictedly a part by bodily membership, while, in so far as it has also some participation in the All-Soul, it possesses in that degree spiritual membership as well, perfect where participation is in the All-Soul alone, partial where there is also a union with a lower soul.

But, with all this gradation, each several thing is affected by all else in virtue of the common participation in the All, and to the degree of its own participation.

This One-All, therefore, is a sympathetic total and stands as one living being; the far is near; it happens as in one animal with its separate parts: talon, horn, finger, and any other member are not continuous and yet are effectively near; intermediate parts feel nothing, but at a distant point the local experience is known. Correspondent things not side by side but separated by others placed between, the sharing of experience by dint of like condition—this is enough to ensure that the action of any distant member be transmitted to its distant fellow. Where all is a living thing summing to a unity there is nothing so remote in point of place as not to be near by virtue of a nature which makes of the one living being a sympathetic organism.

Where there is similarity between a thing affected and the thing affecting it, the affection is not alien; where the affecting cause is dissimilar the affection is firm and unpleasant.

Such hurtful action of member upon member within one living being need not seem surprising: within ourselves, in our own activities, one constituent can be harmed by another; bile and animal spirit seem to press and goad other members of the human total: in the vegetal realm one part hurts another by sucking the moisture from it. And in the All there is something analogous to bile and animal spirit, as to other such constituents. For visibly it is not merely one living organism; it is also a manifold. In virtue of the unity the individual is preserved by the All: in virtue of the multiplicity of things having various contacts, difference often brings about mutual hurt; one thing, seeking its own need, is detrimental to another; what is at once related and different is seized as food; each thing, following its own natural path, wrenches from something else what is serviceable to itself, and destroys or checks in its own interest whatever is becoming a menace to it: each, occupied with its peculiar function, assists no doubt anything able to profit by that, but harms or destroys what is too weak to withstand the onslaught of its action, like fire withering things round it or greater animals in their march thrusting aside or trampling under foot the smaller.

The rise of all these forms of being, their destruction, and their modification, whether to their loss or gain, all goes to the fulfillment of the natural unhindered life of that one living being: for it was not possible for the single thing to be as if it stood alone; the final purpose could not serve to that only end, intent upon the partial: the concern must be for the whole to which each item is member: things are different both from each other and in their own stages, therefore cannot be complete in one unchanging form of life; nor could anything remain utterly without modification if the All is to be durable; for the permanence of an All demands varying forms.

33. The Circuit does not go by chance but under the Reason-Principle of the living whole; therefore there must be a harmony between cause and caused; there must be some order ranging things to each other's purpose, or in due relation to each other: every several configuration within the Circuit must be accompanied by a change in the position and condition of things subordinate to it, which thus by their varied rhythmic movement make up one total dance-play.

In our dance-plays there are outside elements contributing to the total effect—fluting, singing, and other linked accessories—and each of these changes in each new movement: there is no need to dwell on these; their significance is obvious. But besides this there is the fact that the limbs of the dancer cannot possibly keep the same positions in every figure; they adapt themselves to the plan, bending as it dictates, one lowered, another raised, one active, another resting as the set pattern changes. The dancer's mind is on his own purpose; his limbs are submissive to the dance-movement which they accomplish to the end, so that the connoisseur can explain that this or that figure is the motive for the lifting, bending, concealment, effacing, of the various members of the body; and in all this the executant does not choose the particular motions for their own sake; the whole play of the entire person dictates the necessary position to each limb and member as it serves to the plan.

Now this is the mode in which the heavenly beings (the diviner members of the All) must be held to be causes wherever they have any action, and, when they do not act, to indicate.

Or, a better statement: the entire Cosmos puts its entire life into act, moving its major members with its own action and unceasingly setting them in new positions; by the relations thus established, of these members to each other and to the whole, and by the different figures they make together, the minor members in turn are brought under the system as in the movements of some one living being, so that they vary according to the relations, positions, configurations: the beings thus co-ordinated are not the causes; the cause is the co-ordinating All; at the same time it is not to be thought of as acting upon a material distinct from itself, for there is nothing external to it since it is the cause by actually being all: on the one side the configurations, on the other the inevitable effects of those configurations upon a living being moving as a unit and, again, upon a living being (an All) thus by its nature conjoined and concomitant and, of necessity, at once subject and object to its own activities.

38. Whatever springs automatically from the All out of that distinctive life of its own, and, in addition to that self-moving activity, whatever is due to some specific agency—for example, to prayers, simple or taking the form of magic incantations—this entire range of production is to be referred, not to some one of

the heavenly bodies, but to the nature of the thing produced (i.e. to a certain natural tendency in the product to exist with its own quality).

All that forwards life or some other useful purpose is to be ascribed to the transmission characteristic of the All; it is something flowing from the major of an integral to its minor. Where we think we see the transmission of some force unfavorable to the production of living beings, the flaw must be found in the inability of the subject to take in what would serve it: for what happens does not happen upon a void; there is always specific form and quality; anything that could be affected must have an underlying nature definite and characterized. The inevitable blendings, further, have their constructive effect, every element adding something contributory to the life. Then again some influence may come into play at the time when the forces of a beneficent nature are not acting: the co-ordination of the entire system of things does not always allow to each several entity everything that it needs: and further we ourselves add a great deal to what is transmitted to us.

None the less all entwines into a unity: and there is something wonderful in the agreement holding among these various things of varied source, even of sources frankly opposite; the secret lies in a variety within a unity. When by the standard of the better kind among things of process anything falls short—the reluctance of its material substratum having prevented its perfect shaping under Idea—it may be thought of as being deficient in that noble element whose absence brings to shame: the thing is a blend, something due to the high beings, an alloy from the underlying nature, something added by the self.

Because all is ever being knit, all brought to culmination in unity, therefore all events are indicated; but "virtue is not a matter of compulsion"; its spontaneity is equally inwoven into the ordered system by the general law that the things of this sphere are pendant from the higher, that the content of our universe lies in the hands of the diviner beings in whom our world is participant.

40. But magic spells; how can their efficacy be explained?

By the reigning sympathy and by the fact in Nature that there is an agreement of like forces and an opposition of unlike, and by the diversity of those multitudinous powers which converge in the one living universe.

There is much drawing and spell-binding dependent on no interfering machination; the true magic is internal to the All, its attractions and, not less, its repulsions. Here is the primal mage and sorcerer—discovered by men who thenceforth turn those same ensorcellations and magic arts upon one another.

Love is given in Nature; the qualities inducing love induce mutual approach: hence there has arisen an art of magic love-drawing whose practitioners apply by contact certain substances adapted to diverse temperaments and so informed with love as to effect a bond of union; they knit soul to soul as they might train two separate trees towards each other. The magician, too, draws on these patterns of power, and by ranging himself also into the pattern is able tranquilly to possess himself of these forces with whose nature and purpose he has become identified. Supposing the mage to stand outside the All, his evocations and invocations would no longer avail to draw up or to call down; but as things are he operates from no outside standground, he pulls knowing the pull of everything towards any other thing in the living system.

The tune of an incantation, a significant cry, the mien of the operator, these too have a natural leading power over the Soul upon which they are directed, drawing it with the force of mournful patterns or tragic sounds; for it is the reasonless soul, not the will or wisdom, that is beguiled by music, a form of sorcery which raises no question, whose enchantment, indeed, is welcomed, though not demanded, from the performers. Similarly with regard to prayers; there is no question of a will that grants; the powers that answer to incantations do not act by will; a human being fascinated by a snake has neither perception nor sensation of what is happening; he knows only after he has been caught, and his highest mind is never caught. In other words, some influence falls from the being addressed upon the petitioner—or upon someone else—but that being itself, sun or star, perceives nothing of it all.

41. The prayer is answered by the mere fact that part and other part are wrought to one tone like a musical string which, plucked at one end, vibrates at the other also. Often, too, the sounding of one string awakens what might pass for a perception in another, the result of their being in harmony and tuned to one musical scale; now, if the vibration in a lyre affects another by virtue of the sympathy existing between them, then certainly in the All—even though it is constituted in contraries—there must be one melodic system; for it contains its unisons as well, and its entire content, even to those contraries, is a kinship.

Thus, too, whatever is hurtful to man—the passionate spirit, for example, drawn by the medium of the gall into the principle seated in the liver—comes with no intention of hurt; it is simply as one transferring fire to another might innocently burn him: no doubt, since he actually set the other on fire he is a cause, but only as the attacking fire itself is a cause, that is by the merely accidental fact that the person to whom the fire was being brought blundered in taking it.

45. From this discussion it becomes perfectly clear that the individual member of the All contributes to that All in the degree of its kind and condition; thus it acts and is acted upon. In any particular animal each of the limbs and organs, in the measure of its kind and purpose, aids the entire being by service performed and counts in rank and utility: it gives what is in its gift and takes from its fellows in the degree of receptive power belonging to its kind; there is something like a common sensitiveness linking the parts, and in the orders in which each of the parts is also animate, each will have, in addition to its rank as part, the very particular functions of a living being.

We have learned, further, something of our human standing; we know that we too accomplish within the All a work not confined to the activity and receptivity of body in relation to body;

we know that we bring to it that higher nature of ours, linked as we are by affinities within towards the answering affinities outside us; becoming by our soul and the conditions of our kind thus linked—or, better, being linked by Nature—with our next highest in the celestial or daemonic realm, and thence onwards with those above the Celestials, we cannot fail to manifest our quality. Still, we are not all able to offer the same gifts or to accept identically: if we do not possess good, we cannot bestow it; nor can we ever purvey any good thing to one that has no power of receiving good. Anyone that adds his evil to the total of things is known for what he is and, in accordance with his kind, is pressed down into the evil which he has made his own, and hence, upon death, goes to whatever region fits his quality—and all this happens under the pull of natural forces.

For the good man, the giving and the taking and the changes of state go quite the other way; the particular tendencies of the nature, we may put it, transpose the cords (so that we are moved by that only which, in Plato's metaphor of the puppets, draws towards the best).

Thus this universe of ours is a wonder of power and wisdom, everything by a noiseless road coming to pass according to a law which none may elude—which the base man never conceives though it is leading him, all unknowingly, to that place in the All where his lot must be cast—which the just man knows, and, knowing, sets out to the place he must, understanding, even as he begins the journey, where he is to be housed at the end, and having the good hope that he will be with gods.

In a living being of small scope the parts vary but slightly, and have but a faint individual consciousness, and, unless possibly in a few and for a short time, are not themselves alive. But in a living universe, of high expanse, where every entity has vast scope and many of the members have life, there must be wider movement and greater changes. We see the sun and the moon and the other stars shifting place and course in an ordered progression. It is therefore within reason that the souls, also, should have their changes, not retaining unbrokenly the same quality, but ranged in some analogy with their action and experience—some taking rank as head and some as foot in a disposition consonant with the Universal Being which has its degrees in better and less good. A soul, which neither chooses the highest that is here, nor has lent itself to the lowest, is one which has abandoned another, a purer, place, taking this sphere in free election.

The punishments of wrongdoing are like the treatment of diseased parts of the body—here, medicines to knit sundered flesh; there, amputations; elsewhere, change of environment and condition—and the penalties are planned to bring health to the All by settling every member in the fitting place: and this health of the All requires that one man be made over anew and another, sick here, be taken hence to where he shall be weakly no longer.

Ennead IV
Eighth Tractate

THE SOUL'S DESCENT INTO BODY

This early treatise tries to reconcile two different perspectives of viewing the physical universe, i.e., that of the *Phaedo* and the *Timaeus*, which may be regarded simply as two "pedagogical strategies" of Plato. The soul's descent is not only a "fall," but also a "mission," therefore the soul must be benefited by its descent and, waking up from the body, return to the noetic realm. Plotinus maintains (against the later views of Iamblichus and Proclus) that the highest part of the human soul remains in the intelligible world, though we, in our embodied state, are not always conscious of it. According to Pierre Hadot:

> For Plotinus, the human soul is constantly united to the divine intellect through its summit. Although the human soul has fallen into a body, it is always present in the intelligible world through its own parts. In other words, it unceasingly participates, through one of its own parts, in the activity of the divine intellect. . . .
>
> What is this intelligible world, then, in which the summit of the soul dwells continually without usually being conscious of it? It is, first of all, the world of Forms or the Platonic Ideas, but, according to an interpretation of Plato that had developed in Middle Platonism, it is the world of Ideas that has become internal to the divine intellect so that each Form, each Idea, is itself intellect, is itself alive and conscious. The intelligible world thus forms a system of essences mutually implying each other and at the same time a system of intellects that are mutually conscious of each other: everything is in the whole and each part is in the whole, in accordance with its proper mode as part. . . .
>
> All of the Form-Intellects are at the same time themselves and the divine Intellect. Souls as well have the same type of existence. Despite their multiplicity, the soul of the world, the souls of the stars, and human souls are all one soul: they are joined in a

single origin which is the essence of the soul. They form a system
in which each part is identical with the whole.[14]

1. Many times it has happened: lifted out of the body into
myself; becoming external to all other things and self-encentered;
beholding a marvelous beauty; then, more than ever, assured of
community with the loftiest order; enacting the noblest life, acquiring identity with the divine; stationing within It by having attained
that activity; poised above whatsoever within the Intellectual is less
than the Supreme: yet, there comes the moment of descent from
intellection to reasoning, and after that sojourn in the divine, I ask
myself how it happens that I can now be descending, and how did
the Soul ever enter into my body, the Soul which, even within the
body, is the high thing it has shown itself to be.

Heraclitus, who urges the examination of this matter, tells
of "compulsory alternation from contrary to contrary," speaks of
ascent and descent, says that "change reposes," and that "it is weariness to keep toiling at the same things and to be always overcome
by them"; but he seems to teach by metaphor, not concerning himself about making his doctrine clear to us, probably with the idea
that it is for us to seek within ourselves as he sought for himself
and found.

Empedocles—where he says that it is law for faulty souls to
descend to this sphere, and that he himself was here because he
turned "a deserter, wandered from God, in slavery to a raving discord"—reveals neither more nor less than Pythagoras and his school
seem to me to convey on this as on many other matters; but in this
case, versification has some part in the obscurity.

We have to fall back on the illustrious Plato, who uttered many
noble sayings about the Soul, and has in many places dwelt upon
its entry into body, so that we may well hope to get some light
from him.

---

[14] Pierre Hadot, "Plotinus and Porphyry," in *Classical Mediterranean Spirituality:
Egyptian, Greek, Roman*, ed. A.H. Armstrong (London: Routledge & Kegan Paul,
1986), pp. 235-236.

What do we learn from this philosopher?

We will not find him so consistent throughout that it is easy to discover his mind.

Everywhere, no doubt, he expresses contempt for all that is of sense, blames the commerce of soul with body as an enchainment, an entombment, and upholds as a great truth the saying of the Mysteries that the Soul is here a prisoner. In the Cavern of Plato and in the Cave of Empedocles, I discern this universe, where the "breaking of the fetters" and the "ascent" from the depths are figures of the wayfaring towards the Intellectual Realm.

In the Phaedrus he makes a failing of the wings the cause of the entry to this realm: and there are Periods which send back the Soul after it has risen; there are judgments and lots and fates and necessities driving other souls down to this order.

In all these explanations he finds guilt in the arrival of the Soul at body. But treating, in the Timaeus, of our universe he exalts the Cosmos and entitles it "a blessed god," and holds that the Soul was given by the goodness of the Creator to the end that the total of things might be possessed of intellect, for thus intellectual it was planned to be, and thus it cannot be except through soul. There is a reason, then, why the Soul of this All should be sent into it from God: in the same way the Soul of each single one of us is sent, that the universe may be complete; it was necessary that all beings of the Intellectual should be tallied by just so many forms of living creatures here in the realm of sense.

2. Inquiring, then, of Plato as to our own soul, we find ourselves forced to inquire into the nature of soul in general—to discover what there can be in its character to bring it into partnership with body, and, again, what this Cosmos must be in which, willing unwilling or in any way at all, soul has its activity.

We have to face also the question as to whether the Creator has planned well, or whether the World-Soul, it may be, resembles our human souls which, in governing their inferior, the body, must sink deeper and deeper into it if they are to control it.

No doubt the individual body—though in all cases appropriately placed within the universe—is of itself in a state of dissolution,
always on the way to its natural terminus, demanding much irksome
forethought to save it from every kind of outside assailant, always
gripped by need, requiring every help against constant difficulty:
but the body inhabited by the World-Soul—complete, competent,
self-sufficing, exposed to nothing contrary to its nature—this needs
no more than a brief word of command, while the governing soul
is undeviatingly what its nature makes it wish to be, and, amenable
neither to loss nor to addition, knows neither desire nor distress.

This is how we come to read that our soul, entering into association with that complete soul and itself thus made perfect, "walks
the lofty ranges, administering the entire Cosmos," and that as
long as it does not secede and is neither inbound to body nor held
in any sort of servitude, so long it tranquilly bears its part in the
governance of the All, exactly like the World-Soul itself; for in fact
it suffers no hurt whatever by furnishing body with the power to
existence, since not every form of care for the inferior need wrest
the providing soul from its own sure standing in the highest.

The Soul's care for the universe takes two forms: there is the
supervising of the entire system, brought to order by deedless command in a kingly presidence, and there is that over the individual,
implying direct action, the hand to the task, one might say, in
immediate contact: in the second kind of care the agent absorbs
much of the nature of its object.

Now in its comprehensive government of the heavenly system,
the Soul's method is that of an unbroken transcendence in its highest phases, with penetration by its lower power: at this, God can no
longer be charged with lowering the All-Soul, which has not been
deprived of its natural standing and from eternity possesses and will
unchangeably possess that rank and habit which could never have
been intruded upon it against the course of nature but must be its
characteristic quality, neither failing ever nor ever beginning.

Where we read that the souls of stars stand to their bodily
forms as the All-Soul to the body of the All—for these starry bodies are declared to be members of the Soul's circuit—we are given

to understand that the star-souls also enjoy the blissful condition of transcendence and immunity that becomes them.

And so we might expect: commerce with the body is repudiated for two only reasons, as hindering the Soul's intellective act and as filling it with pleasure, desire, pain; but neither of these misfortunes can befall a soul which has never deeply penetrated into the body, is not a slave but a sovereign ruling a body of such an order as to have no need and no shortcoming and therefore to give ground for neither desire nor fear.

There is no reason why it should be expectant of evil with regard to such a body nor is there any such preoccupied concern, bringing about a veritable descent, as to withdraw it from its noblest and most blessed vision; it remains always intent upon the Supreme, and its governance of this universe is effected by a power not calling upon act.

3. The Human Soul, next:

Everywhere we hear of it as in bitter and miserable durance in body, a victim to troubles and desires and fears and all forms of evil, the body its prison or its tomb, the Cosmos its cave or cavern.

Now this does not clash with the first theory (that of the impassivity of soul as in the All); for the descent of the human Soul has not been due to the same causes (as that of the All-Soul).

All that is Intellectual-Principle has its being—whole and all—in the place of Intellection, what we call the Intellectual Cosmos: but there exist, too, the intellective powers included in its being, and the separate intelligences—for the Intellectual-Principle is not merely one; it is one and many. In the same way there must be both many souls and one, the one being the source of the differing many just as from one genus there rise various species, better and worse, some of the more intellectual order, others less effectively so.

In the Intellectual-Principle a distinction is to be made: there is the Intellectual-Principle itself, which like some huge living organism contains potentially all the other forms; and there are the forms thus potentially included now realized as individuals. We may think of it as a city which itself has soul and life, and includes, also, other forms of life; the living city is the more perfect and powerful, but those lesser forms, in spite of all, share in the one same living quality: or, another illustration, from fire, the universal, proceed both the great fire and the minor fires; yet all have the one common essence, that of fire the universal, or, more exactly, participate in that from which the essence of the universal fire proceeds.

No doubt the task of the Soul, in its more emphatically reasoning phase, is intellection: but it must have another as well, or it would be undistinguishable from the Intellectual-Principle. To its quality of being intellective it adds the quality by which it attains its particular manner of being: it ceases to be an Intellectual-Principle, and has thenceforth its own task, as everything must that exists in the Intellectual Realm.

It looks towards its higher and has intellection; towards itself and orders, administers, governs its lower.

The total of things could not have remained stationary in the Intellectual Cosmos, once there was the possibility of continuous variety, of being inferior but as necessarily existent as their superiors.

4. So it is with the individual souls; the appetite for the divine In-tellect urges them to return to their source, but they have, too, a power apt to administration in this lower sphere; they may be compared to the light attached upwards to the sun, but not grudging its bounty to what lies beneath it. In the Intellectual, then, they remain with the All-Soul, and are immune from care and trouble; in the heavenly sphere, inseparable from the All-Soul, they are administrators with it just as kings, associated with the supreme ruler and governing with him, do not descend from their kingly stations: the souls indeed are thus far in the one place; but there comes a stage at which they descend from the universal to become partial and self-centered; in a weary desire of standing apart they find their way, each to a place of its very own. This state long maintained, the Soul is a deserter from the totality; its differentiation has severed it; its vision is no longer set in the Intellectual; it is a partial thing, isolated, weakened, full of care, intent upon the fragment; severed

from the whole, it nestles in one form of being; for this it abandons all else, entering into and caring for only the one, for a thing buffeted about by a worldful of things: thus it has drifted away from the universal and, by an actual presence, it administers the particular; it is caught into contact now, and tends to the outer to which it has become present and into whose inner depths it henceforth sinks far.

With this comes what is known as the casting of the wings, the enchaining in body: the Soul has lost that innocency of conducting the higher which it knew when it stood with the All-Soul, that earlier state to which all its interest would bid it hasten back.

It has fallen: it is at the chain: debarred from expressing itself now through its intellectual phase, it operates through sense; it is a captive; this is the burial, the encavernment, of the Soul.

But in spite of all it has, for ever, something transcendent: by a conversion towards the intellective act, it is loosed from the shackles and soars—when only it makes its memories the starting-point of a new vision of essential being. Souls that take this way have place in both spheres, living of necessity the life there and the life here by turns, the upper life reigning in those able to consort more continuously with the divine Intellect, the lower dominant where character or circumstances are less favorable.

All this is indicated by Plato, without emphasis, where he distinguishes those of the second mixing-bowl, describes them as "parts," and goes on to say that, having in this way become partial, they must of necessity experience birth.

Of course, where he speaks of God sowing them, he is to be understood as when he tells of God speaking and delivering orations; what is rooted in the nature of the All is figuratively treated as coming into being by generation and creation: stage and sequence are transferred, for clarity of exposition, to things whose being and definite form are eternal.

5. It is possible to reconcile all these apparent contradictions— the divine sowing to birth, as opposed to a voluntary descent aiming at the completion of the universe; the judgment and the cave;

necessity and free choice—in fact the necessity includes the choice; embodiment as an evil; the Empedoclean teaching of a flight from God, a wandering away, a sin bringing its punishment; the "solace by fight" of Heraclitus; in a word, a voluntary descent which is also involuntary.

All degeneration is no doubt involuntary, yet when it has been brought about by an inherent tendency, that submission to the inferior may be described as the penalty of an act.

On the other hand these experiences and actions are determined by an eternal law of nature, and they are due to the movement of a being which in abandoning its superior is running out to serve the needs of another: hence there is no inconsistency or untruth in saying that the Soul is sent down by God; final results are always to be referred to the starting-point even across many intervening stages.

Still there is a twofold flaw: the first lies in the motive of the Soul's descent (its audacity, its Tolma), and the second in the evil it does when actually here: the first is punished by what the Soul has suffered by its descent: for the faults committed here, the lesser penalty is to enter into body after body—and soon to return—by judgment according to desert, the word judgment indicating a divine ordinance; but any outrageous form of ill-doing incurs a proportionately greater punishment administered under the surveillance of chastising daimons.

Thus, in sum, the Soul, a divine being and a dweller in the loftier realms, has entered body: it is a god, a later phase of the divine: but, under stress of its powers and of its tendency to bring order to its next lower, it penetrates to this sphere in a voluntary plunge: if it turns back quickly all is well; it will have taken no hurt by acquiring the knowledge of evil and coming to understand what sin is, by bringing its force into manifest play, by exhibiting those activities and productions which, remaining merely potential in the unembodied, might as well never have been even there, if destined never to come into actuality, so that the Soul itself would never have known that suppressed and inhibited total.

The act reveals the power, a power hidden, and we might almost say obliterated or non-existent, unless at some moment it became effective: in the world as it is, the richness of the outer stirs us all to the wonder of the inner whose greatness is displayed in acts so splendid.

6. Something besides a unity there must be or all would be indiscernibly buried, shapeless within that unbroken whole: none of the real beings (of the Intellectual Cosmos) would exist if that unity remained at halt within itself: the plurality of these beings, offspring of the unity, could not exist without their own nexts taking the outward path; these are the beings holding the rank of souls.

In the same way the outgoing process could not end with the souls, their issue stifled: every Kind must produce its next; it must unfold from some concentrated central principle as from a seed, and so advance to its term in the varied forms of sense. The prior in its being will remain unalterably in the native seat; but there is the lower phase, begotten to it by an ineffable faculty of its being, native to soul as it exists in the Supreme.

To this power we cannot impute any halt, any limit of jealous grudging; it must move for ever outward until the universe stands accomplished to the ultimate possibility. All, thus, is produced by an inexhaustible power giving its gift to the universe, no part of which it can endure to see without some share in its being.

There is, besides, no principle that can prevent anything from partaking, to the extent of its own individual receptivity, in the nature of Good. If, therefore, Matter has always existed, that existence is enough to ensure its participation in the being which, according to each receptivity, communicates the supreme Good universally: if on the contrary, Matter has come into being as a necessary sequence of the causes preceding it, that origin would similarly prevent it standing apart from the scheme as though it were out of reach of the principle to whose grace it owes its existence.

In sum: the loveliness that is in the sense-realm is an index of the nobleness of the Intellectual sphere, displaying its power and its goodness alike: and all things are for ever linked; the one order Intellectual in its being, the other of sense; one self-existent, the other eternally taking its being by participation in that first, and to the full of its power reproducing the Intellectual nature.

7. The Kind, then, with which we are dealing is twofold, the Intellectual against the sensible: better for the Soul to dwell in the Intellectual, but, given its proper nature, it is under compulsion to participate in the sense-realm also. There is no grievance in its not being, through and through, the highest; it holds mid-rank among the authentic existences, being of divine station but at the lowest extreme of the Intellectual and skirting the sense-known nature; thus, while it communicates to this realm something of its own store, it absorbs in turn whenever—instead of employing in its government only its safeguarded Phase—it plunges in an excessive zeal to the very midst of its chosen sphere; then it abandons its status as whole soul with whole soul, though even thus it is always able to recover itself by turning to account the experience of what it has seen and suffered here, learning, so, the greatness of rest in the Supreme, and more clearly discerning the finer things by comparison with what is almost their direct antithesis. Where the faculty is incapable of knowing without contact, the experience of evil brings the clearer perception of Good.

The outgoing that takes place in the Intellectual-Principle is a descent to its own downward ultimate: it cannot be a movement to the transcendent; operating necessarily outwards from itself, where it may not stay inclosed, the need and law of Nature bring it to its extreme term, to soul—to which it entrusts all the later stages of being while itself turns back on its course.

The Soul's operation is similar: its next lower act is this universe: its immediate higher is the contemplation of the Authentic Existences. To individual souls such divine operation takes place only at one of their phases and by a temporal process when from the lower in which they reside they turn towards the noblest; but that soul, which we know as the All-Soul, has never entered the lower activity, but, immune from evil, has the property of knowing its lower by inspection, while it still cleaves continuously to the beings above itself; thus its double task becomes possible; it takes hence and, since as soul it cannot escape touching this sphere, it gives hither.

8. And—if it is desirable to venture the more definite statement of a personal conviction with the general view—even our human Soul has not sunk entire; something of it is continuously in the Intellectual Realm, though if that part, which is in this sphere of sense, hold the mastery, or rather be mastered here and troubled, it keeps us blind to what the upper phase holds in contemplation.

The object of the Intellectual Act comes within our ken only when it reaches downward to the level of sensation: for not all that occurs at any part of the Soul is immediately known to us; a thing must, for that knowledge, be present to the total soul; thus desire locked up within the desiring faculty remains unknown except when we make it fully ours by the central faculty of perception, or by deliberate choice, or by both at once. Once more, every soul has something of the lower on the body side and something of the higher on the side of the Intellectual-Principle.

The Soul of the All, as an entirety, governs the universe through that part of it which leans to the body side, but since it does not exercise a will based on calculation as we do—but proceeds by purely intellectual act as in the execution of an artistic conception—its ministrance is that of a laborless overpoising, only its lowest phase being active upon the universe it embellishes.

The souls that have gone into division and become appropriated to some thing partial have also their transcendent phase, but are preoccupied by sensation, and in the mere fact of exercising perception they take in much that clashes with their nature and brings distress and trouble since the object of their concern is partial, deficient, exposed to many alien influences, filled with desires of its own and taking its pleasure, that pleasure which is its lure.

But there is always the other (the transcendent phase of soul), that which finds no savor in passing pleasure, but holds its own even way.

Ennead V
Eighth Tractate

ON THE INTELLIGIBLE BEAUTY

This treatise is a second section of the great work of Plotinus comprising *Enn.* III.8, V.5, and II.9. The Platonic distinction between the sensible and the intelligible remains decisive for Plotinus, and he thus discerns sensible from noetic beauty. All beauty and order here below are due to the living Forms of the noetic realm. The creative activity of *Nous* is non-discursive, hence the higher wisdom of *Nous* knows realities more like images than propositions. Plotinus maintains that Egyptian hieroglyphs are an example of the expression of such symbolic and non-discursive thought. According to Werner Beierwaltes:

> Beautiful is what participates in form and *logos* and is shaped by form and *logos* into a single ordered whole, whether by nature or by art. If form and *logos* mean not the external form of a thing but its inner structural principle—its intelligible foundation—then the identification of form and "idea" is justified. Through itself, that is, through its immanent activity, the "form" or *logos* that is added to unformed matter gives the formless material visible shape or form. The idea thus becomes the cause of the form that appears. . . .
>
> The process of abstraction and purification, an anamnestic return of the soul into itself, leading to self-certainty, thus makes the soul itself the *eidos* and *logos*. The soul as a whole becomes intelligible and transforms itself into intellect. Because intellect gives rise to beauty through its act of reflection, the soul itself also becomes beautiful in this abstractive transformation and attains its own proper beauty; only then does it become truly *itself*. If in this return into itself, the soul rises to *nous* as its own ground or true self, then by becoming like such true *being*, which manifests itself as the unity of "good" and "beautiful," the soul itself becomes in a true sense *being*—good and beautiful.[15]

---

[15] Werner Beierwaltes, "The Love of Beauty and the Love of God," in *Classical Mediterranean Spirituality: Egyptian, Greek, Roman*, ed. A.H. Armstrong (London:

1. It is a principle with us that one who has attained to the vision of the Intellectual Cosmos and grasped the beauty of the Authentic Intellect will be able also to come to understand the Father and Transcendent of that Divine Being. It concerns us, then, to try to see and say, for ourselves and as far as such matters may be told, how the Beauty of the divine Intellect and of the Intellectual Cosmos may be revealed to contemplation.

Let us go to the realm of magnitudes: suppose two blocks of stone lying side by side: one is unpatterned, quite untouched by art; the other has been minutely wrought by the craftsman's hands into some statue of god or man, a Grace or a Muse, or if a human being, not a portrait but a creation in which the sculptor's art has concentrated all loveliness.

Now it must be seen that the stone thus brought under the artist's hand to the beauty of form is beautiful not as stone—for so the crude block would be as pleasant—but in virtue of the Form or Idea introduced by the art. This form is not in the material; it is in the designer before ever it enters the stone; and the artificer holds it not by his equipment of eyes and hands but by his participation in his art. The beauty, therefore, exists in a far higher state in the art; for it does not come over integrally into the work; that original beauty is not transferred; what comes over is a derivative and a minor: and even that shows itself upon the statue not integrally and with entire realization of intention but only in so far as it has subdued the resistance of the material.

Art, then, creating in the image of its own nature and content, and working by the Idea or Reason-Principle of the beautiful object it is to produce, must itself be beautiful in a far higher and purer degree since it is the seat and source of that beauty, indwelling in the art, which must naturally be more complete than any comeliness of the external. In the degree in which the beauty is diffused by entering into matter, it is so much the weaker than that concentrated in unity; everything that reaches outwards is the less for it,

Routledge & Kegan Paul, 1986), pp. 299-300.

strength less strong, heat less hot, every power less potent, and so beauty less beautiful.

Then again every prime cause must be, within itself, more powerful than its effect can be: the musical does not derive from an unmusical source but from music; and so the art exhibited in the material work derives from an art yet higher.

Still the arts are not to be slighted on the ground that they create by imitation of natural objects; for, to begin with, these natural objects are themselves imitations; then, we must recognize that they give no bare reproduction of the thing seen but go back to the Reason-Principles from which Nature itself derives, and, furthermore, that much of their work is all their own; they are holders of beauty and add where nature is lacking. Thus Pheidias wrought the Zeus upon no model among things of sense but by apprehending what form Zeus must take if he chose to become manifest to sight.

2. But let us leave the arts and consider those works produced by Nature and admitted to be naturally beautiful which the creations of art are charged with mutating, all reasoning life and unreasoning things alike, but especially the consummate among them, where the molder and maker has subdued the material and given the form he desired. Now what is the beauty here? It has nothing to do with the blood or the menstrual process: either there is also a color and form apart from all this or there is nothing unless sheer ugliness or (at best) a bare recipient, as it were the mere Matter of beauty.

Whence shone forth the beauty of Helen, battle-sought; or of all those women like in loveliness to Aphrodite; or of Aphrodite herself; or of any human being that has been perfect in beauty; or of any of these gods manifest to sight, or unseen but carrying what would be beauty if we saw?

In all these is it not the Idea, something of that realm but communicated to the produced from within the producer, just as in works of art, we held, it is communicated from the arts to their creations? Now we can surely not believe that, while the made thing and the Idea thus impressed upon Matter are beautiful, yet the Idea not so alloyed but resting still with the creator—the Idea primal, immaterial, firmly a unity—is not Beauty.

If material extension were in itself the ground of beauty, then the creating principle, being without extension, could not be beautiful: but beauty cannot be made to depend upon magnitude since, whether in a large object or a small, the one Idea equally moves and forms the mind by its inherent power. A further indication is that as long as the object remains outside us we know nothing of it; it affects us by entry; but only as an Idea can it enter through the eyes which are not of scope to take an extended mass: we are, no doubt, simultaneously possessed of the magnitude which, however, we take in not as mass but by an elaboration upon the presented form.

Then again the principle producing the beauty must be, itself, ugly, neutral, or beautiful: ugly, it could not produce the opposite; neutral, why should its product be the one rather than the other? The Nature, then, which creates things so lovely must be itself of a far earlier beauty; we, undisciplined in discernment of the inward, knowing nothing of it, run after the outer, never understanding that it is the inner which stirs us; we are in the case of one who sees his own reflection but not realizing whence it comes goes in pursuit of it.

But that the thing we are pursuing is something different and that the beauty is not in the concrete object is manifest from the beauty there is in matters of study, in conduct and custom; briefly, in soul or mind. And it is precisely here that the greater beauty lies, perceived whenever you look to the wisdom in a man and delight in it, not wasting attention on the face, which may be hideous, but passing all appearance by and catching only at the inner comeliness, the truly personal; if you are still unmoved and cannot acknowledge beauty under such conditions, then looking to your own inner being you will find no beauty to delight you and it will be futile in that state to seek the greater vision, for you will be questing it through the ugly and impure.

This is why such matters are not spoken of to everyone; you, if you are conscious of beauty within, remember.

3. Thus there is in the Nature-Principle itself an Ideal archetype of the beauty that is found in material forms and, of that archetype again, the still more beautiful archetype in Soul, source of that in Nature. In the proficient soul this is brighter and of more advanced loveliness: adorning the soul and bringing to it a light from that greater light which is Beauty primally, its immediate presence sets the soul reflecting upon the quality of this prior, the archetype which has no such entries, and is present nowhere but remains in itself alone, and thus is not even to be called a Reason-Principle but is the creative source of the very first Reason-Principle which is the Beauty to which Soul serves as Matter.

This prior, then, is the Intellectual-Principle, the veritable, abiding and not fluctuant since not taking intellectual quality from outside itself. By what image, thus, can we represent it? We have nowhere to go but to what is less. Only from itself can we take an image of it; that is, there can be no representation of it, except in the sense that we represent gold by some portion of gold—purified, either actually or mentally, if it be impure—insisting at the same time that this is not the total thing gold, but merely the particular gold of a particular parcel. In the same way we learn in this matter from the purified Intellect in ourselves, or, if you like, from the gods and the glory of the Intellect in them.

For assuredly all the gods are august and beautiful in a beauty beyond our speech. And what makes them so? Intellect; and especially Intellect operating within them (divine sun and stars) to visibility. It is not through the loveliness of their corporeal forms: even those that have body are not gods by that beauty; it is in virtue of Intellect that they, too, are gods, and as gods beautiful. They do not veer between wisdom and folly: in the immunity of Intellect unmoving and pure, they are wise always, all-knowing, taking cognizance not of the human but of their own being and of all that lies within the contemplation of Intellect. Those of them whose dwelling is in the heavens are ever in this meditation—what task prevents them?—and from afar they look, too, into that further heaven by a lifting of the head. The gods belonging to that higher Heaven itself, they whose station is upon it and in it, see and know in virtue of their omnipresence to it. For all There is heaven; earth is heaven, and sea heaven; and animal and plant and man; all is the heavenly content of that heaven and the gods in it, despising neither men nor anything else that is there where all is of the heavenly order, traverse all that country and all space in peace.

4. To "live at ease" is There; and to these divine beings verity is mother and nurse, existence and sustenance; all that is not of process but of authentic being they see, and themselves in all: for all is transparent, nothing dark, nothing resistant; every being is lucid to every other, in breadth and depth; light runs through light. And each of them contains all within itself, and at the same time sees all in every other, so that everywhere there is all, and all is all and each and infinite the glory. Each of them is great; the small is great; the sun, There, is all the stars; and every star, again, is all the stars and sun. While some one manner of being is dominant in each, all are mirrored in every other.

Movement There is pure (as self-caused), for the moving principle is not a separate thing to complicate it as it speeds.

So, too, Repose is not troubled, for there is no admixture of the unstable; and the Beauty is all beauty since it is not resident in what is not beautiful. Each There walks upon no alien soil; its place is its essential self; and, as each moves so to speak, towards what is Above, it is attended by the very ground from which it starts: there is no distinguishing between the Being and the Place; all is Intellect, the Principle and the ground on which it stands, alike. Thus we might think that our visible sky (the ground or place of the stars), lit as it is, produces the light which reaches us from it, though of course this is really produced by the stars (as it were, by the Principles of light alone, not also by the ground as the analogy would require).

In our realm all is part rising from part and nothing can be more than partial; but There each being is an eternal product of a whole and is at once a whole and an individual manifesting as part but, to the keen vision There, known for the whole it is.

The myth of Lynceus seeing into the very deeps of the earth tells us of those eyes in the divine. No weariness overtakes this vision which yet brings no such satiety as would call for its ending; for there never was a void to be filled so that, with the fullness and the attainment of purpose, the sense of sufficiency be induced: nor is there any such incongruity within the divine that one Being There could be repulsive to another: and of course all There are unchangeable. This absence of satisfaction means only a satisfaction leading to no distaste for that which produces it; to see is to look the more, since for them to continue in the contemplation of an infinite self and of infinite objects is but to acquiesce in the bidding of their nature.

Life, pure, is never a burden; how then could there be weariness There where the living is most noble? That very life is wisdom, not a wisdom built up by reasonings but complete from the beginning, suffering no lack which could set it inquiring, a wisdom primal, unborrowed, not something added to the Being, but its very essence. No wisdom, thus, is greater; this is the authentic knowing, assessor to the divine Intellect as projected into manifestation simultaneously with it; thus, in the symbolic saying, justice is assessor to Zeus.

(Perfect wisdom:) for all the Principles of this order, dwelling There, are as it were visible images projected from themselves, so that all becomes an object of contemplation to contemplators immeasurably blessed. The greatness and power of the wisdom There we may know from this, that it embraces all the real Beings, and has made all and all follow it, and yet that it is itself those beings, which sprang into being with it, so that all is one and the essence There is wisdom. If we have failed to understand, it is that we have thought of knowledge as a mass of theorems and an accumulation of propositions, though that is false even for our sciences of the sense-realm. But in case this should be questioned, we may leave our own sciences for the present, and deal with the knowing in the Supreme at which Plato glances where he speaks of "that knowledge which is not a stranger in something strange to it"—though in what sense, he leaves us to examine and declare, if we boast ourselves worthy of the discussion. This is probably our best starting-point.

5. All that comes to be, work of nature or of craft, some wisdom has made: everywhere a wisdom presides at a making.

No doubt the wisdom of the artist may be the guide of the work; it is sufficient explanation of the wisdom exhibited in the arts; but the artist himself goes back, after all, to that wisdom in Nature which is embodied in himself; and this is not a wisdom built up of theorems but one totality, not a wisdom consisting of manifold detail co-ordinated into a unity but rather a unity working out into detail.

Now, if we could think of this as the primal wisdom, we need look no further, since, at that, we have discovered a principle which is neither a derivative nor a "stranger in something strange to it." But if we are told that, while this Reason-Principle is in Nature, yet Nature itself is its source, we ask how Nature came to possess it; and, if Nature derived it from some other source, we ask what that other source may be; if, on the contrary, the principle is self-sprung, we need look no further: but if (as we assume) we are referred to the Intellectual-Principle we must make clear whether the Intellectual-Principle engendered the wisdom: if we learn that it did, we ask whence: if from itself, then inevitably it is itself Wisdom.

The true Wisdom, then (found to be identical with the Intellectual-Principle), is Real Being; and Real Being is Wisdom; it is wisdom that gives value to Real Being; and Being is Real in virtue of its origin in wisdom. It follows that all forms of existence not possessing wisdom are, indeed, Beings in right of the wisdom which went to their forming, but, as not in themselves possessing it, are not Real Beings.

We cannot, therefore, think that the divine Beings of that sphere, or the other supremely blessed There, need look to our apparatus of science: all of that realm (the very Beings themselves), all is noble image, such images as we may conceive to lie within the soul of the wise—but There not as inscription but as authentic existence. The ancients had this in mind when they declared the Ideas (Forms) to be Beings, Essentials.

6. Similarly, as it seems to me, the wise of Egypt—whether in precise knowledge or by a prompting of nature—indicated the truth where, in their effort towards philosophical statement, they left aside the writing-forms that take in the detail of words and sentences—those characters that represent sounds and convey the propositions of reasoning—and drew pictures instead, engraving in the temple-inscriptions a separate image for every separate item: thus they exhibited the absence of discursiveness in the Intellectual Realm.

For each manifestation of knowledge and wisdom is a distinct image, an object in itself, an immediate unity, not an aggregate of discursive reasoning and detailed willing. Later from this wisdom in unity there appears, in another form of being, an image, already less compact, which announces the original in terms of discourse and unravels the causes by which things are such that the wonder rises how a generated world can be so excellent.

For, one who knows must declare his wonder that this wisdom, while not itself containing the causes by which Being exists and takes such excellence, yet imparts them to the entities produced according to its canons. This excellence, whose necessity is scarcely or not at all manifest to search, exists, if we could but find it out, before all searching and reasoning.

What I say may be considered in one chief thing, and thence applied to all the particular entities:

7. Consider the universe: we are agreed that its existence and its nature come to it from beyond itself; are we, now, to imagine that its maker first thought it out in detail—the earth, and its necessary situation in the middle; water and, again, its position as lying upon the earth; all the other elements and objects up to the sky in due place and order; living beings with their appropriate forms as

we know them, their inner organs and their outer limbs—and that having thus appointed every item beforehand, he then set about the execution?

Such designing was not even possible; how could the plan for a universe come to one that had never looked outward? Nor could he work on material gathered from elsewhere as our craftsmen do, using hands and tools; feet and hands are of the later order.

One way, only, remains: all things must exist in something else; of that prior—since there is no obstacle, all being continuous within the realm of reality—there has suddenly appeared a sign, an image, whether given forth directly or through the ministry of soul or of some phase of soul matters nothing for the moment: thus the entire aggregate of existence springs from the divine world, in greater beauty There because There unmingled but mingled here.

From the beginning to end all is gripped by the Forms of the Intellectual Realm: Matter itself is held by the Ideas of the elements and to these Ideas are added other Ideas and others again, so that it is hard to work down to crude Matter beneath all that sheathing of Idea. Indeed since Matter itself is, in its degree, an Idea—the lowest—all this universe is Idea and there is nothing that is not Idea as the archetype was. And all is made silently, since nothing had part in the making but Being and Idea—a further reason why creation went without toil. The Exemplar was the Idea of an All and so an All must come into being.

Thus nothing stood in the way of the Idea, and even now it dominates, despite all the clash of things: the creation is not hindered on its way even now; it stands firm in virtue of being All. To me, moreover, it seems that if we ourselves were archetypes, Ideas, veritable Being, and the Idea with which we construct here were our veritable Essence, then our creative power, too, would toillessly effect its purpose: as man now stands, he does not produce in his work a true image of himself: become man, he has ceased to be the All; ceasing to be man—we read—"he soars aloft and administers the Cosmos entire"; restored to the All he is maker of the All.

But—to our immediate purpose—it is possible to give a reason why the earth is set in the midst and why it is round and why the ecliptic runs precisely as it does, but, looking to the creating principle, we cannot say that because this was the way therefore things were so planned: we can say only that because the Exemplar is what it is, therefore the things of this world are good; the causing principle, we might put it, reached the conclusion before all formal reasoning and not from any premises, not by sequence or plan but before either, since all of that order is later, all reason, demonstration, persuasion.

Since there is a Source, all the created must spring from it and in accordance with it; and we are rightly told not to go seeking the causes impelling a Source to produce, especially when this is the perfectly sufficient Source and identical with the Term: a Source which is Source and Term must be the All-Unity, complete in itself.

8. This then is Beauty primally: it is entire and omnipresent as an entirety; and therefore in none of its parts or members lacking in beauty; beautiful thus beyond denial. Certainly it cannot be anything (be, for example, Beauty) without being wholly that thing; it can be nothing which it is to possess partially or in which it utterly fails (and therefore it must entirely be Beauty entire).

If this principle were not beautiful, what other could be? Its prior does not deign to be beautiful; that which is the first to manifest itself—Form and object of vision to the intellect—cannot but be lovely to see. It is to indicate this that Plato, drawing on something well within our observation, represents the Creator as approving the work he has achieved: the intention is to make us feel the lovable beauty of the archetype and of the Divine Idea; for to admire a representation is to admire the original upon which it was made.

It is not surprising if we fail to recognize what is passing within us: lovers, and those in general that admire beauty here, do not stay to reflect that it is to be traced, as of course it must be, to the Beauty There. That the admiration of the Demiurge is to be referred to the Ideal Exemplar is deliberately made evident by the rest of the passage: "He admired; and determined to bring the work into still closer likeness with the Exemplar": he makes us feel the magnificent beauty of the Exemplar by telling us that the Beauty sprung from this world is, itself, a copy from That.

And indeed if the divine did not exist, the transcendently beautiful, in a beauty beyond all thought, what could be lovelier than the things we see? Certainly no reproach can rightly be brought against this world save only that it is not That.

9. Let us, then, make a mental picture of our universe: each member shall remain what it is, distinctly apart; yet all is to form, as far as possible, a complete unity so that whatever comes into view, say the outer orb of the heavens, shall bring immediately with it the vision, on the one plane, of the sun and of all the stars with earth and sea and all living things as if exhibited upon a transparent globe.

Bring this vision actually before your sight, so that there shall be in your mind the gleaming representation of a sphere, a picture holding all the things of the universe moving or in repose or (as in reality) some at rest, some in motion. Keep this sphere before you, and from it imagine another, a sphere stripped of magnitude and of spatial differences; cast out your inborn sense of Matter, taking care not merely to attenuate it: call on God, maker of the sphere whose image you now hold, and pray Him to enter. And may He come bringing His own Universe with all the gods that dwell in it—He who is the one God and all the gods, where each is all, blending into a unity, distinct in powers but all one god in virtue of that one divine power of many facets.

More truly, this is the one God who is all the gods; for, in the coming to be of all those, this, the one, has suffered no diminishing. He and all have one existence, while each again is distinct. It is distinction by state without interval: there is no outward form to set one here and another there and to prevent any from being an entire identity; yet there is no sharing of parts from one to another. Nor is each of those divine wholes a power in fragment, a power totaling to the sum of the measurable segments: and so great is God that his very members are infinites. What place can be named to which He does not reach?

Great, too, is this firmament of ours and all the powers constellated within it, but it would be greater still, unspeakably, but that there is inbound in it something of the petty power of body; no doubt the powers of fire and other bodily substances might themselves be thought very great, but in fact, it is through their failure in the true power that we see them burning, destroying, wearing things away, and slaving towards the production of life; they destroy because they are themselves in process of destruction, and they produce because they belong to the realm of the produced.

The power in that other world has merely Being and Beauty of Being. Beauty without Being could not be, nor Being voided of Beauty: abandoned by Beauty, Being loses something of its essence. Being is desirable because it is identical with Beauty; and Beauty is loved because it is Being. How then can we debate which is the cause of the other, where the nature is one? The very figment of Being needs some imposed image of Beauty to make it passable, and even to ensure its existence; it exists to the degree in which it has taken some share in the beauty of Idea; and the more deeply it has drawn on this, the less imperfect it is, precisely because the nature which is essentially the beautiful has entered into it the more intimately.

10. This is why Zeus, although the oldest of the gods and their sovereign, advances first (in the Phaedrus myth) towards that vision, followed by gods and demigods and such souls as are of strength to see. That Being appears before them from some unseen place and rising loftily over them pours its light upon all things, so that all gleams in its radiance; it upholds some beings, and they see; the lower are dazzled and turn away, unfit to gaze upon that sun, the trouble falling the more heavily on those most remote.

Of those looking upon that Being and its content, and able to see, all take something but not all the same vision always: intently gazing, one sees the fount and principle of justice, another is filled with the sight of Moral Wisdom, the original of that quality as found, sometimes at least, among men, copied by them in their degree from the divine virtue which, covering all the expanse, so to speak, of the Intellectual Realm is seen, last attainment of all, by those who have known already many splendid visions.

The gods see, each singly and all as one. So, too, the souls; they see all There in right of being sprung, themselves, of that universe and therefore including all from beginning to end and having their existence There if only by that phase which belongs inherently to the Divine, though often too they are There entire, those of them that have not incurred separation.

This vision Zeus takes and it is for such of us, also, as share his love and appropriate our part in the Beauty There, the final object of all seeing, the entire beauty upon all things; for all There sheds radiance, and floods those that have found their way thither so that they too become beautiful; thus it will often happen that men climbing heights where the soil has taken a yellow glow will themselves appear so, borrowing color from the place on which they move. The color flowering on that other height we speak of is Beauty; or rather all There is light and beauty, through and through, for the beauty is no mere bloom upon the surface.

To those that do not see entire, the immediate impression is alone taken into account; but those drunken with this wine, filled with the nectar, all their soul penetrated by this beauty, cannot remain mere gazers: no longer is there a spectator outside gazing on an outside spectacle; the clear-eyed hold the vision within themselves, though, for the most part, they have no idea that it is within but look towards it as to something beyond them and see it as an object of vision caught by a direction of the will.

All that one sees as a spectacle is still external; one must bring the vision within and see no longer in that mode of separation but as we know ourselves; thus a man filled with a god—possessed by Apollo or by one of the Muses—need no longer look outside for his vision of the divine being; it is but finding the strength to see divinity within.

11. Similarly any one, unable to see himself, but possessed by that God, has but to bring that divine-within before his consciousness and at once he sees an image of himself, himself lifted to a better beauty: now let him ignore that image, lovely though it is, and sink into a perfect self-identity, no such separation remaining; at once he forms a multiple unity with the God silently present; in the degree of his power and will, the two become one; should he turn back to the former duality, still he is pure and remains very near to the God; he has but to look again and the same presence is there.

This conversion brings gain: at the first stage, that of separation, a man is aware of self, but retreating inwards, he becomes possessor of all; he puts sense away behind him in dread of the separated life and becomes one in the Divine; if he plans to see in separation, he sets himself outside.

The novice must hold himself constantly under some image of the Divine Being and seek in the light of a clear conception; knowing thus, in a deep conviction, whither he is going—into what a sublimity he penetrates—he must give himself forthwith to the inner and, radiant with the Divine Intellections (with which he is now one), be no longer the seer, but, as that place has made him, the seen.

Still, we will be told, one cannot be in beauty and yet fail to see it. The very contrary: to see the divine as something external is to be outside of it; to become it is to be most truly in beauty: since sight deals with the external, there can here be no vision unless in the sense of identification with the object.

And this identification amounts to a self-knowing, a self-consciousness, guarded by the fear of losing the self in the desire of a too wide awareness.

It must be remembered that sensations of the ugly and evil impress us more violently than those of what is agreeable and yet leave less knowledge as the residue of the shock: sickness makes the rougher mark, but health, tranquilly present, explains itself better; it takes the first place, it is the natural thing, it belongs to our being; illness is alien, unnatural, and thus makes itself felt by its very incongruity, while the other conditions are native and we take no notice. Such being our nature, we are most completely aware of ourselves when we are most completely identified with the object of our knowledge.

This is why in that other sphere, when we are deepest in that knowledge by intellection, we are aware of none; we are expecting some impression on sense, which has nothing to report since it has seen nothing and never could in that order see anything. The unbelieving element is sense; it is the other, the Intellectual-Principle, that sees; and if this too doubted, it could not even credit its own existence, for it can never stand away and with bodily eyes apprehend itself as a visible object.

12. We have told how this vision it to be procured, whether by the mode of separation or in identity: now, seen in either way, what does it give to report?

The vision has been of God in travail of a beautiful offspring, God engendering a universe within himself in a painless labor and—rejoiced in what he has brought into being, proud of his children—keeping all closely by Him, for the pleasure He has in his radiance and in theirs.

Of this offspring—all beautiful, but most beautiful those that have remained within—only one has become manifest without; from him (Zeus, sovereign over the visible universe), the youngest born, we may gather, as from some image, the greatness of the Father and of the Brothers that remain within the Father's house.

Still the manifested God cannot think that he has come forth in vain from the father; for through him another universe has arisen, beautiful as the image of beauty, and it could not be lawful that Beauty and Being should fail of a beautiful image.

This second Cosmos at every point copies the archetype: it has life and being in copy, and has beauty as springing from that diviner world. In its character of image it holds, too, that divine perpetuity without which it would only at times be truly representative and sometimes fail like a construction of art; for every image whose existence lies in the nature of things must stand during the entire existence of the archetype.

Hence it is false to put an end to the visible sphere as long as the Intellectual endures, or to found it upon a decision taken by its maker at some given moment.

That teaching shirks the penetration of such a making as is here involved: it fails to see that as long as the Supreme is radiant there can be no failing of its sequel but, that existing, all exists. And—since the necessity of conveying our meaning compels such terms—the Supreme has existed for ever and for ever will exist.

13. The God fettered (as in the Kronos Myth) to an unchanging identity leaves the ordering of this universe to his son (to Zeus), for it could not be in his character to neglect his rule within the divine sphere, and, as though sated with the Authentic-Beauty, seek a lordship too recent and too poor for his might. Ignoring this lower world, Kronos (Intellectual-Principle) claims for himself his own father (Ouranos, the Absolute, or One) with all the upward-tending between them: and he counts all that tends to the inferior, beginning from his son (Zeus, the All-Soul), as ranking beneath him. Thus he holds a mid-position determined on the one side by the differentiation implied in the severance from the very highest and, on the other, by that which keeps him apart from the link between himself and the lower: he stands between a greater father and an inferior son. But since that father is too lofty to be thought of under the name of Beauty, the second God remains the primally beautiful.

Soul also has beauty, but is less beautiful than Intellect as being its image and therefore, though beautiful in nature, taking increase of beauty by looking to that original. Since then the All-Soul—to use the more familiar term—since Aphrodite herself is so beautiful, what name can we give to that other? If Soul is so lovely in its own right, of what quality must that prior be? And since its being is derived, what must that power be from which the Soul takes the double beauty, the borrowed and the inherent?

We ourselves possess beauty when we are true to our own being; our ugliness is in going over to another order; our self-knowledge, that is to say, is our beauty; in self-ignorance we are ugly.

Thus beauty is of the Divine and comes Thence only.

Do these considerations suffice to a clear understanding of the Intellectual Sphere or must we make yet another attempt by another road?

Ennead VI
Fifth Tractate: 1-2; 4-7

ON THE INTEGRAL OMNIPRESENCE
OF THE AUTHENTIC EXISTENT (II)

This treatise is the second part of a larger work divided into two treatises by Porphyry. The first part is *Enn.* VI.4. Plotinus discusses man's common awareness of the presence of God, i.e., "what it means to be incorporeal and how an incorporeal divine being which is fullness of life and thought and power must be present immediately and as a whole in and to everyone and everything here below, at every point in space-time diffusion and dispersion."[16] Plotinus is not merely expounding a doctrine, but inviting his reader to seek liberation from the limitations of the empirical ego and attain to salvation, which means to reestablish the divine unity and return to one's real Self. Accordingly, Plotinus aims at "philosophical death" by which the soul is "separated" from the body, thus seeing and living on the level of true Being even during its earthly sojourn. The soul must be at the same time transcendent and immanent, though its real life goes on at the higher level and the lower activities are a mere by-product of the higher Self and express its life at a lower level. Plotinus emphasizes a way in which we can escape from the body whilst being still embodied. Andrew Smith says:

> We can return to our higher selves even whilst attached to individual bodies. We can imitate the way in which the whole Soul transcends the cosmos whilst still attending to its duties there.[17]

In the final analysis, however, for Plotinus there are not two different worlds (namely, the intelligible and the sensible), but one real world,

---

[16] A.H. Armstrong, "Introductory Notes," in Plotinus, *The Enneads*, vol. VI (Cambridge, Mass.: Harvard University Press, 1988), p. 270.

[17] Andrew Smith, *Porphyry's Place in the Neoplatonic Tradition: A Study in Post-Plotinian Neoplatonism* (The Hague: Martinus Nijhoff, 1974), pp. 38-39.

or rather one single Reality, apprehended in different ways on different levels.

1. The integral omnipresence of a unity numerically identical is in fact universally received; for all men instinctively affirm the god in each of us to be one, the same in all. It would be taken as certain if no one asked how or sought to bring the conviction to the test of reasoning; with this effective in their thought, men would be at rest, finding their stay in that oneness and identity, so that nothing would wrench them from this unity. This principle, indeed, is the most solidly established of all, proclaimed by our very souls; we do not piece it up item by item, but find it within beforehand; it precedes even the principle by which we affirm unquestionably that all things seek their good; for this universal quest of good depends on the fact that all aim at unity and possess unity and that universally effort is towards unity.

Now this unity in going forth, so far as it may, towards the Other Order must become manifest as multiplicity and in some sense become multiple; but the primal nature and the appetition of the good, which is appetition of unity, lead back to what is authentically one; to this every form of Being is urged in a movement towards its own reality. For the good to every nature possessing unity is to be self-belonging, to be itself, and that means to be a unity.

In virtue of that unity the Good may be regarded as truly inherent. Hence the Good is not to be sought outside; it could not have fallen outside of what is; it cannot possibly be found in non-Being; within Being the Good must lie, since it is never a non-Being.

If that Good has Being and is within the realm of Being, then it is present, self-contained, in everything; we, therefore, are not separated from Being; we are in it; nor is Being separated from us: therefore all beings are one.

2. Now the reasoning faculty which undertakes this problem is not a unity but a thing of parts; it brings the bodily nature into the inquiry, borrowing its principles from the corporeal: thus it thinks

of the Essential Existence as corporeal and as a thing of parts; it baulks at the unity because it does not start from the appropriate convincing principles to the discussion of the Unity, of perfect Being: we must hold to the Intellectual principles which alone apply to the Intellectual Order and to Real Being.

On the one hand there is the unstable, exposed to all sorts of change, distributed in place, not so much Being as Becoming: on the other, there is that which exists eternally, not divided, subject to no change of state, neither coming into being nor falling from it, set in no region or place or support, emerging from nowhere, entering into nothing, fast within itself.

In dealing with that lower order we would reason from its own nature and the characteristics it exhibits; thus, on a plausible foundation, we achieve plausible results by a plausible system of deduction: similarly, in dealing with the Intellectual, the only way is to grasp the nature of the essence concerned and so lay the sure foundations of the argument, not forgetfully straying over into that other order but basing our treatment on what is essential to the Nature with which we deal.

In every entity the essential nature is the governing principle and, as we are told, a sound definition brings to light many even of the concomitants: where the essential nature is the entire being, we must be all the more careful to keep to that, to look to that, to refer all to that.

4. Then consider this god (in man) whom we cannot think to be absent at some point and present at another. All that have insight into the nature of the divine beings hold the omnipresence of this god and of all the gods, and reason assures us that so it must be.

Now all-pervasion is inconsistent with partition; that would mean no longer the god throughout but part of the god at one point and part at another; the god ceases to be one god, just as a mass cut up ceases to be a mass, the parts no longer giving the first total. Further, the god becomes corporeal.

If all this is impossible, the disputed doctrine presents itself again; holding the god to pervade the Being of man, we hold the omnipresence of an integral identity.

Again, if we think of the divine nature as infinite—and certainly it is confined by no bounds—this must mean that it nowhere fails; its presence must reach to everything; at the point to which it does not reach, there it has failed; something exists in which it is not.

Now, admitting any sequent to the unity itself, that sequent must be bound up with it; any third will be about that second and move towards it, linked to it as its offspring. In this way all participants in the later will have share in the first. The Beings of the Intellectual are thus a plurality of firsts and seconds and thirds attached like one sphere to one center, not separated by interval but mutually present; where, therefore, the Intellectual tertiaries are present the secondaries and firsts are present too.

5. Often for the purpose of exposition—as a help towards stating the nature of the produced multiplicity—we use the example of many lines radiating from one center; but while we provide for individualization we must carefully preserve mutual presence. Even in the case of our circle we need not think of separated radii; all may be taken as forming one surface: where there is no distinction even upon the one surface but all is power and reality undifferentiated, all the beings may be thought of as centers uniting at one central center: we ignore the radial lines and think of their terminals at that center, where they are at one. Restore the radii; once more we have lines, each touching a generating center of its own, but that center remains coincident with the one first center; the centers all unite in that first center and yet remain what they were, so that they are as many as are the lines to which they serve as terminals; the centers themselves appear as numerous as the lines starting from them and yet all those centers constitute a unity.

Thus we may liken the Intellectual Beings in their diversity to many centers coinciding with the one center and themselves at one in it but appearing multiple on account of the radial lines—lines which do not generate the centers but merely lead to them. The radii, thus, afford a serviceable illustration for the mode of contact by which the Intellectual Unity manifests itself as multiple and multipresent.

6. The Intellectual Beings, thus, are multiple and one; in virtue of their infinite nature their unity is a multiplicity, many in one and one over many, a unit-plurality. They act as entire upon entire; even upon the partial thing they act as entire; but there is the difference that at first the partial accepts this working only partially though the entire enters later. Thus, when Man enters into human form there exists a particular man who, however, is still Man. From the one thing Man—man in the Idea—material man has come to constitute many individual men: the one identical thing is present in multiplicity, in multi-impression, so to speak, from the one seal.

This does not mean that Man Absolute, or any Absolute, or the Universe in the sense of a Whole, is absorbed by multiplicity; on the contrary, the multiplicity is absorbed by the Absolute, or rather is bound up with it. There is a difference between the mode in which a color may be absorbed by a substance entire and that in which the soul of the individual is identically present in every part of the body: it is in this latter mode that Being is omnipresent.

7. To Real Being we go back, all that we have and are; to that we return as from that we came. Of what is There we have direct knowledge, not images or even impressions; and to know without image is to be; by our part in true knowledge we are those Beings; we do not need to bring them down into ourselves, for we are There among them. Since not only ourselves but all other things also are those Beings, we all are they; we are they while we are also one with all: therefore we and all things are one.

When we look outside of that on which we depend we ignore our unity; looking outward we see many faces; look inward and all is the one head. If a man could but be turned about—by his own motion or by the happy pull of Athene—he would see at once God and himself and the All. At first no doubt all will not be seen as one whole, but when we find no stop at which to declare a limit to our being we cease to rule ourselves out from the total of reality; we reach to the All as a unity—and this not by any stepping forward, but by the fact of being and abiding there where the All has its being.

Ennead VI
Seventh Tractate: 5-7; 12-13; 15; 22; 31

HOW THE MULTIPLICITY OF THE IDEAL-FORMS CAME INTO BEING; AND ON THE GOOD

This treatise is regarded as the largest of the single works of Plotinus and is devoted to the spiritual ascent and the soul's union with the One, or the Good, which transcends Intellect and any thought altogether. Plotinus describes the ascent guided by *eros* in the symbolic language of Plato's *Phaedrus*. The soul's desire for full participation in the noetic cosmos is an essential stage in its mystical ascent to the One, because in the realm of Intellect the soul discovers its true noetic Self. The noetic realm is not the ultimate reality, and thus the intense love for the Good shifts the "intellectualized" soul's attention from contemplation of Forms to an awareness that intelligible entities are only a medium for the transcendent light radiating from the Good. Thus the soul realizes that the beauty of the noetic world is not its final goal. While participating in Intellect's erotic aspiration for the Good, the soul reaches the final stage of the mystical ascent, that is, the ineffable One itself. Only the "loving intellect" (*nous eron*), i.e., the most unified form of *nous*, can

> overcome thought as its original possibility and then to join in an *ekstasis* with the One or Good itself. The union with the One as the "truly beloved," the God, is also explicitly called an effect of *eros*. . . . The One, or the truly existing Good that is above the beautiful . . . is no abstract neuter but a substance that is itself capable of attracting. . . . It is itself *eros*, that is, as the purely transcendent it remains in itself self-related: "love of itself" (*autou eros*). As such it is also the absolute goal of human striving . . . which is in fact universally present but whose presence must also be realized by the human person through reflection and practice.[18]

[18] Werner Beierwaltes, "The Love of Beauty and the Love of God," in *Classical*

Becoming simple and unified, the soul is one with the Good. Hence, the union with the supreme God is the end of the spiritual journey.

5. Man, thus, must be some Reason-Principle other than soul. But why should he not be some conjoint—a soul in a certain Reason-Principle—the Reason-Principle being, as it were, a definite activity which however could not exist without that which acts?

This is the case with the Reason-Principles in seed which are neither soulless nor entirely soul. For these productive principles cannot be devoid of soul and there is nothing surprising in such essences being Reason-Principles.

But these principles producing man, of what phase of soul are they activities? Of the vegetal soul? Rather of that which produces animal life, a brighter soul and therefore one more intensely living.

The soul of that order, the soul that has entered into Matter of that order, is man by having, apart from body, a certain disposition; within body it shapes all to its own fashion, producing another form of Man, man reduced to what body admits, just as an artist may make a reduced image of that again.

It is this other (lower) form of Man that holds the pattern and Reason-Principles of Man, the natural tendencies, the dispositions and powers—all feeble since this is not the Primal Man—and it contains also its own kinds of sensation, different from those in the archetype, bright to all seeming, but images and dim in comparison with those of the earlier order.

The higher Man, above this sphere, rises from the more godlike soul, a soul possessed of a nobler humanity and brighter perceptions. This must be the Man of Plato's definition ("Man is Soul") where the addition (Soul as using body) marks the distinction between the soul which uses body directly and the soul, poised above, which touches the body only through that intermediary.

The Man of the realm of birth has sense-perception: the higher soul enters to bestow a brighter life, or rather does not so much

Mediterranean Spirituality: Egyptian, Greek, Roman, ed. A.H. Armstrong (London: Routledge & Kegan Paul, 1986), p. 305.

enter as simply impart itself; for soul does not leave the Intellectual but maintaining that contact holds the lower life as pendant from it, blending with it by the natural link of Reason-Principle to Reason-Principle: and man, the dimmer, brightens under that illumination.

6. But how can that higher soul have sense-perception?

It is the perception of what falls under perception There, sensation in the mode of that realm: it is the source of the lower soul's perception of the correspondences in the sense-realm. Man as sense-percipient becomes aware of these correspondences and accommodates the sense-realm to the lowest extremity of its counterpart There, proceeding from the fire here to the fire Intellectual which was perceptible to the higher soul in a manner corresponding to its own nature as Intellectual fire. If material things existed There, the soul would perceive them; Man in the Intellectual, Man as Intellectual soul, would be aware of the terrestrial. This is how the secondary Man, copy of Man in the Intellectual, contains the Reason-Principles in copy; and Man in the Intellectual-Principle contained the Man that existed before any man. The diviner shines out upon the secondary and the secondary upon the tertiary; and even the latest possesses them all—not in the sense of identifying itself with them all but as standing in under-parallel to them. Some of us act by this lowest; in another rank there is a double activity, a trace of the next higher being included; in yet another there is a blending of the third (i.e. highest) grade with the others: each is that Man by which he acts while each too contains all the grades, though in some sense not so. On the separation of the third life and third Man from the body, then if the second also departs—of course not losing hold on the Above—the two, as we are told, will occupy the same place. No doubt it seems strange that a soul which has been the Reason-Principle of a man should come to occupy the body of an animal: but the soul has always been all, and will at different times be this and that.

Pure, not yet fallen to evil, the soul chooses man and is man, for this is the higher and it produces the higher. It produces also the still loftier beings, the Celestials (Daimons), who are of one Form with

the soul that makes Man: higher still stands that Being more entirely
of the Celestial rank, in truth a god; and God is reproduced in the
Celestial who is as closely bound to God as man to the Celestial.
For that Being to which man is bound is not to be called a god;
there remains the difference which distinguishes souls, all of the
same race though they be. This is taking "Celestial" ("Daimon") in
the sense of Plato.

When a soul which in the human state has been thus attached
chooses animal nature and descends to that, it is giving forth the
Reason-Principle—necessarily in it—of the animal as it was in
the Intellectual: this it contained and the activity has been to the
lower.

7. But if it is by becoming evil and inferior that the soul produces the animal nature, the making of ox or horse was not at the
outset in its character; the Reason-Principle of the animal, and the
animal itself, must lie outside of the natural plan?

Inferior, yes; but outside of nature, no. The thing There (Soul
in the Intellectual) was in some sense horse and dog from the
beginning; given the condition, it produces the higher kind; let the
condition fail, then since produce it must, it produces what it may:
it is like a skilful craftsman competent to create all kinds of works
of art but reduced to making what is ordered and what the aptitude
of his material indicates.

The power of the All-Soul, as Reason-Principle of the universe,
may be considered as laying down a pattern before the effective
separate powers go forth from it: this plan would be something like
a tentative illumining of Matter; the elaborating soul would give
minute articulation to these representations of itself; every separate
effective soul would become that towards which it tended, assuming that particular form as the choral dancer adapts himself to the
action set down for him.

But this is to anticipate: our inquiry was, how there can be
sense-perception in man without the implication that the Divine
addresses itself to the realm of process. We maintained, and proved,
that the Divine does not look to this realm but that things here are

dependent upon those and represent them and that man here holding his powers from Thence is directed Thither, so that, while sense
makes the environment of what is of sense in him, the Intellectual
in him is linked to the Intellectual.

What we have called the perceptibles of that realm enter into
cognizance in a way of their own, since they are not material, while
the sensible sense here is fainter than the perception belonging to
that higher world, but gains a specious clarity because its objects
are bodies; the man of this sphere has sense-perception because
apprehending in a less true degree and taking only enfeebled images
of things There: perceptions here are Intellections of the dimmer
order, and the Intellections There are vivid perceptions.

12. Or take it another way: Since in our view this universe
stands to that as copy to original, the living total must exist There
beforehand; that is the realm of complete Being and everything
must exist There.

The sky There must be living and therefore not bare of stars,
here known as the heavens—for stars are included in the very
meaning of the word. Earth too will be There, and not void but
even more intensely living and containing all that lives and moves
upon our earth and the plants obviously rooted in life; sea will be
There and all waters with the movement of their unending life and
all the living things of the water; air too must be a member of that
universe with the living things of air as here.

The content of that living thing must surely be alive—as in this
sphere—and all that lives must of necessity be There. The nature of
the major parts determines that of the living forms they comprise;
by the being and content of the heaven There are determined all
the heavenly forms of life; if those lesser forms were not There, that
heaven itself would not be.

To ask how those forms of life come to be There is simply asking how that heaven came to be; it is asking whence comes the living form, and so, whence comes life, whence the All-Life, whence
the All-Soul, whence collective Intellect: and the answer is that
There no indigence or impotence can exist but all must be teeming,

seething, with life. All flows, so to speak, from one fount not to be thought of as some one breath or warmth but rather as one quality englobing and safeguarding all qualities—sweetness with fragrance, wine-quality, and the savors of everything that may be tasted, all colors seen, everything known to touch, all that ear may hear, all melodies, every rhythm.

13. For Intellectual-Principle is not a simplex, nor is the Soul that proceeds from it: on the contrary things include variety in the degree of their simplicity, that is to say in so far as they are not compounds but Principles and Activities; the activity of the lowest is simple in the sense of being a fading-out, that of the First is the total of all activity. Intellectual-Principle is moved in a movement unfailingly true to one course but its unity and identity are not those of the partial; they are those of its universality; and indeed the partial itself is not a unity but divides to infinity.

We know that Intellectual-Principle has a source and advances to some term as its ultimate; now, is the intermediate between source and term to be thought of as a line or as some distinct kind of body uniform and unvaried?

Where at that would be its worth? If it had no change, if no differentiation woke it into life, it would not be a Force; that condition would in no way differ from mere absence of power and, even calling it movement, it would still be the movement of a life not all-varied but indiscriminate; now it is of necessity that life be all-embracing, covering all the realms, and that nothing fail of life. Intellectual-Principle, therefore, must move in every direction upon all, or more precisely must ever have so moved.

A simplex moving retains its character; either there is no change, movement has been null, or if there has been advance it still remains a simplex and at once there is a permanent duality: if the one member of this duality is identical with the other, then it is still as it was, there has been no advance; if one member differs from the other, it has advanced with differentiation, and, out of a certain identity and difference, it has produced a third unity. This production, based on Identity and Difference, must be in its nature identical and different; it will be not some particular different thing but Collective Difference, as its Identity is Collective Identity.

Being thus at once Collective Identity and Collective Difference, Intellectual-Principle must reach over all different things; its very nature then is to modify itself into a universe. If the realm of different things existed before it, these different things must have modified it from the beginning; if they did not, this Intellectual-Principle produced all, or rather was all.

Beings could not exist save by the activity of Intellectual-Principle; wandering down every way it produces thing after thing, but wandering always within itself in such self-bound wandering as authentic Intellect may know; this wandering permitted to its nature is among real beings which keep pace with its movement; but it is always itself; this is a stationary wandering, a wandering within "the Meadow of Truth" from which it does not stray.

It holds and covers the universe which it has made the space, so to speak, of its movement, itself being also that universe which is space to it. And this Meadow of Truth is varied so that movement through it may be possible; suppose it not always and everywhere varied, the failing of diversity is a failure of movement; failure in movement would mean a failing of the Intellectual Act; halting, it has ceased to exercise its Intellectual Act; this ceasing, it ceases to be.

The Intellectual-Principle is the Intellectual Act, its movement is complete, filling Being complete; and the entire of Being is the Intellectual Act entire, comprehending all life and the unfailing succession of things. Because this Principle contains Identity with Difference its division is ceaselessly bringing the different things to life. Its entire movement is through life and among living things. To a traveler over land all is earth but earth abounding in difference: so in this journey the life through which Intellectual-Principle passes is one life but, in its ceaseless changing, a varied life.

Throughout this endless variation it maintains the one course because it is not, itself, subject to change but on the contrary is present as identical and unvarying Being to the rest of things. For if there be no such principle of unchanging identity to things, all is dead, activity and actuality exist nowhere. These "other things" through which it passes are also Intellectual-Principle itself, otherwise it is not the all-comprehending principle: if it is to be itself, it must be all-embracing; failing that, it is not itself. If it is complete in itself, complete because all-embracing, and there is nothing which does not find place in this total, then there can be nothing belonging to it which is not different; only by difference can there be such co-operation towards a total. If it knew no otherness but was pure identity its essential Being would be the less for that failure to fulfill the specific nature which its completion requires.

15. That Life, the various, the all-including, the primal and one, who can consider it without longing to be of it, disdaining all the other?

All other life is darkness, petty and dim and poor; it is unclean and polluting the clean, for if you do but look upon it you no longer see nor live this life which includes all living, in which there is nothing that does not live and live in a life of purity void of all that is ill. For evil is here where life is in copy and Intellect in copy; There is the archetype (the Intellectual-Principle) which has the form of Good—we read—as holding the Good in its Forms (or Ideas). That Good is distinct from Intellectual-Principle itself which maintains its life by contemplation (of the Good); and it sees also as good the objects of its contemplation because it holds them in its act of contemplating the Principle of Good. But the Good comes to it not as it was in its primal state but in accord with the condition of the Intellectual-Principle. The Good is the source from which the objects of contemplation come to be seen in the Intellectual-Principle; Intellectual-Principle has produced them by its vision of the Good. In the very law, never, looking to That, could it fail of Intellectual Act; never, on the other hand, could its objects be in the Good—otherwise it (the Intellectual-Principle) would not produce them itself. Thence it must draw its power to bring forth, to teem with offspring of itself; but the Good bestows what itself does not possess. From that Unity came multiplicity to Intellectual-Principle; it could not sustain the power poured upon

it and therefore broke it up; it turned that one power into variety
so as to carry it piecemeal.

All its production, effected in the power of The Good, contains
goodness; it is good, itself, since it is constituted by these things of
good; it is Good made diverse. It might be likened to a living sphere
teeming with variety, to a globe of faces radiant with faces all living,
to a unity of souls, all the pure souls, not the faulty but the perfect,
with Intellect enthroned over all so that the place entire glows with
Intellectual splendor.

But this would be to see it from without, one thing seeing
another; the true way is to become Intellectual-Principle and be,
our very selves, what we are to see.

22. That light known, then indeed we are stirred towards
those Beings in longing and rejoicing over the radiance about them,
just as earthly love is not for the material form but for the Beauty
manifested upon it. Every one of those Beings exists for itself but
becomes an object of desire by the color cast upon it from The
Good, source of those graces and of the love they evoke. The soul
taking that outflow from the divine is stirred; seized with a Bacchic
passion, goaded by these goads, it becomes Love. Before that, even
Intellectual-Principle with all its loveliness did not stir the soul; for
that beauty is dead until it take the light of The Good, and the soul
lies supine, cold to all, unquickened even to Intellectual-Principle
there before it. But when there enters into it a glow from the
divine, it gathers strength, awakens, spreads true wings, and however urged by its nearer environing, speeds its buoyant way elsewhere,
to something greater to its memory: so long as there exists anything
loftier than the near, its very nature bears it upwards, lifted by
the giver of that love. Beyond Intellectual-Principle it passes but
beyond The Good it cannot, for nothing stands above That. Let it
remain in Intellectual-Principle and it sees the lovely and august,
but it is not there possessed of all it sought; the face it sees is beautiful no doubt but not of power to hold its gaze because lacking in
the radiant grace which is the bloom upon beauty.

Even here we have to recognize that beauty is that which irradiates symmetry rather than symmetry itself and is that which truly calls out our love.

Why else is there more of the glory of beauty upon the living and only some faint trace of it upon the dead though the face yet retains all its fullness and symmetry? Why are the most living portraits the most beautiful, even though the other happen to be more symmetric? Why is the living ugly more attractive than the sculptured handsome? It is that the one is more nearly what we are looking for, and this because there is soul there, because there is more of the Idea of The Good, because there is some glow of the light of The Good and this illumination awakens and lifts the soul and all that goes with it, so that the whole man is won over to goodness and in the fullest measure stirred to life.

31. But since the beauty and light in all come from That which is before all, it is Thence that Intellectual-Principle took the brilliance of the Intellectual Energy which flashed Nature into being; Thence soul took power towards life, in virtue of that fuller life streaming into it. Intellectual-Principle was raised thus to that Supreme and remains with it, happy in that presence. Soul too, that soul which as possessing knowledge and vision was capable, clung to what it saw; and as its vision so its rapture; it saw and was stricken; but having in itself something of that principle it felt its kinship and was moved to longing like those stirred by the image of the beloved to desire of the veritable presence. Lovers here mould themselves to the beloved; they seek to increase their attraction of person and their likeness of mind; they are unwilling to fall short in moral quality or in other graces lest they be distasteful to those possessing such merit—and only among such can true love be. In the same way the soul loves the Supreme Good, from its very beginnings stirred by it to love.

The soul which has never strayed from this love waits for no reminding from the beauty of our world: holding that love—perhaps unawares—it is ever in quest, and, in its longing to be borne Thither, passes over what is lovely here and with one glance at the beauty of the universe dismisses all; for it sees that all is put together of flesh and Matter, befouled by its housing, made fragmentary by corporal extension, not the Authentic Beauty which could never venture into the mud of body to be soiled, annulled.

By only noting the flux of things it knows at once that from elsewhere comes the beauty that floats upon them and so it is urged Thither, passionate in pursuit of what it loves: never—unless someone robs it of that love—never giving up till it attain.

There indeed all it saw was beautiful and veritable; it grew in strength by being thus filled with the life of the True; itself becoming veritable Being and attaining veritable knowledge, it enters by that neighboring into conscious possession of what it has long been seeking.

Ennead VI
Eighth Tractate: 7; 18-19

ON FREE WILL AND THE WILL OF THE ONE

In this treatise Plotinus speaks about the One and the freedom of the One which underlies the concept of human freedom. The One, or the Good, is paradoxically described in the terms of will, love, and thought, but this kataphatic emphasis in no way diminishes the apophatic, or negative, way of approach to the One. Any experience of the Good transcends language. Though the First Principle may be equated to the center of the circle, it is, in fact, everywhere and nowhere. Human freedom is merely a reflection of transcendent divine freedom. It is always liberation from manifold manifested existence and return to the One. Accordingly, freedom is a sort of divine power which is present in each soul to the extent that all liberation and return to the supreme Source presupposes the power to make oneself free. As Georges Leroux pointed out:

> Human freedom can be imagined only through its original and essential participation in the freedom of the One through the mediation, at once ontological and spiritual, of Intellect. One can speak of an essential freedom, therefore, by which the soul is free as long as it refers back to its source, and of a spiritual freedom by which the soul is free in each spiritual act which liberates it in this life.[19]

7. Soul becomes free when it moves without hindrance, through Intellectual-Principle, towards The Good; what it does in that spirit is its free act; Intellectual-Principle is free in its own right. That principle of Good is the sole object of desire and the source of self-disposal to the rest, to soul when it fully attains, to Intellectual-Principle by connate possession.

---

[19] Georges Leroux, "Human Freedom in the Thought of Plotinus," in *The Cambridge Companion to Plotinus*, ed. L.P. Gerson (Cambridge: Cambridge University Press, 1996), p. 304.

How then can the sovereign of all that august sequence—the first in place, that to which all else strives to mount, all dependent upon it and taking from it their powers even to this power of self-disposal—how can This be brought under the freedom belonging to you and me, a conception applicable only by violence to Intellectual-Principle itself?

It is rash thinking drawn from another order that would imagine a First Principle to be chance-made what it is, controlled by a manner of being imposed from without, void therefore of freedom or self-disposal, acting or refraining under compulsion. Such a statement is untrue to its subject and introduces much difficulty; it utterly annuls the principle of free will with the very conception of our own voluntary action, so that there is no longer any sense in discussion upon these terms, empty names for the non-existent. Anyone upholding this opinion would be obliged to say not merely that free act exists nowhere but that the very word conveys nothing to him. To admit understanding the word is to be easily brought to confess that the conception of freedom does apply where it is denied. No doubt a concept leaves the reality untouched and unappropriated, for nothing can produce itself, bring itself into being; but thought insists upon distinguishing between what is subject to others and what is independent, bound under no allegiance, lord of its own act.

This state of freedom belongs in the absolute degree to the Eternals in right of that eternity and to other beings in so far as without hindrance they possess or pursue The Good which, standing above them all, must manifestly be the only good they can reasonably seek.

To say that The Good exists by chance must be false; chance belongs to the later, to the multiple; since the First has never come to be we cannot speak of it either as coming by chance into being or as not master of its being. Absurd also the objection that it acts in accordance with its being if this is to suggest that freedom demands act or other expression against the nature. Neither does its nature as the unique annul its freedom when this is the result of no compulsion but means only that The Good is no other than itself, is self-complete and has no higher.

The objection would imply that where there is most good there is least freedom. If this is absurd, still more absurd to deny freedom to The Good on the ground that it is good and self-con-centered, not needing to lean upon anything else but actually being the Term to which all tends, itself moving to none.

Where—since we must use such words—the essential act is identical with the being—and this identity must obtain in The Good since it holds even in Intellectual-Principle—there the act is no more determined by the Being than the Being by the Act. Thus "acting according to its nature" does not apply; the Act, the Life, so to speak, cannot be held to issue from the Being; the Being accom-panies the Act in an eternal association: from the two (Being and Act) it forms itself into The Good, self-springing and unspringing.

18. Seeking Him, seek nothing of Him outside; within is to be sought what follows upon Him; Himself do not attempt. He is, Himself, that outer, He the encompassment and measure of all things; or rather He is within, at the innermost depth; the outer, circling round Him, so to speak, and wholly dependent upon Him, is Reason-Principle and Intellectual-Principle—or becomes Intellectual-Principle by contact with Him and in the degree of that contact and dependence; for from Him it takes the being which makes it Intellectual-Principle.

A circle related in its path to a center must be admitted to owe its scope to that center; it has something of the nature of that center in that the radial lines converging on that one central point assimilate their impinging ends to that point of convergence and of departure, the dominant of radii and terminals: the terminals are of one nature with the center, feeble reproductions of it, since the center is, in a certain sense, the source of terminals and radii impinging at every point upon it; these lines reveal the center; they are the development of that undeveloped.

In the same way we are to take Intellectual-Principle and Being. This combined power springs from the Supreme, an outflow and as it were development from That and remaining dependent upon that Intellective nature, showing forth that, so to speak, Intellect-in-Unity which is not Intellectual-Principle since it is no duality. No more than in the circle are the lines or circumference to be identified with that center which is the source of both: radii and circle are images given forth by indwelling power and, as products of a certain vigor in it, not cut off from it.

Thus the Intellective power circles around the Supreme which stands to it as archetype to image; the archetype is Intellect-in-Unity; the image in its manifold movement round about its prior has produced the multiplicity by which it is constituted Intellectual-Principle: that prior has no movement; it generates Intellectual-Principle by its sheer wealth.

Such a power, author of Intellectual-Principle, author of being—how does it lend itself to chance, to hazard, to any "So it happened"?

What is present in Intellectual-Principle is present, though in a far transcendent mode, in the One: so in a light diffused afar from one light shining within itself, the diffused is vestige, the source is the true light; but Intellectual-Principle, the diffused and image light, is not different in kind from its prior; and it is not a thing of chance but at every point is reason and cause.

The Supreme is cause of the cause: it is cause pre-eminently, cause as containing cause in the deepest and truest mode; for in it lie the Intellective causes which are to be unfolded from it, author as it is not of the chance-made but of what the divine willed: and this willing was not apart from reason, was not in the realm of hazard and of what happened to present itself but of what must needs be, since hazard is excluded from that realm.

Thus Plato applies to it the words "necessary" and "appropriate" because he wished to establish beyond a doubt that it is far removed from hazard and that what exists is what must exist: if thus the existence is "necessary" it does not exist without reason: if its manner of being is the "appropriate," it is the utterly self-disposing in comparison with its sequents and, before that, in regard to itself: thus it is not "as it happened to be" but as it willed to be: all this, on the assumption that God wills what should be and that it is impossible to separate right from realization and that this Necessary is not to God an outside thing but is, itself, his first Activity manifesting outwardly in the exactly representative form. Thus we must speak of God since we cannot tell Him as we would.

19. Stirred to the Supreme by what has been told, a man must strive to possess it directly; then he too will see, though still unable to tell it as he would wish.

One seeing That as it really is will lay aside all reasoning upon it and simply state it as the self-existent, such that if it had essence that essence would be subject to it and, so to speak, derived from it; none that has been would dare to talk of its "happening to be," or indeed be able to utter word. With all his courage he would stand astounded, unable at any venture to say where This might be, with the vision everywhere before the eyes of the soul so that, look where one may, there it is seen unless one deliberately look away, ignoring God, thinking no more upon Him. So we are to understand the Beyond-Essence darkly indicated by the ancients: it is not merely that He generated Essence but that He is subject neither to Essence nor to Himself; his Essence is not his Principle; He is Principle to Essence and not for Himself did He make it; producing it He left it outside of Himself. He had no need of being, who brought it to be. Thus his making of being is no "action in accordance with his being."

Ennead VI
Ninth Tractate: 3-4; 7-11

ON THE GOOD, OR THE ONE

This early treatise deals with the One and union with the One as the main goal of the philosophic life. In order to reach the ultimate Principle, one needs to turn inwards, away from sensible phenomena and all other things, even away from oneself. The vision of the One is regarded as mystical union (*henosis*) with no consciousness of duality. According to Pierre Hadot:

> Although in the mystical experience of the Good the soul is with the Intellect, in the state in which it is in contact with the Good, in which it is the loving Intellect, "out of its mind," drunk on the divine nectar that the soul identifies with, the soul remains nonetheless the subject to which the mystical experiences in the Plotinian descriptions are referred. Plotinus is obviously concerned with guiding the human soul towards union with God. This is why the mystical experience is presented as an exceptional phenomenon and as transitory. Although the union of the Intellect with the Good is eternal, the unitive experiences of the soul are exceptional. They appear suddenly, and we cannot induce them ourselves. The exercise of internal purification that prepares for their reception is not enough to induce them; they also disappear abruptly. . . .
>
> Like all lovers, the soul wants to be alone with the one it loves, all the more since the one it loves is the only One. But the soul, following the Intellect, wants to abandon all form and remain with the Good primarily because the Good transcends all forms which might dominate it and determine it, because the Good is not a thing and is external to all things, in a word, because the Good is infinite. The soul refuses, then, to remain in any form, however elevated, and thus it experiences the infinite love of the Infinite. . . . The soul feels the presence of another with which it is identified, and it is no longer itself. It is transposed outside itself and does not know any longer what it is, no longer hav-

ing the opportunity to consider what it is when it considers the Good.[20]

3. What then must The Unity be, what nature is left for it?

No wonder that to state it is not easy; even Being and Form are not easy, though we have a way, an approach through the Ideas.

The soul or mind reaching towards the formless finds itself incompetent to grasp where nothing bounds it or to take impression where the impinging reality is diffuse; in sheer dread of holding to nothingness, it slips away. The state is painful; often it seeks relief by retreating from all this vagueness to the region of sense, there to rest as on solid ground, just as the sight distressed by the minute rests with pleasure on the bold.

Soul must see in its own way; this is by coalescence, unification; but in seeking thus to know the Unity it is prevented by that very unification from recognizing that it has found; it cannot distinguish itself from the object of this intuition. None the less, this is our one resource if our philosophy is to give us knowledge of The Unity.

We are in search of unity; we are to come to know the principle of all, the Good and First; therefore we may not stand away from the realm of Firsts and lie prostrate among the lasts: we must strike for those Firsts, rising from things of sense which are the lasts. Cleared of all evil in our intention towards The Good, we must ascend to the Principle within ourselves; from many, we must become one; only so do we attain to knowledge of that which is Principle and Unity. We shape ourselves into Intellectual-Principle; we make over our soul in trust to Intellectual-Principle and set it firmly in That; thus what That sees the soul will waken to see: it is through the Intellectual-Principle that we have this vision of The Unity; it must be our care to bring over nothing whatever from sense, to allow nothing from that source to enter into Intellectual-

---

[20] Pierre Hadot, "Plotinus and Porphyry," in *Classical Mediterranean Spirituality: Egyptian, Greek, Roman*, ed. A.H. Armstrong (London: Routledge & Kegan Paul, 1986), pp. 245, 246.

The Enneads

Principle: with Intellect pure, and with the summit of Intellect, we are to see the All-Pure.

If the quester has the impression of extension or shape or mass attaching to That Nature he has not been led by Intellectual-Principle which is not of the order to see such things; the activity has been of sense and of the judgment following upon sense: only Intellectual-Principle can inform us of the things of its scope; its competence is upon its priors, its content, and its issue: but even its content is outside of sense; and still purer, still less touched by multiplicity, are its priors, or rather its Prior.

The Unity, then, is not Intellectual-Principle but something higher still: Intellectual-Principle is still a being but that First is no being but precedent to all Being: it cannot be a being, for a being has what we may call the shape of its reality but The Unity is without shape, even shape Intellectual.

Generative of all, The Unity is none of all; neither thing nor quantity nor quality nor intellect nor soul; not in motion, not at rest, not in place, not in time: it is the self-defined, unique in form or, better, formless, existing before Form was, or Movement or Rest, all of which are attachments of Being and make Being the manifold it is.

But how, if not in the movement, can it be otherwise than at rest?

The answer is that movement and rest are states pertaining to Being, which necessarily has one or the other or both. Besides, anything at rest must be so in virtue of Rest as something distinct: Unity at rest becomes the ground of an attribute and at once ceases to be a simplex.

Note, similarly, that when we speak of this First as Cause we are affirming something happening not to it but to us, the fact that we take from this Self-Enclosed: strictly we should put neither a This nor a That to it; we hover, as it were, about it, seeking the statement of an experience of our own, sometimes nearing this Reality, sometimes baffled by the enigma in which it dwells.

211

4. The main source of the difficulty is that awareness of this Principle comes neither by knowing nor by the Intellection that discovers the Intellectual Beings but by a presence overpassing all knowledge. In knowing, soul or mind abandons its unity; it cannot remain a simplex: knowing is taking account of things; that accounting is multiple; the mind thus plunging into number and multiplicity departs from unity.

Our way then takes us beyond knowing; there may be no wandering from unity; knowing and knowable must all be left aside; every object of thought, even the highest, we must pass by, for all that is good is later than This and derives from This as from the sun all the light of the day.

"Not to be told; not to be written": in our writing and telling we are but urging towards it: out of discussion we call to vision: to those desiring to see, we point the path; our teaching is of the road and the traveling; the seeing must be the very act of one that has made this choice.

There are those that have not attained to see. The soul has not come to know the splendor There; it has not felt and clutched to itself that love-passion of vision known to the lover come to rest where he loves. Or struck perhaps by that authentic light, all the soul lit by the nearness gained, we have gone weighted from beneath; the vision is frustrate; we should go without burden and we go carrying that which can but keep us back; we are not yet made over into unity.

From none is that Principle absent and yet from all: present, it remains absent save to those fit to receive, disciplined into some accordance, able to touch it closely by their likeness and by that kindred power within themselves through which, remaining as it was when it came to them from the Supreme, they are enabled to see in so far as God may at all be seen.

Failure to attain may be due to such impediment or to lack of the guiding thought that establishes trust; impediment we must charge against ourselves and strive by entire renunciation to become emancipate; where there is distrust for lack of convincing reason, further considerations may be applied.

7. If the mind reels before something thus alien to all we know, we must take our stand on the things of this realm and strive thence to see. But in the looking beware of throwing outward; this Principle does not lie away somewhere leaving the rest void; to those of power to reach, it is present; to the inapt, absent. In our daily affairs we cannot hold an object in mind if we have given ourselves elsewhere, occupied upon some other matter; that very thing, and nothing else, must be before us to be truly the object of observation. So here also; preoccupied by the impress of something else, we are withheld under that pressure from becoming aware of The Unity; a mind gripped and fastened by some definite thing cannot take the print of the very contrary. As Matter, it is agreed, must be void of quality in order to accept the types of the universe, so and much more must the soul be kept formless if there is to be no infixed impediment to prevent it being brimmed and lit by the Primal Principle.

In sum, we must withdraw from all the extern, pointed wholly inwards; no leaning to the outer; the total of things ignored, first in their relation to us and later in the very idea; the self put out of mind in the contemplation of the Supreme; all the commerce so closely There that, if report were possible, one might become to others reporter of that communion.

Such converse, we may suppose, was that of Minos, thence known as the Familiar of Zeus; and in that memory he established the laws which report it, enlarged to that task by his vision There. Some, on the other hand, there will be to disdain such citizen service, choosing to remain in the higher: these will be those that have seen much.

God—we read—is outside of none, present unperceived to all; we break away from Him, or rather from ourselves; what we turn from we cannot reach; astray ourselves, we cannot go in search of another; a child distraught will not recognize its father; to find ourselves is to know our source.

8. Every soul that knows its history is aware, also, that its movement, unthwarted, is not that of an outgoing line; its natural

course may be likened to that in which a circle turns not upon some external but on its own center, the point to which it owes its rise. The soul's movement will be about its source, to this it will hold, poised intent towards that unity to which all souls should move and the divine souls always move, divine in virtue of that movement; for to be a god is to be integral with the Supreme; what stands away is man still multiple, or beast.

Is then this "center" of our souls the Principle for which we are seeking?

We must look yet further: we must admit a Principle in which all these centers coincide: it will be a center by analogy with the center of the circle we know. The soul is not a circle in the sense of the geometric figure but in that its primal nature (wholeness) is within it and about it, that it owes its origin to what is whole, and that it will be still more entire when severed from body.

In our present state—part of our being weighed down by the body, as one might have the feet under water with all the rest untouched—we bear ourselves aloft by that intact part and, in that, hold through our own center to the center of all the centers, just as the centers of the great circles of a sphere coincide with that of the sphere to which all belong. Thus we are secure.

If these circles were material and not spiritual, the link with the centers would be local; they would lie round it where it lay at some distant point: since the souls are of the Intellectual, and the Supreme still loftier, we understand that contact is otherwise procured, that is by those powers which connect Intellectual agent with Intellectual object; indeed soul is closer to the Supreme than Intellect to its object—such is its similarity, identity, and the sure link of kindred. Material mass cannot blend into other material mass: unbodied beings are not under this bodily limitation; their separation is solely that of otherness, of differentiation; in the absence of otherness, it is similars mutually present.

Thus the Supreme as containing no otherness is ever present with us; we with it when we put otherness away. It is not that the Supreme reaches out to us seeking our communion: we reach towards the Supreme; it is we that become present. We are always before it: but we do not always look: thus a choir, singing set in due order about the conductor, may turn away from that center to which all should attend; let it but face aright and it sings with beauty, present effectively. We are ever before the Supreme—cut off is utter dissolution; we can no longer be—but we do not always attend: when we look, our Term is attained; this is rest; this is the end of singing ill; effectively before Him, we lift a choral song full of God.

9. In this choiring, the soul looks upon the wellspring of Life, wellspring also of Intellect, beginning of Being, fount of Good, root of Soul. It is not that these are poured out from the Supreme, lessening it as if it were a thing of mass. At that the emanants would be perishable; but they are eternal; they spring from an eternal principle, which produces them not by its fragmentation but in virtue of its intact identity: therefore they too hold firm; so long as the sun shines, so long there will be light.

We have not been cut away; we are not separate, what though the body-nature has closed about us to press us to itself; we breathe and hold our ground because the Supreme does not give and pass but gives on for ever, so long as it remains what it is.

Our being is the fuller for our turning Thither; this is our prosperity; to hold aloof is loneliness and lessening. Here is the soul's peace, outside of evil, refuge taken in the place clean of wrong; here it has its Act, its true knowing; here it is immune. Here is living, the true; that of today, all living apart from Him, is but a shadow, a mimicry. Life in the Supreme is the native activity of Intellect; in virtue of that silent converse it brings forth gods, brings forth beauty, brings forth righteousness, brings forth all moral good; for of all these the soul is pregnant when it has been filled with God. This state is its first and its final, because from God it comes, its good lies There, and, once turned to God again, it is what it was. Life here, with the things of earth, is a sinking, a defeat, a failing of the wing.

That our good is There is shown by the very love inborn with the soul; hence the constant linking of the Love-God with the

Psyches in story and picture; the soul, other than God but sprung of Him, must needs love. So long as it is There, it holds the heavenly love; here its love is the baser; There the soul is Aphrodite of the heavens; here, turned harlot, Aphrodite of the public ways: yet the soul is always an Aphrodite. This is the intention of the myth which tells of Aphrodite's birth and Eros born with her.

The soul in its nature loves God and longs to be at one with Him in the noble love of a daughter for a noble father; but coming to human birth and lured by the courtships of this sphere, she takes up with another love, a mortal, leaves her father and falls.

But one day coming to hate her shame, she puts away the evil of earth, once more seeks the father, and finds her peace.

Those to whom all this experience is strange may understand by way of our earthly longings and the joy we have in winning to what we most desire—remembering always that here what we love is perishable, hurtful, that our loving is of mimicries and turns awry because all was a mistake, our good was not here, this was not what we sought; There only is our veritable love and There we may unite with it, not holding it in some fleshly embrace but possessing it in all its verity. Any that have seen know what I have in mind: the soul takes another life as it draws nearer and nearer to God and gains participation in Him; thus restored it feels that the dispenser of true life is There to see, that now we have nothing to look for but, far otherwise, that we must put aside all else and rest in This alone, This become, This alone, all the earthly environment done away, in haste to be free, impatient of any bond holding us to the baser, so that with our being entire we may cling about This, no part in us remaining but through it we have touch with God.

Thus we have all the vision that may be of Him and of ourselves; but it is of a self wrought to splendor, brimmed with the Intellectual light, become that very light, pure, buoyant, unburdened, raised to Godhood or, better, knowing its Godhood, all aflame then—but crushed out once more if it should take up the discarded burden.

10. But how comes the soul not to keep that ground?

Because it has not yet escaped wholly: but there will be the time of vision unbroken, the self hindered no longer by any hindrance of body. Not that those hindrances beset that in us which has veritably seen; it is the other phase of the soul that suffers, and that only when we withdraw from vision and take to knowing by proof, by evidence, by the reasoning processes of the mental habit. Such logic is not to be confounded with that act of ours in the vision; it is not our reason that has seen; it is something greater than reason, reason's Prior, as far above reason as the very object of that thought must be.

In our self-seeing There, the self is seen as belonging to that order, or rather we are merged into that self in us which has the quality of that order. It is a knowing of the self restored to its purity. No doubt we should not speak of seeing; but we cannot help talking in dualities, seen and seer, instead of, boldly, the achievement of unity. In this seeing, we neither hold an object nor trace distinction; there is no two. The man is changed, no longer himself nor self-belonging; he is merged with the Supreme, sunken into it, one with it: center coincides with center, for centers of circles, even here below, are one when they unite, and two when they separate; and it is in this sense that we now (after the vision) speak of the Supreme as separate. This is why the vision baffles telling; we cannot detach the Supreme to state it; if we have seen something thus detached we have failed of the Supreme which is to be known only as one with ourselves.

11. This is the purport of that rule of our Mysteries: "Nothing Divulged to the Uninitiate": the Supreme is not to be made a common story, the holy things may not be uncovered to the stranger, to any that has not himself attained to see. There were not two; beholder was one with beheld; it was not a vision compassed but a unity apprehended. The man formed by this mingling with the Supreme must—if he only remember—carry its image impressed upon him: he is become the Unity, nothing within him or without inducing any diversity; no movement now, no passion, no outlook-

ing desire, once this ascent is achieved; reasoning is in abeyance and all Intellection and even, to dare the word, the very self: caught away, filled with God, he has in perfect stillness attained isolation; all the being calmed, he turns neither to this side nor to that, not even inwards to himself; utterly resting he has become very rest. He belongs no longer to the order of the beautiful; he has risen beyond beauty; he has overpassed even the choir of the virtues; he is like one who, having penetrated the inner sanctuary, leaves the temple images behind him—though these become once more first objects of regard when he leaves the holies; for There his converse was not with image, not with trace, but with the very Truth in the view of which all the rest is but of secondary concern.

There, indeed, it was scarcely vision, unless of a mode unknown; it was a going forth from the self, a simplifying, a renunciation, a reach towards contact and at the same time a repose, a meditation towards adjustment. This is the only seeing of what lies within the holies: to look otherwise is to fail.

Things here are signs; they show therefore to the wiser teachers how the supreme God is known; the instructed priest reading the sign may enter the holy place and make real the vision of the inaccessible.

Even those that have never found entry must admit the existence of that invisible; they will know their source and Principle since by principle they see principle and are linked with it, by like they have contact with like and so they grasp all of the divine that lies within the scope of mind. Until the seeing comes they are still craving something, that which only the vision can give; this Term, attained only by those that have overpassed all, is the All-Transcending.

It is not in the soul's nature to touch utter nothingness; the lowest descent is into evil and, so far, into non-being: but to utter nothing, never. When the soul begins again to mount, it comes not to something alien but to its very self; thus detached, it is in nothing but itself; self-gathered it is no longer in the order of being; it is in the Supreme.

There is thus a converse in virtue of which the essential man outgrows Being, becomes identical with the Transcendent of Being. The self thus lifted, we are in the likeness of the Supreme: if from that heightened self we pass still higher—image to archetype—we have won the Term of all our journeying. Fallen back again, we waken the virtue within until we know ourselves all order once more; once more we are lightened of the burden and move by virtue towards Intellectual-Principle and through the Wisdom in That to the Supreme.

This is the life of gods and of the godlike and blessed among men, liberation from the alien that besets us here, a life taking no pleasure in the things of earth, the passing of solitary to solitary.

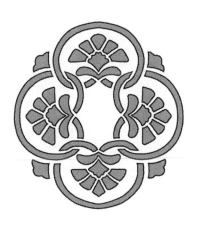

PORPHYRY'S ON *THE CAVE OF THE NYMPHS* AND THE SPIRITUAL EXEGESIS OF HOMER

Porphyry and His Works

Porphyry (c. 233-305) was born in Tyre, Phoenicia, and his Syriac name Malchus means "king." Porphyry (meaning "purple," the royal color) is simply a Greek rendering of his Semitic name, and the disciple of Plotinus was thus sometimes called Basilius. While the influence of Iamblichus predominated in the Greek-speaking Eastern half of the Roman world, Porphyry determined the understanding of Neoplatonism in the Latin (especially Christian) West. Most of his works are lost due to his anti-Christian polemics, including a scholarly analysis of the Biblical texts that was regarded too dangerous by the Christians and therefore almost totally destroyed.

Among the most important works which survived are the *Sentences Leading to the Intelligible World* (*Aphormai pros ta noeta*), a collection of 44 metaphysical statements, based on the *Enneads* of Plotinus but turned into rigid axioms. However, Porphyry is not simply a popularizer of his master. Porphyry's philosophy in many respects goes beyond that of Plotinus, especially regarding metaphysical and soteriological details, and in its interpretation of Aristotle. Porphyry's *Introduction* (*Eisagoge*) to Aristotle's *Categories* became the chief source of inspiration for later Western logicians and largely determined the rise of the quarrel between Realism and Nominalism in Mediaeval European Scholasticism.

Porphyry's Platonic commentaries are lost, though Pierre Hadot attributes some anonymous pieces to Porphyry. The treatises *On the Abstinence from Animal Food* (*De abstinentia*), *Letter to*

Marcella, The Life of Pythagoras, The Life of Plotinus are all intact, but *Philosophy from Oracles, On the Return of the Soul (De regressu anima), Miscellaneous Inquiries,* and many other works survive only in fragments or are entirely lost.

Porphyry's religious and literary interests are reflected in his commentaries on Homer, especially in the surviving examples of an allegorical interpretation of traditional myths. In his remarkable commentary on a mysterious cave described by Homer in the XIIIth book of the *Odyssey*, Porphyry interprets the cave as an image of the cosmos. *On the Cave of the Nymphs (De antro nympharum)* is one of the finest pieces of the Neoplatonic philosophic and allegorical interpretation of Homer surviving from late antiquity.

Odysseus as a Philosopher and Spiritual Hero

The Orphics and Pythagoreans already regarded the epic poems of Homer as spiritual allegories and symbols for the progress of the soul, based on transcendent divine realities. The Cynics in the fifth century B.C. put Odysseus forward as an *exemplum*, or *paradeigma*, of the sage (*sophos*). For instance, they see in Odysseus dressed in rags a model of the life advocated by Cynicism.

Stephen R. Hill, who produced a comparative study of the *Odyssey* and the *Ramayana*, says that the first word of this Homeric poem is *andra*, the accusative of *andros*, meaning "man," whose prime duty is the same as set out in the *Bhagavadgita*: to "surrender himself." Therefore the whole of the *Odyssey* may be viewed as a story of a man who had to be stripped of everything in the process of "surrendering himself":[1]

> "Restless seas" are themselves a symbol of the troubles of man in the iron age, and in one sense Odysseus' journey is to a life beyond the restless seas. Having arrived at Skheria, Odysseus proceeds to outline to his hosts the seven years of his great

---

[1] Stephen R. Hill, *Concordia: The Roots of European Thought. Comparative Studies in Vedic and Greek Ideas* (London: Duckworth, 1992), p. 74.

wanderings that have preceded his arrival on Kalypso's island. During these wanderings Odysseus has had to face twelve major obstacles, which are in fact spiritual tests of his developing powers. At the outset he is surrounded by many companions but they are *nepioi*, meaning "foolish," and they are gradually lost or killed, until Odysseus alone returns to Ithaka.[2]

For the ancient Pythagoreans, the song of the Homeric Sirens symbolized the planetary music of the spheres that enthralls souls after death and agitates them already in this life, if only their ears are not sealed by passions. This interpretation considerably differs from later Neoplatonic exegesis, because here the wax-blocked ears paradoxically stand for the carnal passions. Plutarch relates this Pythagorean interpretation as a piece of Platonic exegesis. He says:

> Now Homer's Sirens, it is true, frighten us, inconsistently with the Platonic myth; but the poet too conveyed a truth symbolically, namely that the power of their music is not inhuman or destructive: as souls depart from this world to the next, so it seems, and drift uncertainly after death, it creates in them a passionate love for the heavenly and divine, and forgetfulness of mortality; it possesses them and enchants them with its spell, so that in joyfulness they follow the Sirens and join them in their circuits. Here on earth a kind of faint echo of that music reaches us, and appealing to our souls through the medium of words, reminds them of what they experienced in an earlier existence. The ears of most souls, however, are plastered over and blocked up, not with wax, but with carnal obstructions and affections (*Quaest. conviv.* IX.14.6 745 DF Sandbach).

For the Pythagoreans, the Sirens represent the harmony of the spheres. Pythagoreans and Neoplatonists revealed a metaphysical dimension of the Homeric poems and regarded Odysseus as a spiritual hero, "the philosopher Odysseus" (*ho philosophos Odusseus*: Eustathius *Comm. ad. Hom. Odysseam* I.51; X.241). The Cynics and the Stoics, who also took into account Odysseus' actions in the *Iliad*, viewed him as a moral ideal. The Neoplatonists concentrated

[2] Ibid., p. 77.

themselves mainly on the figure as represented in the *Odyssey* with his maritime adventures, regarding the sea in which their hero struggles as the symbol of *genesis* and the Sirens (contrary to the Pythagorean account) as the embodiment of temptations. In this they followed Plato who advised to avoid the Sirens (*Phaedr.* 259a). Thus, according to Proclus:

> As to souls, who live in the world of *genesis*, they should "sail past them," imitating Homer's Odysseus—if it is true that the sea also is the image (*eikon*) of genesis—so as not to allow themselves to be bewitched by *genesis* (*In Crat.* 158, p.88.20.23 Pasquali).

After freeing himself from the charms of Circe and Calypso, Odysseus is able to return to his fatherland in the noetic realm, leaving behind the beauties of the sensible world. As regards the union with the divine Intellect—the "mystical harbor of soul," or a place "where the sea is unknown," according to the prediction of Teiresias—this is the true goal of Odysseus, as Proclus explains (*In Euclidem* 55.16-23). Noetic union and salvation can be reached only through his turning back within himself, though this is accomplished by the intervention of grace in the form of Hermes commanding Calypso, i.e. imagination (*phantasia*), to release him.[3]

Thus Odysseus becomes a hero of the renunciation of the material world and its sensible pleasures in favor of the eternal and transcendent beauty of the Forms. Accordingly, Plotinus distinguishes three classes of men: 1) those who do not try to rise above the sensible realm, 2) those who attempt to escape the material world but cannot, and 3) those who succeed to arrive "there" (*ekei*), i.e., the noetic cosmos, "just as a man arrives in his well-governed land after a long journey" (*hosper ek polles planes eis patrida eunomon aphikomenos anthropos: Enn.* V.9.1.20-21). Thus Plotinus argues that the quest for eternal beauty (*to kalon*) requires the abandonment of all the obscurities of matter, thus fleeing to one's own land:

---

[3] Algis Uždavinys, "Through the Idols of Twilight: Postmodernism and Tradition," *Sophia: The Journal of Traditional Studies*, vol. 5, no. 1, Summer 1999, p. 165.

What is this flight and how shall we be borne away? Just as Odysseus says he was delivered from a witch like Circe or Calipso, claiming—and I believe he hints at some further meaning—that it did not please him to stay, though there he enjoyed visual delights and was in the presence of enormous beauty on the level of senses. Our land is that place from which we came and our father is there (*Enn.* I.6.8.17-21).

Hence, Odysseus is a type or a symbol of the highest class of humanity, of the golden race: those mystical philosophers and sages who have reached home, i.e., the realm of Intellect and the One. For Porphyry, Odysseus bears a symbol for one who passes through the stages of becoming (*genesis*) and "returns to those beyond every wave (*kludonos*) who have no knowledge of the sea," i.e., any material substance, so that "his oar is thought to be a winnowing-fan, because of the utter ignorance of nautical instruments and activities" (*De antro nympharum* 34-35).

Porphyry's Allegorical Interpretation of Homer

According to Jean Pepin, the distinctive characteristic of Porphyry's exegesis is found in the sea as symbol, not only of the world of *genesis*, but more widely of matter. However, this symbolism is referred back to Plato, e.g., the famous myth in the *Statesman* (272d-273c), where the universe, at certain moments of its existence and in consequence of its corporeal constitution, is compared to a boat buffeted by the storm and very near to sinking in "the bottomless ocean of unlikeness."[4]

Robert Lamberton says that Porphyry's assertion of the existence of numerous valid possibilities in the interpretation of a single text reflects the paradigm of Neoplatonic epistemology and by no means serves as an evidence of a lack of clearly defined prin-

[4] Jean Pepin, "The Platonic and Christian Ulysses," in *Neoplatonism and Christian Thought*, ed. Dominic J. O'Meara (Norfolk: ISNS, 1982), p. 9.

ciples of exegesis because randomness is intolerable to Porphyry.[5] The Phoenician philosopher is assured that "the cosmos has not come into being in vain or randomly" (*ho kosmos ouk eike oud' hos etuche gegonen: De antro nympharum* 78.11-12). Since the universe (symbolized by the cave: *Odyssey* XIII.102-112) is the result of noetic irradiation and wisdom, its order reveals the divine purpose. Likewise, the hieratic and inspired texts, especially those produced by the theologian (*ho theologos*) Homer—regarded as a divine sage with revealed knowledge of the fate of souls and of the composition of reality—reflect the structure of the intelligible archetypes. When a text is no longer considered as a normal human utterance but as a piece of scripture (e.g., the poems of Orpheus, the *Chaldean Oracles*), all its details, including inadequacies, are to be explained as having another mysterious, allegorical, or inner esoteric meaning.

According to Lamberton, "the tradition of interpretation cultivated by the Neoplatonists generated a model of meaning of these poems—and of the structure of that meaning—that departed extraordinarily from the most obvious meaning, transforming the poem into revelation."[6] Aristotle already placed Homer among "those very ancient people who lived long before the present age and were the first to theologize" (*protous theologesantes: Metaph.* A 983b28-29). Their "theological philosophy" (*theologike*) belongs to the larger class of "contemplative philosophy" (*theoretikai: Metaph.* E 1026a19).

Porphyry stands in the train of a long hermeneutical tradition (*paradosis*). Stobaeus preserved another interpretative piece from Porphyry, without indication as to which of Porphyry's lost works it belongs. This excerpt also concerns the truth about the fate of

---

[5] Robert Lamberton, *Homer the Theologian: Neoplatonist Allegorical Reading and the Growth of the Epic Tradition* (Berkeley: University of California Press, 1986), p. 123.

[6] Ibid., p. 21. See also Algis Uždavinys, "From Homer to the Glorious Qur'an: Hermeneutical Strategies in the Hellenic and Islamic Traditions," *Sacred Web: A Journal of Tradition and Modernity*, no. 11, 2003, pp. 79-114.

souls and imitates the structure of the treatise *On the Cave of the Nymphs.*[7] The part of this intriguing text runs as follows:

> What Homer says about Circe contains an amazing view of things that concern the soul. He says:
> "Their heads and voices, their bristles and their bodies
> were those of pigs, but their minds were solid, as before" (*Od.* X.239-240).
> Clearly this myth is a riddle concealing what Pythagoras and Plato have said about the soul: that it is indestructible by nature and eternal, but not immune to experience and change, and that it undergoes change and transfer into other types of bodies when it goes through what we call "destruction" or "death." It then seeks out, in the pursuit of pleasure, that which is fitting and appropriate to it because it is similar and its way of life is similar in character. At this point, by virtue of what each of us gains through education and philosophy, the soul, remembering the good and repelled by shameful and illicit pleasures, is able to prevail and watch itself carefully and take care lest through inattention it be reborn as a beast and fall in love with a body badly suited for virtue and impure, nurturing an uncultivated and irrational nature and encouraging the appetitive and passionate elements of the soul rather than the rational. Empedocles calls the fate and nature that preside over this transformation a *daimon* "wrapping souls in an alien tunic of flesh" (fr. B 126 DK) and giving them new clothes.
> Homer, for his part, calls the cyclical progress and rotation of metensomatosis "Circe," making her a child of the Sun, which is constantly linking destruction with birth and birth back again with destruction and stringing them together. The island of Aiaia is both the fate that awaits the dead and a place in the upper air. When they have first fallen into it, the souls wander about disoriented and wail and do not know where the west is "Or where the Sun that lights mortal men goes beneath the earth" (*Od.* X.191).
> The urge for pleasure makes them long for their accustomed way of life in and through the flesh, and so they fall back in the witch's brew of *genesis*, which truly mixes and brews together the immortal and mortal, the rational and emotional, the Olympian and the terrestrial. The souls are bewitched and softened by the pleasures that lead them back again into *genesis*, and at this point

---

[7] Robert Lamberton, *Homer the Theologian*, p. 115.

they have special need of great good fortune and self-restraint lest they follow and give in to their worst parts and emotions and take on an accursed and beastly life.

The "meeting of three roads" that is imagined as being among the shades in Hades is actually in this world, in the three divisions of the soul, the rational, the passionate, and the appetitive. Each path or division starts from the same source but leads to a life of a specific sort appropriate to it. We are no longer talking about a myth or a poem but about truth and a description of things as they are (*kai ouk eti tauta muthon oude poiesis, all' aletheia kai psuchikos logos*). . . .

. . . Therefore where death is concerned, purity is just as important as in an initiation (*telete*), and you must keep all base emotion from the soul, put all painful desire to sleep, and keep as far from the mind as possible all jealousy, ill will, and anger, as you leave the body. Hermes with his golden staff—in reality, *logos*—meets the soul and clearly points the way to the good. He either bars the soul's way and prevents its reaching the witch's brew or, if it drinks, watches over it and keeps it as long as possible in a human form (Stob. *Ecl.* 1.41.60).

Titus Burckhardt, in his famous essay "The Return of Ulysses"[8] also interprets the poem of Homer as a symbolic account of the path leading towards spiritual realization, partly basing his explanation on Porphyry's exegesis.

Numenius and His Pythagorean Philosophy

Since Porphyry's interpretation on the Homeric poems partly depends on the lost works of Numenius of Apamea (the Syrian city in the Orontes valley) we will give a short description of his philosophy, based not only on the teachings of Pythagoras and Plato, but also on the ancient wisdom of Syria, Mesopotamia, and Egypt.

Numenius makes distinction between the first and second God. In one of the surviving fragments he says:

---

[8] Titus Burckhardt, *Mirror of the Intellect: Essays on Traditional Science and Sacred Art,* trans. and ed. William Stoddart (Cambridge: Quinta Essentia, 1987), pp. 156-163.

The First God, existing in His own place, is simple and, con-
sorting as He does with Himself alone, can never be divisible.
The Second and Third God, however, are in fact one; but in the
process of coming into contact with Matter, which is the Dyad,
He gives unity to it, but is Himself divided by it, since Matter
has a character prone to desire and is in flux. So in virtue of not
being in contact with the Intelligible (which would mean being
turned in upon Himself), by reason of looking towards Matter
and taking thought for it, He becomes unregarding (*apeirioptos*)
of Himself. And He seizes upon the sense realm and ministers
to it and yet draws it up to His own character, as a result of this
yearning towards Matter (fr. 11).

The Good, or the One, is regarded as the first principle of
Being by Numenius and sometimes (contrary to the later position
of Plotinus, to whom the One as such is beyond Being, Life, and
Intelligence) is called the Absolute Living Creature and Primal
Intellect (*Nous*). The Demiurge, as the god of *genesis*, is only the
imitator (*mimetes*) of the Good by participating in it:

If the Demiurge of Generation (*genesis*) is good, then in truth the
Demiurge of Being will be the Good Itself, this being inherent
in His essence. For the Second, being double, creates His own
form and the cosmos as well, being a Demiurge, since the First is
wholly contemplative (fr. 16).

Since the Demiurge is only good by participation, John Dillon
regards this feature of the Numenian theology as the closest
approximation to the Gnostic notion of the "ignorant Demiurge."
Dillon says:

Certainly, there are suggestions that the Demiurge creates as a
result of a lust (*orexis*) for Matter (fr. 11), by which he is "split"
(perhaps even rent asunder, in the manner of Dionysus or Osiris).
In the heat of his enthusiasm for Matter, he becomes forgetful
of himself.[9]

[9] John Dillon, *The Middle Platonists: A Study of Platonism 80 B.C. to A.D.220*
(London: Duckworth, 1996), p. 369.

However, to see the Demiurge of Numenius as "an evil principle" would be incorrect. Though the Demiurge, in a sense, leads the subsequent manifestations away from the Father, he is Intellect proper, equated with the universal Helmsman. Numenius argues as follows:

> A helmsman, after all, sailing on the high sea seated high above the tiller, directs the ship from his perch, and his eyes and his intellect are straining upwards to the aether, towards the heights of heaven, and his route comes down to him from above through heavens, while he sails below on the sea; even so the Demiurge, binding Matter fast by harmony, so that it may not break loose or wander astray, himself takes his seat above it, as if above a ship upon the sea; and he directs the harmony, steering it with the Forms, and he looks, as upon the heavens, at the God above who attracts his eyes, and takes his critical faculty (*kritikon*) from this contemplation, while he derives his impulsive faculty (*hormetikon*) from his desire (*orexis*) (fr. 18).

Numenius maintains that there are alternating world cycles of order and disorder, "according to whether God has his hand on the tiller of the cosmos or has retired into his conning-tower, leaving the ship to drift where it may."[10] In fact, this notion is based on the interpretation of Plato's *Statesman* (272c). Numenius argues:

> The First God is inactive in respect of all works, and is King (*Rep.* X.597e; *Leg.* X.904a), while the demiurgic God "takes command in his progress through Heaven" [thus being equated with the Zeus of the *Phaedrus* myth]. And it is through him that our journey takes place also, when intellect (*nous*) is sent down through the spheres (*en diexodai*) to all those who are ready to participate in it. When the God looks and directs himself towards each one of us, it then comes about that bodies live and flourish, since the God fosters them with his rays (*akrobolismoi*); but when the God turns back into his conning-tower (*periope*), these things are extinguished, and *nous* lives in enjoyment of a happy life (fr. 12).

[10] Ibid., p. 370.

The Third God of Numenius is, in fact, the Demiurge as divided up by Matter (the Dyad). This division is analogous to the dismemberment of Osiris. The Third God is not a World Soul in the strict sense, but rather an aspect of the Demiurge or *Logos.*[11] In addition, Numenius speaks of two World Souls. The beneficent World Soul has the same function as the Third God, and, in this respect, may be compared to the Egyptian goddess Isis, the consort of Osiris. The evil World Soul, which is like Typhon (the Egyptian Seth), is postulated following Plato's hints in the *Laws.*

According to Numenius, before descending through the planetary spheres to earthly bodies, the souls gather in the Milky Way. The milk and honey symbolize the lure of pleasure which leads into the realm of *genesis.* This motif belongs to the Numenian exegesis of the *Cave of the Nymphs* and is analogous to the Hermetic motif of the "unmixed wine of Ignorance."

In Egypt, the northern way is that which leads to the Imperishable Stars, the Intelligible Archetypes. This path is aimed at final liberation and the eternal noetic life, while the southern path leads to the realm of becoming or that of reincarnation into a mortal body. Thus the southern sky is governed by Osiris (Orion) and Isis (Sothis, Sirius), along with the thirty-six decans, that is, the constellations which are periodically rising and setting, dying and coming into existence again, thereby symbolizing the psycho-somatic world of becoming. The rising of each decan occurs after it has passed seventy days of invisibility in the Duat, the Osirian Netherworld, a period corresponding to that of mummification— the process supervised by Anubis, the initiator into the mysteries of death and rebirth. Therefore the openings in the Pyramid of Khufu (Cheops) leads (1) towards the Circumpolar Stars in the north and (2) the constellation of Orion (*Sah,* Osiris) in the south. The Horus-like Pharaoh, being son of Ra, the perfect *imago dei* (and all initiates who are modeled upon this paradigm) climbs to the sky,

---

[11] Ibid., pp. 374-375.

since his soul's (*ba*) aim is to become a Star, to be re-united with the supreme God. According to Lucie Lamy:

> Corresponding to Horus, Master of the North, is the dilation of the heart, the spiritual quest for transcendent light symbolized by the search for the "Eye." It is therefore in the north the mummy, receptacle of the divine spark during existence, now freed from decomposition, was respectfully buried.
>
> Corresponding to Seth, Lord of the South, are the contractive functions assimilated to those of semen (the testicles are his symbol): those of physical, terrestrial continuity. Thus in the south the *ka* can exercise to the maximum its capacity of "calling" and manifest its appetite, the reason that it was symbolically offered food items. The south then was the burial place for the vital organs, the animal parts of man.[12]

Contrary to Egyptian cosmography, the accounts of both Numenius and Porphyry depict the northern path as that of descent and the southern path as that of ascent. While discussing the problems of locating the place of judgment, described in the Platonic myth of Er (*Rep.* X), Proclus relates the position of Numenius as follows:

> Numenius says that this place is the center of the entire cosmos, and likewise of the earth, because it is at once in the middle of heaven and in the middle of earth. There the judges sit and send some souls to heaven, some to the region beneath the earth and to the rivers there. By "heaven" he means the sphere of the fixed stars, and he says there are two holes in this, Capricorn and Cancer, the one a path down (*kathodou*) into *genesis*, the other a path of ascent (*anodou*), and the rivers under the earth he calls the planets, for he associates the rivers and even Tartarus with these, and introduces a further enormous fantasy with leaping of souls from the tropics to the solstices and returns from these back to the tropics—leapings that are all his own and that he transfers to these matters, stitching the Platonic utterances together with astrological concerns and these with the mysteries. He invokes the poem of Homer as a witness to the two chasms—

---

[12] Lucie Lamy, *Egyptian Mysteries: New Light on Ancient Knowledge* (London: Thames and Hudson, 1991), p. 28.

not only when he calls "the one from the north a path for man to descend" (*Od.* XIII.110) since Cancer brings to completion by advancing into Capricorn, [and says] "the other, toward the south [is divine]" (*Od.* XIII.111), through which it is impossible for men to [enter], for that path belongs exclusively to immortals, since Capricorn, as it draws the soul upward, undoes their life in the human realm and accepts only the immortal and divine— but also when it sings of "the gates of sun and the people of dreams" (*Od.* XXIV.12) calling the two tropical signs the "gates of the sun" and the Milky Way the "people of dreams," as he claims. For he also says that Pythagoras in his obscure language called the Milky Way "Hades" and "a place of souls," for souls are crowded together there, whence among some peoples they pour libations of milk to the gods that cleanse souls, and when souls have just fallen into *genesis* milk is their first food. Furthermore, he claims that Plato, as mentioned, is describing the gates in speaking of two "chasms" and that in describing the light that he calls the "bond of heaven" he is really referring to the Milky Way, into which souls ascend in twelve days from the place of the judges, for that place was in the center and, starting from there, the dodecad is completed in heaven. This consists of the center, the earth, water, air, the seven planets, and the fixed sphere itself. He claims the signs of the Tropics, the double chasms, and the two gates are different only in name, and again that the Milky Way, the "light like a rainbow," and the "people of dreams" are all one—for the poet elsewhere compares disembodied souls to dreams. . . (*In Remp.* 2.128.26ff).

Cronius, the Companion of Numenius

Another author, to whom Porphyry refers regarding Homeric exegesis, is Cronius, the companion of Numenius. Our knowledge about Cronius is close to nothing, though he is mentioned by Longinus as the author read in Plotinus' school (Porph. *Vita Plot.* 14). It seems that Cronius' theory of the soul is the same as that held by Numenius, since Cronius and Numenius are twice mentioned together by Iamblichus in his *De anima*, on the questions of the origin of evil in the soul and the soul's entry into the body. According to John Dillon:

Cronius' only named work is one On *Reincarnation* (mentioned by Nemesius of Emesa, *Nat. Hom.* p.116, 3ff. Matthei), in which he apparently denied metempsychosis into animals, but he is quoted by Porphyry, along with Numenius, as an exegete of the *Cave of the Nymphs*, and by Proclus as commenting on at least the Nuptial Number (*In Remp.* II.22.20ff Kroll) and the Myth of Er (*In Remp.* II.109.7ff) of the *Republic*.[13]

Cronius thought that Er, described in Plato's myth, really existed and was the teacher of Zoroaster.

Remarks on Thomas Taylor's Translation

The translation of Porphyry's *De antro nympharum* was made by Thomas Taylor (1758-1835) and was first published as part of his dissertation On *the Restoration of the Platonic Theology by the Late Platonists* in his *The Philosophical and Mathematical Commentaries of Proclus*, vol. II, 1792. It was later included in *Select Works of Porphyry* (1823). Thomas Taylor the Platonist,[14] who called himself "the modern Pletho" and the follower of "that sublime theology which was first obscurely promulgated by Orpheus, Pythagoras, and Plato," spent his life laboring at the task of the first English translation of Plato's and Aristotle's works, as well as most of Plotinus and the other Neoplatonists.

Since Thomas Taylor followed the eighteenth century fashion of changing the names of the Hellenic gods into those of the Roman, we have been obliged to restore the original Greek spelling, for example, Zeus instead of Jupiter, Odysseus instead of Ulysses, and so on. However, we have preserved intact Taylor's notes to the text, making some corrections where necessary.

Algis Uždavinys

---

[13] John Dillon, *The Middle Platonists*, p. 380.

[14] See Thomas Taylor the Platonist, *Selected Writings*, eds. Kathleen Raine and George Mills Harper (Princeton: Princeton University Press, 1969).

Porphyry the Phoenician

ON THE CAVE OF THE NYMPHS

1. What does Homer obscurely signify by the cave in Ithaca, which he describes in the following verses?

High at the head a branching olive grows,
And crowns the pointed cliffs with shady boughs.
A cavern pleasant, though involv'd in night,
Beneath it lies, the Naiades' delight:
Where bowls and urns of workmanship divine
And massy beams in native marble shine;
On which the Nymphs amazing webs display,
Of purple hue, and exquisite array.
The busy bees within the urns secure
Honey delicious, and like nectar pure.
Perpetual waters through the grotto glide,
A lofty gate unfolds on either side;
That to the north is pervious to mankind;
The sacred south t'immortals is consign'd.

[At the head of the harbor is a slender-leaved olive
and nearby it a lovely and murky cave
sacred to the nymphs called Naiads.
Within are kraters and amphoras
of stone, where bees lay up stores of honey.
Inside, too, are massive stone looms and there the nymphs
weave sea-purple cloth, a wonder to see.
The water flows unceasingly. The cave has two gates,
the one from the north, a path for men to descend,
while the other, toward the south, is divine. Men do not
enter by this one, but it is rather a path for immortals.]
(*Odyssey*, XIII.102-112)

That the poet, indeed, does not narrate these particulars from historical information, is evident from this, that those who have given us a description of the island, have, as Cronius[1] says, made no mention of such a cave being found in it. This likewise, says he, is manifest, that it would be absurd for Homer to expect, that in

---

[1] This Cronius, the Pythagorean, is also mentioned by Porphyry, in his *Life of Plotinus*.

describing a cave fabricated merely by poetical license, and thus artificially opening a path to Gods and men in the region of Ithaca, he should gain the belief of mankind. And it is equally absurd to suppose, that nature herself should point out, in this place, one path for the descent of all mankind, and again another path for all the Gods. For, indeed, the whole world is full of Gods and men: but it is impossible to be persuaded, that in the Ithacensian cave men descend, and Gods ascend. Cronius, therefore, having premised thus much, says that it is evident, not only to the wise but also to the vulgar, that the poet, under the veil of allegory, conceals some mysterious signification; thus compelling others to explore what the gate of men is, and also what is the gate of the Gods: what he means by asserting that this cave of the Nymphs has two gates; and why it is both pleasant and obscure, since darkness is by no means delightful, but is rather productive of aversion and horror. Likewise, what is the reason why it is not simply said to be the cave of the Nymphs, but it is accurately added, of the Nymphs which are called Naiades? Why, also, is the cave represented as containing bowls and amphorae, when no mention is made of their receiving any liquor, but bees are said to deposit their honey in these vessels as in hives? Then, again, why are oblong beams adapted to weaving placed here for the Nymphs; and these not formed from wood, or any other pliable matter, but from stone, as well as the amphorae and bowls? Which last circumstance is, indeed, less obscure; but that, on these stony beams, the Nymphs should weave purple garments, is not only wonderful to the sight, but also to the auditory sense. For who would believe that Goddesses weave garments in a cave involved in darkness, and on stony beams, especially while he hears the poet asserting that the purple webs of the Goddesses were visible. In addition to these things likewise, this is admirable, that the cave should have a twofold entrance; one made for the descent of men, but the other for the ascent of Gods. And again, that the gate, which is pervious by men, should be said to be turned towards the north wind, but the portal of the Gods to the south; and why the poet did not rather make use of the west and the east for this purpose; since nearly all temples have their statues and entrances turned towards the east; but those who enter them look towards the west, when standing with their faces turned towards the statues, they honor and worship the Gods. Hence, since this narration is full of such obscurities, it can neither be a fiction casually devised for the purpose of procuring delight, nor an exposition of a topical history; but something allegorical must be indicated in it by the poet, who likewise mystically places an olive near the cave. All which particulars the ancients thought very laborious to investigate and unfold; and we, with their assistance, shall now endeavor to develop the secret meaning of the allegory. Those persons, therefore, appear to have written very negligently about the situation of the place, who think that the cave, and what is narrated concerning it, are nothing more than a fiction of the poet. But the best and most accurate writers of geography, and among these Artemidorus the Ephesian, in the fifth book of his work, which consists of eleven books, thus writes: "The island of Ithaca, containing an extent of eighty-five stadia,[2] is distant from Panormus, a port of Cephalenia, about twelve stadia. It has a port named Phorcys, in which there is a shore, and on that shore a cave, in which the Phaeacians are reported to have placed Odysseus." This cave, therefore, will not be entirely an Homeric fiction. But whether the poet describes it as it really is, or whether he has added something to it of his own invention, nevertheless the same inquiries remain, whether the intention of the poet is investigated, or of those who founded the cave. For, neither did the ancients establish temples without fabulous symbols, nor does Homer rashly narrate the particulars pertaining to things of this kind. But how much the more any one endeavors to show that this description of the cave is not an Homeric fiction, but prior to Homer was consecrated to the Gods, by so much the more will this consecrated cave be found to be full of ancient wisdom. And on this account it deserves to

---

[2] That is, rather more than ten Italian miles and a half, eight stadia making an Italian mile.

be investigated, and it is requisite that its symbolical consecration should be amply unfolded into light.

2. The ancients, indeed, very properly consecrated a cave to the world, whether assumed collectively, according to the whole of itself, or separately, according to its parts. Hence they considered earth as a symbol of that matter of which the world consists, on which account some thought that matter and earth are the same, through the cave indicating the world, which was generated from matter. For caves are, for the most part, spontaneous productions, and connascent with the earth, being comprehended by one uniform mass of stone, the interior parts of which are concave, but the exterior parts are extended over an indefinite portion of land. And the world being spontaneously produced [i.e., being produced by no external, but from an internal cause], and being also self-adherent, is allied to matter; which, according to a secret signification, is denominated a stone and a rock, on account of its sluggish and repercussive nature with respect to form: the ancients, at the same time, asserting that matter is infinite through its privation of form. Since, however, it is continually flowing, and is of itself destitute of the supervening investments of form, through which it participates of *morphe*, and becomes visible, the flowing waters, darkness, or, as the poet says, obscurity of the cavern, were considered by the ancients as apt symbols of what the world contains, on account of the matter with which it is connected. Through matter, therefore, the world is obscure and dark; but through the connecting power, and orderly distribution of form, from which also it is called *world*, it is beautiful and delightful. Hence it may very properly be denominated as a cave; as being lovely, indeed, to him who first enters into it, through its participation of forms, but obscure to him who surveys its foundation, and examines it with an intellectual eye. So that its exterior and superficial parts, indeed, are pleasant, but its interior and profound parts are obscure, [and its very bottom is darkness itself]. Thus also the Persians, mystically signifying the descent of the soul into the sublunary regions, and its regression from it, initiate the mystic [or him who is admitted to the arcane sacred

rites] in a place which they denominate a cavern. For, as Eubulus says, Zoroaster was the first who consecrated, in the neighboring mountains of Persia, a spontaneously produced cave, florid, and having fountains, in honor of Mithra, the maker and father of all things; a cave, according to Zoroaster, bearing a resemblance of the world, which was fabricated by Mithra. But the things contained in the cavern being arranged according to commensurate intervals, were symbols of the mundane elements and climates.

3. After this, Zoroaster likewise, it was usual with others to perform the rites pertaining to the mysteries in caverns and dens, whether spontaneously produced, or made by the hands. For, as they established temples, groves, and altars, to the celestial Gods, but to the terrestrial Gods, and to heroes, altars alone, and to the subterranean divinities pits and cells; so to the world they dedicated caves and dens; as likewise to Nymphs,[3] on account of the water which trickles, or is diffused in caverns, over which the Naiades, as we shall shortly observe, preside. Not only, however, did the ancients make a cavern, as we have said, to be a symbol of the world, or of a generated and sensible nature, but they also assumed it as a symbol of all invisible powers; because, as caverns are obscure and dark, so the essence of these powers is occult. Hence Kronos fabricated a cavern in the ocean itself, and concealed in it his children. Thus, too, Demeter educated Persephone, with her Nymphs, in a cave; and many other particulars of this kind may be found in the writings of theologists. But that the ancients dedicated caverns to Nymphs, and especially to the Naiades, who dwell near fountains, and who are called Naiades from the streams over which they preside, is manifest from the hymn to Apollo, in which it is said: "The Nymphs residing in caves shall deduce fountains of intellectual waters to thee, (according to the divine voice of the Muses,

---

[3] "Nymphs," says Hermias, in his *Scholia on the Phaedrus of Plato*, "are Goddesses who preside over regeneration, and are ministrant to Bacchus, the off-spring of Semele. Hence they dwell near water, that is, they are conversant with generation. But this Bacchus supplies the regeneration of the whole sensible world."

which are the progeny of a terrene spirit. Hence waters, bursting through every river, shall exhibit to mankind perpetual effusions of sweet streams."[4] From hence, as it appears to me, the Pythagoreans, and after them Plato, showed that the world is a cavern and a den. For the powers which are the leaders of souls, thus speak in a verse of Empedocles:

Now at this secret cavern we're arrived.

And by Plato, in the seventh book of his *Republic*, it is said, "Behold men as if dwelling in a subterraneous cavern, and in a den-like habitation, whose entrance is widely expanded to the admission of the light through the whole cave." But when the other person in the Dialogue says, "You adduce an unusual and wonderful similitude," he replies, "The whole of this image, friend Glauco, must be adapted to what has been before said, assimilating this receptacle, which is visible through the sight, to the habitation of a prison; but the light of the fire which is in it to the power of the sun."

4. That theologists therefore considered caverns as symbols of the world, and of mundane powers, is, through this, manifest. And it has been already observed by us that they also considered a cave as a symbol of the intelligible essence; being impelled to do so by different and not the same conceptions. For they were of the opinion that a cave is a symbol of the sensible world, because caverns are dark, stony, and humid; and they asserted that the world is a thing of this kind, through the matter of which it consists, and through its repercussive and flowing nature. But they thought it to be a symbol of the intelligible world, because that world is invisible to sensible perception, and possesses a firm and stable essence. Thus, also, partial powers are unapparent, and especially those which are inherent in matter. For they formed these symbols from surveying the spontaneous production of caves, and their noctur-

---

[4] These lines are not to be found in any of the hymns now extant, ascribed to Homer.

nal, dark, and stony nature; and not entirely, as some suspect, from directing their attention to the figure of a cavern. For every cave is not spherical, as is evident from this Homeric cave with a twofold entrance. But since a cavern has a twofold similitude, the present cave must not be assumed as an image of the intelligible, but of the sensible essence. For in consequence of containing perpetually-flowing streams of water, it will not be a symbol of an intelligible hypostasis, but of a material essence. On this account also, it is sacred to Nymphs, not the mountain, or rural Nymphs, or others of the like kind, but to the Naiades, who are thus denominated from streams of water. For we peculiarly call the Naiades, and the powers that preside over waters, Nymphs; and this term, also, is commonly applied to all souls descending into generation. For the ancients thought that these souls are incumbent on water which is inspired by divinity, as Numenius says, who adds, that on this account, a prophet asserts that the Spirit of God moved on the waters. The Egyptians likewise, on this account, represent all daemons, and also the sun, and, in short, all the planets, not standing on any thing solid, but on a sailing vessel; for souls descending into generation fly to moisture. Hence, also, Heraclitus says, "that moisture appears delightful and not deadly to souls"; but the lapse into generation is delightful to them. And in another place [speaking of unembodied souls], he says, "We live their death, and we die their life." Hence the poet calls those that are in generation humid, because they have souls which are *profoundly* steeped in moisture. On this account, such souls delight in blood and humid seed; but water is the nutriment of the souls of plants. Some likewise are of opinion that the bodies in the air, and in the heavens, are nourished by vapors from fountains and rivers, and other exhalations. But the Stoics assert that the sun is nourished by the exhalation from the sea; the moon from the vapors of fountains and rivers; and the stars from the exhalation of the earth. Hence, according to them, the sun is an intellectual composition formed from the sea; the moon from river waters; and the stars from terrene exhalations.

5. It is necessary, therefore, that souls, whether they are corporeal or incorporeal, while they attract to themselves body, and especially such as are about to be bound to blood and moist bodies, should verge to humidity, and be corporalized, in consequence of being drenched in moisture. Hence the souls of the dead are evocated by the effusion of bile and blood; and souls that are lovers of body, by attracting a moist spirit, condense this humid vehicle like a cloud. For moisture condensed in the air constitutes a cloud. But the pneumatic vehicle being condensed in these souls becomes visible through an excess of moisture. And among the number of these we must reckon those apparitions of images, which, from a spirit colored by the influence of imagination, present themselves to mankind. But pure souls are averse to generation; so that, as Heraclitus says, "a dry soul is the wisest." Hence, here also, the spirit becomes moist and more aqueous through the desire of coition, the soul thus attracting a humid vapor from verging to generation. Souls, therefore, proceeding into generation, are the Nymphs called Naiades. Hence it is usual to call those that are married Nymphs, as being conjoined to generation, and to pour water into baths from fountains, or rivers, or perpetual rills.

6. This world, then, is sacred and pleasant to souls who have now proceeded into nature, and to natal daemons, though it is essentially dark and *obscure* (*eeroides*), from which some have suspected that souls also are of an *obscure* nature (*aerodos*), and essentially consist of air. Hence a cavern, which is both pleasant and dark, will be appropriately consecrated to souls on the earth, conformably to its similitude to the world; in which, as in the greatest of all temples, souls reside. To the Nymphs likewise, who preside over waters, a cavern, in which there are perpetually flowing streams, is adapted. Let, therefore, this present cavern be consecrated to souls, and, among the more partial powers, to nymphs that preside over streams and fountains, and who, on this ac-count, are called *fontal* and *Naiades*. What, therefore, are the different symbols, some of which are adapted to souls, but others to the aquatic powers, in order that we may apprehend that this cavern

is consecrated in common to both? Let the stony bowls, then, and the amphorae, be symbols of the aquatic Nymphs. For these are, indeed, the symbols of Bacchus (i.e., Dionysus), but their composition is fictile, i.e., consists of baked earth; and these are friendly to the vine, the gift of the God, since the fruit of the vine is brought to a proper maturity by the celestial fire of the sun. But the stony bowls and amphorae are in the most eminent degree adapted to the Nymphs who preside over the water that flows from rocks. And to souls that descend into generation, and are occupied in corporeal energies, what symbol can be more appropriate than those instruments pertaining to weaving? Hence, also, the poet ventures to say, "that on these the Nymphs weave purple webs, admirable to the view." For the formation of the flesh is on and about the bones, which in the bodies of animals resemble stones. Hence these instruments of weaving consist of stone, and not of any other matter. But the purple webs will evidently be the flesh which is woven from the blood. For purple woolen garments are tinged from blood; and wool is dyed from animal juice. The generation of flesh, also, is through and from blood. Add, too, that the body is a garment with w hich the soul is invested, a thing wonderful to the sight, whether this refers to the composition of the soul, or contributes to the colligation of the soul [to the whole of a visible essence]. Thus, also, Proserpine, who is the inspective guardian of every thing produced from seed, is represented by Orpheus as weaving a web;[5] and the

---

[5] The theological meaning of this Orphic myth is beautifully unfolded by Proclus, as follows: "Orpheus says that the vivific cause of partible natures [i.e. Persephone], while she remained on high, weaving the order of celestials, was a nymph, as being undefiled; and in consequence of this connected with Zeus, and abiding in her appropriate manners; but that, proceeding from her proper habitation, she left her webs unfinished, was ravished; having been ravished, was married; and that being married she generated, in order that she might animate things which have an adventitious life. For the unfinished state of her webs indicates, I think, that the universe is imperfect or unfinished, as far as to perpetual animals [i.e., the universe would be imperfect if nothing inferior to the celestial Gods was produced]. Hence Plato says, that the one Demiurgus calls on the many Demiurgi to weave together the mortal and immortal natures; after a manner reminding us, that the addition of the mortal genera is the perfection of the textorial life of the universe, and also

heavens are called by the ancients a veil, in consequence of being, as it were, the vestment of the celestial Gods.

7. Why, therefore, are the amphorae said not to be filled with water, but with honey-combs? For in these Homer says the bees deposit their honey. But this is evident from the word (*tithai-bossein*), which signifies (*tithenai ten bosin*); i.e. to deposit aliment. And honey is the nutriment of bees. Theologists, also, have made honey subservient to many and different symbols, because it consists of many powers; since it is both cathartic and preservative. Hence, through honey, bodies are preserved from putrefaction, and inveterate ulcers are purified. Farther still, it is also sweet to the taste, and is collected by bees, who are ox-begotten, from flowers. When, therefore, those who are initiated in the Leontic sacred rites, pour honey instead of water on their hands; they are ordered [by the initiator] to have their hands pure from every thing productive of molestation, and from every thing noxious and detestable. Other initiators [into the same mysteries] employ fire, which is of a cathartic nature, as an appropriate purification. And they likewise purify the tongue from all the defilement of evil with honey. But the Persians, when they offer honey to the guardian of fruits, consider it as the symbol of a preserving and defending power. Hence some persons have thought that the nectar and ambrosia,[6] which

---

exciting our recollection of the divine Orphic myth, and affording us interpretative causes of the unfinished webs of Persephone."

[6] The theological meaning of nectar and ambrosia is beautifully unfolded by Hermias, in his *Scholia on the Phaedrus of Plato* . . . where he informs us, "that *ambrosia* is analogous to dry nutriment, and that, on this account, it signifies an establishment in causes; but that *nectar* is analogous to moist food, and that it signifies the providential attention of the Gods to secondary natures; the former being dominated, according to *a privation of the mortal and corruptible;* but the latter, according to *a privation of the funeral and sepulchral.* And when the Gods are represented as energizing providentially, they are said to drink nectar. Thus Homer, in the beginning of the fourth book of the *Iliad*:

Now with each other, on the golden floor
Seated near Zeus, the Gods converse; to whom

the poet pours into the nostrils of the dead, for the purpose of preventing putrefaction, is honey, since honey is the food of the Gods. On this account, also, the same poet somewhere calls nectar (*eruthron*); for such is the color of honey, [viz. it is a deep yellow]. But whether or not honey is to be taken for nectar, we shall elsewhere more accurately examine. In Orpheus, likewise, Kronos is ensnared by Zeus through honey. For Kronos, being filled with honey, is intoxicated, his senses are darkened, as if from the effects of wine, and he sleeps; just as Poros, in the *Symposium* of Plato, is filled with nectar; for wine was not (says he) yet known. The Goddess Night, too, in Orpheus, advises Zeus to make use of honey as an artifice. For she says to him—

> When stretch'd beneath the lofty oaks you view
> Saturn, with honey by the bees produc'd,
> Sunk in ebriety,[7] fast bind the God.

This, therefore, takes place, and Kronos being bound, is castrated in the same manner as Ouranos (Heaven); the theologist obscurely signifying by this, that divine natures become through pleasure bound, and drawn down into the realms of generation; and also that, when dissolved in pleasure, they emit certain seminal powers. Hence Kronos castrates Ouranos, when descending to earth, through a desire for coition.[8] But the sweetness of honey signi-

> The venerable Hebe nectar bears,
> In golden goblets; and as these flow round,
> Th' immortals turn their careful eyes on Troy.

For then they providentially attend to the Trojans. The possession, therefore, of immutable providence by the Gods is signified by their drinking nectar; the exertion of this providence, by their beholding Troy; and their communicating with each other in providential energies, by receiving the goblets from each other."

[7] Ebriety, when ascribed to divine natures by ancient theologists, signifies a deific superessential energy, or an energy superior to intellect. Hence, when Kronos is said by Orpheus to have been intoxicated with honey or nectar, the meaning is that he then energized providentially, in a deific and super-intellectual manner.

[8] Porphyry, though he excelled in philosophical, was deficient in theological

fies, with theologists, the same thing as the pleasure arising from copulation, by which Kronos, being ensnared, was castrated. For Kronos, and his sphere, are the first of the orbs that move contrary to the course of Coelum, or the heavens. Certain powers, however, descend both from Ouranos [or the inerratic sphere] and the planets. But Kronos receives the powers of Ouranos, and Zeus the powers of Kronos. Since, therefore, honey is assumed in purgations, and as an antidote to putrefaction, and is indicative of the pleasure which draws souls downward to generation, it is a symbol well adapted to aquatic Nymphs, on account of the unputrescent nature of the waters over which they preside, their purifying power, and their co-operation with generation. For water co-operates in the work of generation. On this account the bees are said, by the poet, to deposit their honey in bowls and amphorae; the bowls being a symbol of fountains, and therefore a bowl is placed near to Mithra, instead of a fountain; but the amphorae are symbols of the vessels with which we draw water from fountains. And fountains and streams are adapted to aquatic Nymphs, and still more so to the Nymphs that are souls, which the ancients peculiarly called bees, as the efficient causes of sweetness. Hence Sophocles does not speak inappropriately when he says of souls—

> In swarms while wandering, from the dead,
> A humming sound is heard.

8. The priestesses of Demeter, also, as being initiated into the mysteries of the terrene Goddess, were called by the ancients bees;

---

knowledge; of which what he now says of the castrations of Kronos and Ouranos is a remarkable instance. For ancient theologists, by things preternatural, adumbrated the transcendent nature of the Gods; by such as are irrational, a power more divine than all reason; and by things apparently base, incorporeal beauty. Hence, in the fabulous narrations to which Porphyry now alludes; the genital parts must be considered as symbols of prolific power; and the castration of these parts as signifying the progression of this power into a subject order. So that the myth means that the prolific powers of Kronos are called forth into progression by Zeus, and those of Ouranos by Kronos; Zeus being inferior to Kronos, and Kronos to Ouranos.

and Persephone herself was denominated by them honied. The moon, likewise, who presides over generation, was called by them a bee, and also a bull. And Taurus is the exaltation of the moon. But bees are ox-begotten. And this appellation is also given to souls proceeding into generation. The God, likewise, who is occultly connected with generation, is a stealer of oxen. To which may be added that honey is considered as a symbol of death, and on this account, it is usual to offer libations of honey to the terrestrial Gods; but gall is considered as a symbol of life; whether it is obscurely signified by this, that the life of the soul dies through pleasure, but through bitterness the soul resumes its life, whence, also, bile is sacrificed to the Gods; or whether it is because death liberates from molestation, but the present life is laborious and bitter. All souls, however, proceeding into generation, are not simply called bees, but those who will live in it justly, and who, after having performed such things as are acceptable to the Gods, will again return [to their kindred stars]. For this insect loves to return to the place from whence it first came, and is eminently just and sober. Whence, also, the libations which are made with honey are called sober. Bees, likewise, do not sit on beans, which were considered by the ancients as a symbol of generation proceeding in a right line, and without flexture; because this leguminous vegetable is almost the only seed-bearing plant, whose stalk is perforated throughout without any intervening knots.[9] We must therefore admit, that honey-combs and bees are appropriate and common symbols of the aquatic Nymphs, and of souls that are married [as it were] to [the humid and fluctuating nature of] generation.

9. Caves, therefore, in the most remote periods of antiquity, were consecrated to the Gods, before temples were erected to them. Hence, the Curetes in Crete dedicated a cavern to Zeus; in Arcadia, a cave was sacred to Selene (the Moon), and to Lycean

---

[9] Hence, when Pythagoras exhorted his disciples to abstain from beans, he intended to signify that they should beware of a continued and perpetual descent into the realms of generation.

The Heart of Plotinus

Pan; and in Naxus, to Bacchus. But wherever Mithra was known, they propitiated the God in a cavern. With respect, however, to this Ithacensian cave, Homer was not satisfied with saying that it had two gates, but adds, that one of the gates was turned towards the north, but the other, which was more divine, to the south. He also says, that the northern gate was pervious to descent, but does not indicate whether this was also the case with the southern gate. For of this, he only says, "It is inaccessible to men, but it is the path of the immortals."

10. It remains, therefore, to investigate what is indicated by this narration, whether the poet describes a cavern which was in reality consecrated by others, or whether it is an enigma of his own invention. Since, however, a cavern is an image and symbol of the world, as Numenius and his familiar Cronius assert, there are two extremities in the heavens, viz. the winter tropic, than which nothing is more southern, and the summer tropic, than which nothing is more northern. But the summer tropic is in Cancer, and the winter tropic in Capricorn. And since Cancer is nearest to us, it is very properly attributed to the Moon, which is the nearest of all the heavenly bodies to the earth. But as the southern pole, by its great distance, is invisible to us, hence Capricorn is attributed to Kronos (Saturn), the highest and most remote of all the planets. Again, the signs from Cancer to Capricorn are situated in the following order: and the first of these is Leo, which is the house of Helios (the Sun); afterwards Virgo, which is the house of Hermes (Mercury); Libra, the house of Aphrodite (Venus); Scorpius, of Ares (Mars), Sagittarius, of Zeus (Jupiter); and Capricornus, of Kronos (Saturn). But from Capricorn in an inverse order, Aquarius is attributed to Kronos; Pisces, to Zeus; Aries, to Ares; Taurus, to Aphrodite; Gemini, to Hermes; and, in the last place, Cancer to Selene (the Moon).

11. Theologists therefore assert that these two gates are Cancer and Capricorn; but Plato calls them entrances. And of these theologists say that Cancer is the gate through which souls descend, but Capricorn that through which they ascend. Cancer is indeed northern, and adapted to descent; but Capricorn is southern, and

254

adapted to ascent.[10] The northern parts, likewise, pertain to souls

[10] Macrobius, in the twelfth chapter of his *Commentary on the Dream of Scipio*, has derived some of the ancient arcana which it contains from what is here said by Porphyry. A part of what he has further added, I shall translate, on account of its excellence and connection with the above passage. "Pythagoras thought that the empire of Pluto began downwards from the milky way, because souls falling from thence appear to have already receded from the Gods. Hence he asserts that the nutriment of milk is first offered to infants, because their first motion commences from the galaxy, when they begin to fall into terrene bodies. On this account, since those who are about to descend are yet in Cancer, and have not left the milky way, they rank in the order of the Gods. But when, by falling, they arrive at the Lion, in this constellation they enter on the exordium of their future condition. And because, in the Lion, the rudiments of birth, and certain primary exercises of human nature, commence; but Aquarius is opposite to the Lion, and presently sets after the Lion rises; hence, when the sun is in Aquarius, funeral rites are performed to departed souls, because he is then carried in a sign which is contrary or adverse to human life. From the confine, therefore, in which the zodiac and galaxy touch each other, the soul, descending from a round figure, which is the only divine form, is produced into a cone by its defluxion. And as a line is generated from a point, and proceeds into length from an indivisible, so the soul, from its own point, which is a monad, passes into the duad, which is the first extension. And this is the essence which Plato, in the *Timaeus*, calls impartible, and at the same time partible, when he speaks of the nature of the mundane soul. For as the soul of the world, so likewise that of man, will be found to be in one respect without division, if the simplicity of a divine nature is considered; and in another respect partible, if we regard the diffusion of the former through the world, and of the latter through the members of the body.

"As soon, therefore, as the soul gravitates towards body in this first production of herself, she begins to experience a material tumult, that is, matter flowing into her essence. And this is what Plato remarks in the *Phaedo*, that the soul is drawn into body staggering with recent intoxication; signifying by this, the new drink of matter's impetuous flood, through which the soul, becoming defiled and heavy, is drawn into a terrene situation. But the starry cup placed between Cancer and the Lion, is a symbol of this mystic truth, signifying that descending souls first experience intoxication in that part of the heavens through the influx of matter. Hence oblivion, the companion of intoxication, there begins silently to creep into the recesses of the soul. For if souls retained in their descent to bodies the memory of divine concerns, of which they were conscious in the heavens, there would be no discussion among men about divinity. But all, indeed, in descending, drink of oblivion; though some more, and others less. On this account, though truth is not apparent to all men on the earth, yet all exercise their opinions about it, because *a defect of memory is the origin of opinion*. But those discover most have drunk least

descending into generation. And the gates of the cavern which are
turned to the north are rightly said to be pervious to the descent of
men; but the southern gates are not the avenues of the Gods, but
of souls ascending to the Gods. On this account, the poet does not

of oblivion, because they easily remember what they had known before in the
heavens.

"The soul, therefore, falling with this first weight from the zodiac and milky
way into each of the subject spheres, is not only clothed with the accession of a
luminous body, but produces the particular motions which it is to exercise in the
respective orbs. Thus in Saturn, it energizes according to a ratiocinative and intellective power; in the sphere of Jove, according to a practic power; in the orb of the
Sun, according to a sensitive and imaginative nature; but according to the motion
of desire in the planet Venus; of pronouncing and interpreting what it perceives
in the orb of Mercury; and according to a plantal or vegetable nature, and a power
of acting on body, when it enters into the lunar globe. And this sphere, as it is the
last among the divine orders, so it is the first in our terrene situation. For this body,
as it is the dregs of divine natures, so it is the first animal substance. And this is
the difference between terrene and supernal bodies (under the latter of which I
comprehend the heaven, the stars, and the more elevated elements) that the latter
are called upwards to be the seat of the soul, and merit immortality from the very
nature of the region, and an imitation of sublimity; but the soul is drawn down to
these terrene bodies, and is on this account said to die when it is enclosed in this
fallen region, and the seat of mortality. Nor ought it to cause any disturbance that
we have so often mentioned the death of the soul, which we have pronounced to
be immortal. For the soul is not extinguished by its own proper death, but is only
overwhelmed for a time. Nor does it lose the benefit of perpetuity by its temporal demersion. Since, when it deserves to be purified from the contagion of vice,
through its entire refinement from body, it will be restored to the light of perennial life, and will return to its pristine integrity and perfection."

The powers, however, of the planets, which are the causes of the energies of the
soul in the several planetary spheres, are more accurately described by Proclus, in
p. 260 of his admirable *Commentary on the Timaeus*, as follows: "If you are willing,
also, you may say, that of the beneficent planets, Selene (the Moon) is the cause to
mortals of nature, being herself the visible statue of fontal nature. But Helios (the
Sun) is the Demiurgus of every thing sensible, in consequence of being the cause
of sight and visibility. Hermes is the cause of the motions of the phantasy; for of
the imaginative essence itself, so far as sense and phantasy are one, Helios is the
producing cause. But Aphrodite is the cause of epithymetic appetites [or of the appetites pertaining to desire]; and Ares, of the irascible motions which are conform-
able to nature. Of all vital powers, however, Zeus is the common cause; but of all
gnostic powers, Kronos. For all the irrational forms are divided into these."

say that they are the avenues of the Gods, but of immortals; this appellation being also common to our souls, which are *per se*, or essentially, immortal. It is said that Parmenides mentions these two gates in his treatise *On the Nature of Things;* as likewise, that they are not unknown to the Romans and Egyptians. For the Romans celebrate their Kronia (Saturnalia) when the Sun is in Capricorn; and during this festivity, slaves wear the shoes of those who are free, and all things are distributed among them in common; the legislator obscurely signifying by this ceremony, that, through this gate of the heavens, those who are now born slaves will be liberated through the Kronian festival, and the house attributed to Kronos, i.e. Capricorn, when they live again, and return to the fountain of life. Since, however, the path from Capricorn is adapted to ascent, hence the Romans denominate that month in which the Sun, turning from Capricorn to the east, directs his course to the north, Januarius, or January, from *janua,* a gate. But with the Egyptians, the beginning of the year is not Aquarius, as with the Romans, but Cancer. For the star Sothis, which the Greeks call the Dog, is near to Cancer. And the rising of Sothis is the new moon with them, this being the principle of generation to the world. On this account, the gates of the Homeric cavern are not dedicated to the east and west, nor to the equinoctial signs, Aries and Libra, but to the north and south, and to those celestial signs which, towards the south, are most southerly, and, towards the north, are most northerly; because this cave was sacred to souls and aquatic Nymphs. But these places are adapted to souls descending into generation, and afterwards separating themselves from it. Hence, a place near to the equinoctial circle was assigned to Mithra as an appropriate seat. And on this account he bears the sword of Aries, which is a martial sign. He is likewise carried in the Bull, which is the sign of Aphrodite. For Mithra, as well as the Bull, is the demiurgus and lord of generation.[11] But he is placed near the equinoctial circle,

---

[11] Hence Phanes, or Protogonus, who is the paradigm of the universe, and who was absorbed by Zeus, the Demiurgus, is represented by Orpheus as having the head of a *bull* among other heads with which he is adorned. And in the Orphic hymn to him, he is called *bull-roarer.*

257

having the northern parts on his right hand, and the southern on his left. They likewise arranged towards the south the southern hemisphere, because it is hot; but the northern hemisphere towards the north, through the coldness of the north wind.

12. The ancients, likewise, very reasonably connected winds with souls proceeding into generation, and again separating themselves from it, because, as some think, souls attract a spirit, and have a pneumatic essence. But the north wind is adapted to souls falling into generation; and, on this account, the northern blasts refresh those who are dying, and when they can scarcely draw their breath. On the contrary, the southern gales dissolve life. For the north wind, indeed, from its superior coldness, congeals [as it were, the animal life], and detains it in the frigidity of terrene generation. But the south wind being hot, dissolves this life, and sends it upward to the heat of a divine nature. Since, however, our terrene habitation is more northern, it is proper that souls which are born in it should be familiar with the north wind; but those that exchange this life for a better, with the south wind. This also is the cause why the north wind is at its commencement great; but the south wind, at its termination. For the former is situated directly over the inhabitants of the northern part of the globe; but the latter is at a great distance from them; and the blast from places very remote is more tardy than from such as are near. But when it is coacervated, then it blows abundantly, and with vigor. Since, however, souls proceed into generation through the northern gate, hence this wind is said to be amatory. For, as the poet says,

> Boreas, enamour'd of the sprightly train,
> Conceal'd his godhead in a flowing mane.
> With voice dissembled, to his loves he neigh'd,
> And coursed the dappled beauties o'er the mead:
> Hence sprung twelve others of unrivall'd kind,
> Swift as their mother mares, and father wind
> (*Iliad*, XX.223 ff).

It is also said that Boreas ravished Orithya,[12] from whom he begot Zetis and Calais. But as the south is attributed to the Gods, hence, when the Sun is at his meridian, the curtains in temples are drawn before the statues of the Gods; in consequence of observing the Homeric precept, "that it is not lawful for men to enter

---

[12] This myth is mentioned by Plato in the *Phaedrus*, and is beautifully unfolded as follows, by Hermias, in his Scholia on that Dialogue: "A twofold solution may be given of this myth; one from history, more ethical; but the other, transferring us [from parts] to wholes. And the former of these is as follows: Orithya was the daughter of Erectheus, and the priestess of Boreas; for each of the winds has a presiding deity, which the telestic art, or the art pertaining to sacred mysteries, religiously cultivates. To this Orithya, then, the God was so very propitious, that he sent the north wind for the safety of the country; and besides this, he is said to have assisted the Athenians in their naval battles. Orithya, therefore, becoming enthusiastic, being possessed by her proper God Boreas, and no longer energizing as a human being (for animals cease to energize according to their own peculiarities when possessed by superior causes), died under the inspiring influence, and thus was said to have been ravished by Boreas. And this is the more ethical explanation of the fable.

"But the second, which transfers the narration to wholes, and does not entirely subvert the former, is the following: for divine fables often employ transactions and histories, in subserviency to the discipline of wholes. It is said then that Erectheus is the God that rules over the three elements, air, water, and earth. Sometimes, however, he is considered as alone the ruler of the earth, and sometimes as the presiding deity of Attica alone. Of this deity Orithya is the daughter; and she is the prolific power of the Earth, which is indeed coextended with the word *Erectheus*, as the unfolding of the name signifies. For it is *the prolific power of the Earth, flourishing and restored, according to the seasons*. But Boreas is the providence of the Gods, supernally illuminating secondary natures. For the providence of the Gods in the world is signified by Boreas, because this divinity blows from lofty places. And the elevating power of the Gods is signified by the south wind, because this wind blows from low to lofty places; and besides this, *things situated towards the south are more divine*. The providence of the Gods, therefore, causes the prolific power of the Earth, or of the Attic land, to ascend and become visible.

"Orithya also may be said to be a soul aspiring after things above, from (*orouo*) and (*theio*), according to the Attic custom of adding a letter at the end of a word, which letter is here an 'ω.' Such a soul, therefore, is ravished by Boreas supernally blowing. But if Orithya was hurled from a precipice, this also is appropriate, for such a soul dies a philosophic, not receiving a physical death, and abandons a life pertaining to her own deliberate choice, at the same time that she lives a physical life. And philosophy, according to Socrates in the *Phaedo*, is nothing else than a meditation of death."

temples when the Sun is inclined to the south," for this is the path of the immortals. Hence, when the God is at his meridian altitude, the ancients placed a symbol of mid-day and of the south in the gates of the temples; and, on this account, in other gates also, it was not lawful to speak at all times, because gates were considered as sacred. Hence, too, the Pythagoreans, and the wise men among the Egyptians, forbade speaking while passing through doors or gates; for then they venerated in silence that God who is the principle of wholes [and, therefore of all things].

13. Homer likewise knew that gates are sacred, as is evident from his representing Oeneus, when supplicating, shaking the gate:

The gates he shakes, and supplicates the son (*Iliad*, XI.579).

He also knew the gates of the heavens which are committed to the guardianship of the Hours; which gates originate in cloudy places, and are opened and shut by the clouds. For he says,

Whether dense clouds they close, or wide unfold (*Iliad*, VIII.395).

And on this account, these gates emit a bellowing sound, because thunders roar through the clouds:

Heaven's gates spontaneous open to the powers;
Heaven's bellowing portals, guarded by the Hours (*Iliad*, VIII.393).

He likewise elsewhere speaks of the gates of the Sun, signifying by these Cancer and Capricorn; for the Sun proceeds as far as to these signs, when he descends from the north to the south, and from thence ascends again to the northern parts. But Capricorn and Cancer are situated about the galaxy, being allotted the extremities of this circle; Cancer, indeed, the northern, but Capricorn the southern extremity of it. According to Pythagoras, also, the people of dreams[13] are the souls which are said to be collected in the galaxy, this circle being so called from the milk with which souls are nourished when they fall into generation. Hence, those who evocate departed souls, sacrifice to them by a libation of milk mingled with honey; because, through the allurements of sweetness, they will proceed into generation; with the birth of man, milk being naturally produced. Farther still, the southern regions produce small bodies; for it is usual with heat to attenuate them in the greatest degree. But all bodies generated in the north are large, as is evident in the Celtae, the Thracians, and the Scythians; and these regions are humid, and abound with pasture. For the word Boreas is derived from (*bora*), which signifies nutriment. Hence, also, the wind which blows from a land abounding in nutriment, is called (*Borras*), as being of a nutritive nature. From these causes, therefore, the northern parts are adapted to the mortal tribe, and to souls that fall into the realms of generation. But the southern parts are adapted to that which is immortal, just as the eastern parts of the world are attributed to the Gods, but the western to daemons. For, in consequence of nature originating from diversity, the ancients every where made that which has a twofold entrance to be a symbol of the nature of things. For the progression is either through that which is intelligible, or through that which is sensible. And if through that which is sensible, it is either through the sphere of the fixed stars, or through the sphere of the planets. And again, it is either through an immortal, or through a mortal progression. One center, likewise, is above, but the other beneath the earth; and the one is eastern, but the other western. Thus, too, some parts of the world are situated on the left, but others on the right hand: and night is opposed to day. On this account, also, harmony consists of and proceeds through contraries. Plato also says that there are two openings, one of which affords a passage to souls ascending to the heavens, but the other to souls descending to the

[13] The souls of the suitors are said by Homer, in the twenty-fourth book of the *Odyssey* (v. 11), to have passed, in their descent to the regions of spirits, beyond *the people of dreams.*

earth. And, according to theologists, the Sun and Moon are the gates of souls, which ascend through the Sun, and descend through the Moon. With Homer, likewise, there are two tubs,

> From which the lot of every one he fills,
> Blessings to these, to those distributes ills (*Iliad*, XXIV.528).

But Plato, in the *Gorgias*, by tubs intends to signify souls, some of which are malefic, but other beneficent, and some of which are rational, but others irrational.[14] Souls, however, are [analogous to]

---

[14] The passage in the *Gorgias* of Plato, to which Porphyry here alludes, is as follows: "Socrates. But indeed, as you also say, life is a grievous thing. For I should not wonder if Euripides spoke the truth when he says: 'Who knows whether to live is not to die, and to die is not to live?' And we, perhaps, are in reality dead. For I have heard from one of the wise, that we are now dead; and that the body is our sepulcher; but that the part of the soul in which the desires are contained, is of such a nature that it can be persuaded, and hurled upwards and downwards. Hence a certain elegant man, perhaps a Sicilian, or an Italian, denominated, mythologizing, this part of the soul a tub, by a derivation from the probable and the persuasive; and, likewise, he called those that are stupid, or deprived of intellect, uninitiated. He further said, that the intemperate and uncovered nature of that part of the soul in which the desires are contained, was like a pierced tub, through its insatiable greediness."

What is here said by Plato is beautifully unfolded by Olympiodorus, in his MS. *Commentary on the Gorgias*, as follows: "Euripides (in *Phryxo*) says, that to live is to die, and to die to live. For the soul coming hither, as she imparts life to the body, so she partakes [through this] of a certain privation of life; but this is an evil. When separated, therefore, from the body, she lives in reality; for she dies here, through participating a privation of life, because the body becomes the source of evils. And hence it is necessary to subdue the body.

"But the meaning of the Pythagoric myth, which is here introduced by Plato, is this: We are said to be dead, because, as we have before observed, we partake of a privation of life. The sepulcher which we carry about with us is, as Plato himself explains it, the body. But Hades is the unapparent, because we are situated in obscurity, the soul being in a state of servitude to the body. The tubs are the desires; whether they are so called from our hastening to fill them, as if they were tubs, or from desire persuading us that it is beautiful. The initiated, therefore, i.e. those that have a perfect knowledge, pour into the entire tub: for these have their tub full; or, in other words, have perfect virtue. But the uninitiated, namely those that possess nothing perfect, have perforated tubs. For those that are in a state of servitude to desire always wish to fill it, and are more inflamed; and on this account they have tubs, because they contain in themselves energies and habits, as in a vessel. In Hesiod too, we find one tub closed, but the other opened by Pleasure, who scatters its contents every where, Hope alone remaining behind. For in those things in which a depraved soul, being dispersed about matter, deserts the proper order of its essence; in all these, it is accustomed to feed itself with [the pleasing prospects of] auspicious hope.

14. Since, therefore, every twofold entrance is a symbol of nature, this Homeric cavern has, very properly, not one portal only, but two gates, which differ from each other conformably to things themselves; of which one pertains to Gods and good [daemons], but the other to mortals, and depraved natures. Hence, Plato took occasion to speak of bowls, and assumes tubs instead of amphorae, and two openings, as we have already observed, instead of two gates. Pherecydes Syrus also mentions recesses and trenches, caverns, doors, and gates; and through these obscurely indicates the generations of souls, and their separation from these material realms. And thus much for an explanation of the Homeric cave, which we think we have sufficiently unfolded without adducing any farther testimonies from ancient philosophers and theologists, which would give a needless extent to our discourse.

15. One particular, however, remains to be explained, and that is the symbol of the olive planted at the top of the cavern, since

perforated tubs, as being never full. But the sieve is the rational soul mingled with the irrational. For the [rational] soul is called a circle, because it seeks itself, and is itself sought; finds itself, and is itself found. But the irrational soul imitates a right line, since it does not revert to itself like a circle. So far, therefore, as the sieve is circular, it is an image of the rational soul; but, as it is placed under the right lines formed from the holes, it is assumed for the irrational soul. Right lines, therefore, are in the middle of the cavities. Hence, by the sieve, Plato signifies the rational in subjection to the irrational soul. But the water is the flux of nature: for, as Heraclitus says, *moisture* is *the death of the soul.*"

In this extract the intelligent reader will easily perceive that the occult signification of the *tubs* is more scientifically unfolded by Olympiodorus than by Porphyry.

Homer appears to indicate something very admirable by giving it such a position. For he does not merely say that an olive grows in this place, but that it flourishes on the summit of the cavern.

> High at the head a branching olive grows,
> Beneath, a gloomy grotto's cool recess.

But the growth of the olive in such a situation is not fortuitous, as some one may suspect, but contains the enigma of the cavern. For since the world was not produced rashly and casually, but is the work of divine wisdom and an intellectual nature, hence an olive, the symbol of this wisdom, flourishes near the present cavern, which is an image of the world. For the olive is the plant of Athena; and Athena is wisdom. But this Goddess being produced from the head of Zeus, the theologist has discovered an appropriate place for the olive, by consecrating it at the summit of the port; signifying by this that the universe is not the effect of a casual event, and the work of irrational fortune, but that it is the offspring of an intellectual nature and divine wisdom, which is separated, indeed, from it [by a difference of essence], but yet is near to it, through being established on the summit of the whole port; [i.e. from the dignity and excellence of its nature governing the whole with consummate wisdom]. Since, however, an olive is ever-flourishing, it possesses a certain peculiarity in the highest degree adapted to the revolutions of souls in the world; for to such souls this cave [as we have said] is sacred. For in summer, the white leaves of the olive tend upward, but in winter, the whiter leaves are bent downward. On this account, also, in prayers and supplications, men extend the branches of an olive, ominating from this that they shall exchange the sorrowful darkness of danger for the fair light of security and peace. The olive, therefore, being naturally ever-flourishing, bears fruit which is the auxiliary of labor [by being its reward]; it is also sacred to Athena, supplies the victors in athletic labors with crowns, and affords a friendly branch to the suppliant petitioner. Thus, too, the world is governed by an intellectual nature, and is conducted by a wisdom eternal and ever-flourishing; by which the rewards of victory are conferred on the conquerors in the athletic race of life, as the reward of severe toil and patient perseverance. And the Demiurgus, who connects and contains the world [in ineffable comprehensions], invigorates miserable and suppliant souls.

16. In this cave, therefore, says Homer, all external possessions must be deposited. Here, naked, and assuming a suppliant habit, afflicted in body, casting aside every thing superfluous, and being averse to the energies of sense, it is requisite to sit at the foot of the olive, and consult with Athena by what means we may most effectually destroy that hostile rout of passions which insidiously lurk in the secret recesses of the soul. Indeed, as it appears to me, it was not without reason that Numenius and his followers thought the person of Odysseus in the *Odyssey* represented to us a man who passes in a regular manner over the dark and stormy sea of generation, and thus at length arrives at that region where tempest and seas are unknown, and finds a nation

Who ne'er knew salt, or heard the billows roar.

17. Again, according to Plato, the deep, the sea, and a tempest are images of a material nature. And on this account, I think, the poet called the port by the name of Phorcys. For he says, "It is the port of the ancient marine Phorcys."[15] The daughter, likewise, of this God is mentioned in the beginning of the *Odyssey*. But from Thoosa the Cyclops was born, whom Odysseus deprived of sight. And this deed of Odysseus became the occasion of reminding him of his errors, till he was safely landed in his native country. On this

---

[15] Phorcys is one among the ennead of Gods who, according to Plato in the *Timaeus*, fabricate generation. Of this deity, Proclus observes, "that as the Zeus in this ennead causes the unapparent divisions and separation of forms made by Kronos to become apparent, and as Rhea calls them forth into motion and generation, so Phorcys inserts them in matter, produces sensible natures and adorns the visible essence, in order that there may not only be divisions of productive principles [or forms] in natures and in souls, and in intellectual essences prior to these, *but likewise in sensibles. For this is the peculiarity of fabrication.*"

account, too, a seat under the olive is proper to Odysseus, as to one who implores divinity, and would appease his natal daemon with a suppliant branch. For it will not be simply, and in a concise way, possible for any one to be liberated from this sensible life, who blinds this daemon, and renders his energies inefficacious; but he who dares to do this, will be pursued by the anger[16] of the marine and material Gods, whom it is first requisite to appease by sacrifices, labors, and patient endurance; at one time, indeed, contending with the passions, and at another employing enchantments and deceptions, and by these, transforming himself in an all-various manner; in order that, being at length divested of the torn garments [by which his true person was concealed], he may recover the ruined empire of his soul. Nor will he even then be liberated from labors; but this will be effected when he has entirely passed over the raging sea, and, though still living, becomes so ignorant of marine and material works [through deep attention to intelligible concerns], as to mistake an oar for a corn-van.

18. It must not, however, be thought, that interpretations of this kind are forced, and nothing more than the conjectures of ingenious men; but when we consider the great wisdom of antiquity, and how much Homer excelled in intellectual prudence, and in an accurate knowledge of every virtue, it must not be denied that he has obscurely indicated the images of things of a more divine nature in the fiction of a fable. For it would not have been possible to devise the whole of this hypothesis, unless the figment had been transferred [to an appropriate meaning] from established truths. But reserving the discussion of this for another treatise, we shall here finish our explanation of the present Cave of the Nymphs.

---

[16] "The anger of the Gods," says Proclus, "is not an indication of any passion in them, but demonstrates our inaptitude to participate of their illuminations."

SELECTED BIBLIOGRAPHY

Armstrong, A.H. *The Architecture of the Intelligible Universe in the Philosophy of Plotinus: An Analytical and Historical Study.* Amsterdam: Adolf M. Hakkert Publisher, 1967.

————. "Platonic Mirrors." *Eranos 1989, Jahrbuch* 55:147-181. Insel Verlag Frankfurt am Main, 1988.

————. "Aristotle in Plotinus: The Continuity and Discontinuity of Psyche and Nous." In *Aristotle and the Later Tradition,* edited by Henry Blumenthal and Howard Robinson, 117-127. Oxford: Clarendon Press, 1991.

————. "Plotinus and Christianity." In *Platonism in Late Antiquity,* edited by Stephen Gersh and Charles Kannenguisser, 115-130. Notre Dame, Indiana: University of Notre Dame Press, 1992.

Blumenthal, H.J. "Plotinus in Later Platonism." In *Neoplatonism and Early Christian Thought: Essays in Honor of A.H. Armstrong,* edited by H.J. Blumenthal and R.A. Markus, 33-49. London: Variorum, 1981.

————. "On Soul and Intellect." In *The Cambridge Companion to Plotinus,* edited by Lloyd P. Gerson, 82-104. Cambridge: Cambridge University Press, 1996.

————. "The Psychology of Plotinus and Later Platonism." In *The Perennial Tradition of Neoplatonism,* edited by J.J. Cleary, 269-290. Leuven: Leuven University Press, 1997.

Bussanich, J. "Plotinus's Metaphysics of the One." In *The Cambridge Companion to Plotinus,* edited by Lloyd P. Gerson, 38-65. Cambridge: Cambridge University Press, 1996.

Charrue, J.M. *Plotin lecteur de Platon.* Paris: Les Belles Lettres, 1978.

Dillon, J.M. *The Middle Platonists: A Study of Platonism 80 B.C. to A.D. 220,* revised edition with new afterword. London: Duckworth, 1996.

————. "Harpocration's Commentary on Plato: Fragments of a Middle Platonic Commentary." *California Studies in Classical Antiquity* 4:125-146. Berkeley, 1971.

———. "Plotinus at Work on Platonism." *Greece & Rome* XXXIX:189-204, no. 2, October, 1992.

———. "The Descent of the Soul in Middle Platonic and Gnostic Thought." In *The Rediscovery of Gnosticism*, vol. 1, edited by B. Layton, 357-364. Leiden: E.J. Brill, 1980.

———. "*Aisthesis Noete*: A Doctrine of Spiritual Senses in Origen and in Plotinus." In *Hellenica et Judaica: Hommage à Valentin Nikiprowetsky*, edited by A. Caquot et al, 443-455. Leuven-Paris: Editions Peeters, 1986.

———. "Plotinus and the Transcendental Imagination." In *Religious Imagination*, edited by J.P. Mackey, 55-64. Edinburgh: University of Edinburgh Press, 1986.

———. "An Ethic for the Late Antique Sage." In *The Cambridge Companion to Plotinus*, edited by Lloyd P. Gerson, 315-335. Cambridge: Cambridge University Press, 1996.

Dodds, E.R. "Numenius and Ammonius." *Entretiens sur l'Antiquité classique*, no. 5:3-61. Vandoeuvres-Geneve, 1960.

Evangeliou, C. *The Hellenic Philosophy: Between Europe, Asia, and Africa*. Binghamton University: Institute of Global Cultural Studies, 1997.

Findlay, J.N. "The Neoplatonism of Plato." In *The Significance of Neoplatonism*, edited by R. Baine Harris, 23-40. Norfolk: ISNS, 1976.

Gatti, M.L. "Plotinus: The Platonic Tradition and the Foundation of Neoplatonism." In *The Cambridge Companion to Plotinus*, edited by Lloyd P. Gerson, 10-37. Cambridge: Cambridge University Press, 1996.

Gerson, L.P. "Introduction." In *The Cambridge Companion to Plotinus*, edited by Lloyd P. Gerson, 1-9. Cambridge: Cambridge University Press, 1996.

———. "The Study of Plotinus Today." *American Catholic Philosophical Quarterly* LXXI, no. 3:293-300.

———. "Plotinus's Metaphysics: Emanation or Creation?" *The Review of Metaphysics* XLVI, no. 3:559-574. Issue no. 183, 1993.

Glucker, J. *Antiochus and the Late Academy*. Hypomnemata, Gottingen: Vandenhocck & Ruprecht, 1978.

Hadot, P. *Philosophy as a Way of Life: Spiritual Exercises from Socrates to Foucault*, edited with an introduction by Arnold I. Davidson, translated by Michael Chase. Oxford: Blackwell, 1995.

———. "Ouranos, Kronos and Zeus in Plotinus' Treatise *Against Gnostics*." In *Neoplatonism and Early Christian Thought: Essays in Honor of A.H. Armstrong*, edited by H.J. Blumenthal and R.A. Marcus, 33-49. London: Variorum, 1981.

———. "Neoplatonist Spirituality: Plotinus and Porphyry." In *Classical Mediterranean Spirituality: Egyptian, Greek, Roman*, edited by A.H. Armstrong, 230-249. London: Routledge and Kegan Paul, 1986.

Henry, P. "The Place of Plotinus in the History of Thought." In Plotinus, *The Enneads*, translated by Stephen MacKenna, xlii-lxxxiii. London: Penguin Books, 1991.

Kenney, J.P. *Mystical Monotheism: A Study in Ancient Platonic Theology.* Hanover & London: Brown University Press, 1991.

Kingsley, P. *Ancient Philosophy, Mystery, and Magic: Empedocles and Pythagorean Tradition.* Oxford: Clarendon Press, 1995.

Leroux, G. "Human Freedom in the Thought of Plotinus." In *The Cambridge Companion to Plotinus*, edited by Lloyd P. Gerson, 292-314. Cambridge: Cambridge University Press, 1996.

Lloyd, A.C. *The Anatomy of Neoplatonism.* Oxford: Clarendon Press, 1991.

Merlan, P. *From Platonism to Neoplatonism.* Third edition, revised. The Hague: Martinus Nijhoff, 1968.

Moutsopoulos, E. *Le problème de l'imaginaire chez Plotin.* Athenes: Editions Grigoris, 1980.

O'Brien, D. "Plotinus and the Secrets of Ammonius." *Hermathena: A Trinity College Dublin Review* CLVII:137-153, 1994.

O'Meara, D.J. *Pythagoras Revived: Mathematics and Philosophy in Late Antiquity.* Oxford: Clarendon Press, 1997.

———. "Indian Wisdom and Porphyry's Search for a Universal Way." In *Neoplatonism and Indian Thought*, edited by R. Baine Harris, 5-25. Norfolk, Virginia: International Society for Neoplatonic Studies, 1982.

————. "The Hierarchical Ordering of Reality in Plotinus." In *The Cambridge Companion to Plotinus*, edited by Lloyd P. Gerson, 66-81. Cambridge: Cambridge University Press, 1996.

Pépin, J. "Porphyre, exégète d'Homer." *Porphyre: Entretiens sur l'Antiquité classique* XII:229-272. Vandoeuvres-Genève, 1960.

————. "The Platonic and Christian Ulysses." In *Neoplatonism and Christian Thought*, edited by Dominic J. O'Meara, 3-18. Norfolk: ISNS, 1982.

Rappe, S. "Self-Knowledge and Subjectivity in the Enneads." In *The Cambridge Companion to Plotinus*, edited by Lloyd P. Gerson, 250-274. Cambridge: Cambridge University Press, 1986.

Rist, J.M. *Plotinus: The Road to Reality*. Cambridge: Cambridge University Press, 1967.

————. "Mysticism and Transcendence in Later Neoplatonism." In *Platonism and its Christian Heritage*, 213-225. London: Variorum Reprints, 1985.

Schroeder, F.M. "Light and the Active Intellect in Alexander and Plotinus." *Hermes: Zeitschrift für klassische Philologie* 112:239-248. Band, Stuttgart: Franz Steiner Verlag Wiesbaden, 1984.

Smith, A. *Porphyry's Place in the Neoplatonic Tradition: A Study in Post-Plotinian Neoplatonism*. The Hague: Martinus Nijhoff, 1974.

Tarrant, H. *Thrasyllan Platonism*. Ithaca and London: Cornell University Press, 1993.

Tigerstedt, E.N. "The Decline and Fall of the Neoplatonic Interpretation of Plato: An Outline and Some Observations." *Commentationes Humanarum Litterarum* 52. Helsinki, 1974.

Trouillard, J. *La purification plotinienne*. Paris: Presses Universitaires de France, 1955.

Wallis, R.T. *Neoplatonism*. Second edition with a foreword and bibliography by Lloyd P. Gerson. London: Duckworth, 1995.

Warren, E.W. "Imagination in Plotinus." *The Classical Quarterly* 16:277-285. Oxford: Clarendon Press, 1966.

BIOGRAPHICAL NOTES

ALGIS UŽDAVINYS was Professor and Head of the Department of Humanities at Vilnius Academy of Fine Arts, Kaunas Faculty, and a Senior Research Fellow at the Lithuanian State Institute of Culture, Philosophy, and Arts in his native Lithuania. He is a published scholar in English and Lithuanian. His most recent books include (in English): *Philosophy as a Rite of Rebirth: From Ancient Egypt to Neoplatonism* (2008), *Sufism and Ancient Wisdom* (forthcoming), *Philosophy and Theurgy in Late Antiquity* (forthcoming), and (in Lithuanian): *Sufism in Islamic Civilization* (2007), *Understanding of Symbols and Images in Ancient Civilizations* (2006), *Hermes Trismegistus: The Way of Wisdom* (2005), *Hellenic Philosophy from Numenius to Syrianus* (2003), and *Egyptian Book of the Dead* (2003). He has also edited *The Golden Chain: An Anthology of Pythagorean and Platonic Philosophy* (World Wisdom, 2004). His research includes work on Hellenic philosophy, especially Platonism and Neoplatonism, as well as traditional mythology and metaphysics, Sufism, and traditional art. In 2005 he was awarded the Andrew Mellon fellowship to the American Center of Oriental Research in Amman, Jordan. Dr. Uždavinys has also translated the works of Frithjof Schuon into Russian. Dr. Uždavinys died in 2010.

JAY BREGMAN is Professor of History at the University of Maine, Orono. His research has focused on the religious transformation of the Hellenic world in the centuries leading up to and following the Christianization of the Roman Empire. More recently his work has focused on the influence of the late antique "philosophical religion," Neoplatonism, on American thought, especially New England Transcendentalism and its offshoots. He sits on the board of directors of the International Society for Neoplatonic Studies and is a member of the American Academy of Religion. Dr. Bregman is author of *Synesius of Cyrene, Philosopher Bishop* and the article on Synesius for *The Cambridge History of Philosophy in Late Antiquity* (2008). He is also co-editor (with Melanie Mineo) of *Platonic Traditions in American Thought* (2008).

INDEX

Advaita Vedanta, 39
alchemy, 4
Alexandria, 5, 7, 10, 13
All-Soul, 43, 80, 82, 102, 121-
    122, 148, 150, 161-164, 167,
    185, 196, 197
Amelius Gentilianus, 2, 6, 9,
    13
Ammonius (Saccas), 1, 2, 5-9,
    11, 14, 16, 17
amorphon, 22. *See also* formless
Antiochus, of Ascalon, 2
apeiron, 22. *See also* infinite
Aphrodite, 64, 96, 99-104,
    108-109, 171, 185, 216, 254-
    257
arche, 15, 26, 27. *See also* One,
    The
archetypes, 3, 29, 33, 41, 178,
    228. *See also* Forms
Aristotle, 1, 3, 6, 9, 14, 17, 19,
    28, 30, 37, 38, 41, 47, 87,
    223, 228, 236-237
Arithmetic, 12, 62
Armstrong, A.H., 5-6, 15, 23,
    26, 28, 30, 35, 39-41, 43, 86,
    97, 111, 118, 119, 137, 159,
    169, 187, 194, 210
Ascension, 31
Athena, 6, 264-265
Atticus, 2, 17
Atum-Ra, 15, 21
Augustine, of Hippo, 35

AUM, 38, 39
Authentic-Existence, 61, 127
Authentic-Existent, 59, 60, 141
awareness, 19, 23-24, 32-34,
    127, 147, 183, 187, 193,
    212. *See also sunesis*

ba, 136, 234
Bacchus, 245, 249, 254
Basilius, 223. *See also* Porphyry
Beauty, 11, 29, 32, 43, 50, 59,
    60, 64-75, 97-100, 108-109,
    159, 169-174, 178-186, 193,
    201-203, 215, 218, 226-227,
    252. *See also kalon*
Bhagavadgita, 39, 40, 137, 224
birth, 58, 75, 88, 97, 99, 102-
    105, 109, 122-123, 136, 164,
    194, 216, 229, 255, 261
Brahman, 38, 39

Calvenus Taurus, 2
Celestials, 103, 104, 105, 156,
    195. *See also* Daimons
Chaldean Oracles, 33, 228
Christ, 2
Christianity, 1, 2, 35, 77
Civic Virtues, 47-51
Contemplation, 21, 26-29, 55,
    62, 64, 84, 86, 101, 118-129,
    136, 145, 167-168, 170, 173,
    175, 193, 200, 213, 232. See
    also *theoria*

Light of Lights, 20, 35
logic, 19, 58, 61, 217
logos, 5, 17, 86, 169, 230
Love, 96-107, 110, 127, 154,
    169, 193, 201, 215. See
    also *eros*
Lycopolis, 4, 5, 17

MacKenna, Stephen, 43
Malchus, 6, 223. *See also*
    Porphyry
Mass, 43, 86, 111, 115, 187
Mathematics, 60
Matter, 23, 28-29, 50-51, 62,
    67-69, 71, 88, 91, 100, 105,
    110-117, 120, 121, 133, 166,
    171-173, 178, 180, 194, 196,
    203, 213, 231-233
Memory, 110, 141-142, 145
memory, 60, 98, 140-145, 147-
    149, 201, 213, 255
metaphysics, 1, 2, 15, 18, 20,
    27
Moral-Balance, 48. See
    also *Sophrosune*
Muses, The, 182, 245
mystical union, 8, 18, 33-34,
    209. See also *henosis*
mysticism, 2, 20, 26, 35-36,
    40, 64
myth, 3, 15, 74, 96, 175, 181,
    216, 225, 227, 229-230,
    232-234, 236, 249-250, 252,
    259, 262

Nature, 24, 29, 38, 79, 92, 97-
    98, 107, 112, 118-128, 134,

139, 154, 156, 167, 171-173,
    176, 189, 202, 211, 257
Nature-Principle, 120, 121,
    122, 123, 173
Neoplatonism, 1-3, 10, 15, 19,
    21, 23, 26, 30, 32-33, 36,
    39, 40-42, 64, 77, 87, 137,
    187, 223, 227
Neoplatonists, 2, 3, 5, 16, 17,
    19, 30, 225, 226, 228, 236
Nichomachean Ethics, 47
noesis, 23, 24, 28, 33, 35. See
    also intellection
Nominalism, 223
Nous, 23-30, 32-35, 39, 47,
    58, 118, 136, 169, 231. *See
    also* Intellect *and* Intelligible
    Matter
Numenius, of Apamea, 5-8,
    16-17, 230-236, 247, 254,
    265

Odysseus, 74, 224-227, 236,
    243, 265-266
Odyssey, 224, 226, 228, 241,
    261, 265
omnipresence, 22, 174, 188,
    189, 190
One, The, 8, 12, 14-17, 21-23,
    25-27, 29, 30, 33-40, 42-43,
    47, 52, 58, 60, 65, 86, 89,
    96, 97, 118, 129, 130, 132,
    133, 150, 178, 185, 193,
    204, 207-209, 227, 231, 261,
    263
oracle of Apollo, 4
oral teachings, 2, 8-9

For a glossary of all key foreign words used in books published by World
Wisdom, including metaphysical terms in English, consult:
www.DictionaryofSpiritualTerms.org.
This on-line Dictionary of Spiritual Terms provides extensive
definitions, examples, and related terms in other languages.

Introduction to Traditional Islam, Illustrated:
Foundations, Art, and Spirituality,
by Jean-Louis Michon, 2008

Introduction to Sufism: The Inner Path of Islam,
by Éric Geoffroy, 2010

Islam, Fundamentalism, and the Betrayal of Tradition:
Essays by Western Muslim Scholars,
edited by Joseph E.B. Lumbard, 2004, 2009

Journeys East:
20th Century Western Encounters with Eastern Religious
Traditions, by Harry Oldmeadow, 2004

Light From the East: Eastern Wisdom for the Modern West,
edited by Harry Oldmeadow, 2007

Living in Amida's Universal Vow: Essays in Shin Buddhism,
edited by Alfred Bloom, 2004

Maintaining the Sacred Center: The Bosnian City of Stolac,
by Rusmir Mahmutćehajić, 2011

The Mystery of Individuality:
Grandeur and Delusion of the Human Condition,
by Mark Perry, 2012

Of the Land and the Spirit:
The Essential Lord Northbourne on Ecology and Religion,
edited by Christopher James and Joseph A. Fitzgerald, 2008

On the Origin of Beauty:
Ecophilosophy in the Light of Traditional Wisdom,
by John Griffin, 2011

Outline of Sufism: The Essentials of Islamic Spirituality,
by William Stoddart, 2012

Paths to the Heart: Sufism and the Christian East,
edited by James S. Cutsinger, 2002

Remembering in a World of Forgetting:
Thoughts on Tradition and Postmodernism, by William Stoddart, 2008

Returning to the Essential: Selected Writings of Jean Biès,
translated by Deborah Weiss-Dutilh, 2004

Science and the Myth of Progress,
edited by Mehrdad M. Zarandi, 2003

Seeing God Everywhere: Essays on Nature and the Sacred,
edited by Barry McDonald, 2003

Singing the Way: Insights in Poetry and Spiritual Transformation,
by Patrick Laude, 2005

The Spiritual Legacy of the North American Indian:
Commemorative Edition, by Joseph E. Brown, 2007

Sufism: Love & Wisdom,
edited by Jean-Louis Michon and Roger Gaetani, 2006

The Timeless Relevance of Traditional Wisdom,
by M. Ali Lakhani, 2010

Touchstones of the Spirit: Essays on Religion, Tradition & Modernity,
by Harry Oldmeadow, 2012

The Underlying Religion: An Introduction to the Perennial Philosophy,
edited by Martin Lings and Clinton Minnaar, 2007

Universal Aspects of the Kabbalah and Judaism,
by Leo Schaya, 2014

Unveiling the Garden of Love:
Mystical Symbolism in Layla Majnun and Gita Govinda,
by Lalita Sinha, 2008

What Does Islam Mean in Today's World:
Religion, Politics, Spirituality,
by William Stoddart, 2012

The Wisdom of Ananda Coomaraswamy:
Selected Reflections on Indian Art, Life, and Religion,
edited by S. Durai Raja Singam and Joseph A. Fitzgerald, 2011

Wisdom's Journey: Living the Spirit of Islam in the Modern World,
by John Herlihy, 2009

Ye Shall Know the Truth: Christianity and the Perennial Philosophy,
edited by Mateus Soares de Azevedo, 2005